Ethno-Politics and Power Sharing in Guyana

Also by New Academia Publishing

History / Political Science

PAN-AFRICANISM, PAN-AFRICANISTS, AND AFRICAN LIBERATION IN THE 21ST CENTURY, by Horace Campbell and Rodney Worrell

PAN-AFRICANISM IN BARBADOS: An Analysis of the Activities of the Major 20th-Century Pan-African Formations in Barbados, by Rodney Worrell

DOOMED TO REPEAT?: Terrorism and the Lessons of History, edited by Sean Brawley

FROM PIETY TO POLITICS: The Evolution of Sufi Brotherhoods
by Barbara DeGorge

GOD, GREED, AND GENOCIDE: The Holocaust through the Centuries
by Arthur Grenke

THE SOVIETIZATION OF EASTERN EUROPE: New Perspectives on the Postwar Period, edited by Balázs Apor, Péter Apor, and E. A. Rees, eds.

NATIONALISM, HISTORIOGRAPHY AND THE (RE)CONSTRUCTION OF THE PAST, edited by Claire Norton

TURKEY'S MODERNIZATION: Refugees from Nazism and Atatürk's Vision
by Arnold Reisman

RED ATTACK WHITE RESISTANCE: Civil War in South Russia, 1918
by Peter Kenez
Peter Kenez

RED ADVANCE WHITE DEFEAT: Civil War in South Russia, 1919-1920
by Peter Kenez

To read an excerpt, visit: www.newacademia.com

Ethno-Politics and Power Sharing in Guyana
History and Discourse

David Hinds

Washington, DC

Copyright © 2010 by David Hinds

New Academia Publishing, 2011

All rights reserved. No part of this book may be reproduced or transmitted in any form or by any means, electronic or mechanical, including photocopying, recording, or by any information storage and retrieval system.

Printed in the United States of America

Library of Congress Control Number: 2010930938
ISBN 978-0-9828061-0-4 paperback (alk. paper)

 New Academia Publishing
P.O. Box 27420, Washington, DC, 20038-7420
Info@newacademia.com - www.newacademia.com

I dedicate this book

To Bro Eusi Kwayana for his foresight and courage in publicly traversing this messy terrain of race and ethnicity.

And to the memory of Clarence Ellis, economist, African Man and Village Man, for passionately believing.

Contents

Preface ix

1 Political History 1
2 Political Mobilization, Political Economy and Political Behavior 29
3 The Discourse on Race and Ethnicity 1955-92 57
4 Post-1992 Discourse on Race and Ethnicity 75
5 Power Sharing Proposals and Discourse 117
6 The PPP's Betrayal of Power Sharing and National Reconciliation in Guyana 1990-92 147
7 Benefits, Concerns and Prospects 161
8 Conclusion 173

Appendix 1 179
Appendix 2 185
Appendix 3 191
Notes 197
Bibliography 200
Index 207

Preface

One of the major global problems at the beginning of the twenty-first century is the escalation of ethnic conflicts. While this problem is not new, its growing impact on the political economy at the national, regional and global levels is cause for concern. It is most urgent in those countries which have been described as ethnically divided, bipolar or extreme plural societies. In these societies, the contending ethnic groups are, among other things, of almost equal strength in terms of population size and dominance of strategic sectors of the society and state, such as the economy, the military and the public service. The consequence is that these groups have the capacity, which they often use, to prevent the other from effectively governing the country.

It follows, therefore, that in such societies political instability is often the rule rather than the exception. This instability is often reflected in a combination of non-cooperation and open political and economic sabotage by the group that finds itself outside of the formal institutions of decision-making in the state. Competition for control of the executive branch becomes important especially in situations where each contending group dominates one of the other strategic centers of power. The group, which wins control of the executive, gains the advantage over the other group by virtue of the fact that such control gives it sole authority to determine the distribution of political, economic and cultural resources. Not only are those societies prone to political instability, they are also often susceptible to authoritarian rule and economic underdevelopment. Finally, the preoccupation with ethnic rivalry often takes precedence over national considerations thus frustrating the development of a national ethos.

The Caribbean is home to two of these societies- Guyana and Trinidad and Tobago- where descendants of formerly enslaved Africans and indentured East Indians have been locked in a political struggle for control of the state for all of their post- colonial experience. This has had serious implications not only for the internal politics of the countries but for regional politics. The first challenge is how to achieve ethnic peace based on an equality that is acceptable to both groups or guarantees the satisfaction of their core interests. The second challenge is to find an electoral formula that retains electoral competition without shutting out the losing group from meaningfully influencing decision making.

This book starts from the premise that while the Westminster winner- take- all model has been somewhat effective in more homogenous societies, it has been less effective in ethnically divided societies. Rather, it has often led to a less than democratic outcome as it creates a permanent majority and minority, which in the long run leads to the perception and reality of ethnic domination. The fear or experience of such a situation leads the minority ethnic group to subvert the democratic process, which often causes the government to reach for authoritarian methods of governance. Democracy, therefore, ultimately becomes a victim of the ethnic conflict.

This book focuses on Guyana, which attracted the attention of part of the US media on January 26, 2008 when eleven people of East Indian descent, including five children, were murdered by gunmen as they slept. Two weeks later the same gunmen carried out a similar attack in another town; this time killing fifteen people. The East Indian-dominated government condemned the attacks as designed to create terror in the society and vowed to bring the attackers to justice, but after one month the police had only arrested one suspect. But it scoffed at calls by a Jesuit priest, Fr Malcolm Rodrigues, a veteran political leader, Eusi Kwayana and an ex-soldier Oliver Hinckson for dialogue between the government and the gunmen. The African-dominated major opposition party also condemned the attacks, but argued that their genesis lay in the government's neglect of communities that supported its political rival. It subsequently refused to sign an all-party communiqué that called for a new crime-fighting strategy. The country remained in a state of fear as citizens braced themselves for the next attack. The

USA State Department issued an official caution to its citizens to be careful when traveling to Guyana while the regional Caribbean organization, the Caribbean Community and Common Market (CARICOM), expressed its concern.

On the surface it appeared as if the problem was caused by a group of criminals roaming the country in search of loot. But a casual conversation with Guyanese would reveal that the attacks were politically motivated. In fact this was the latest in a string of ethnic eruptions, estimated to have claimed more than two hundred lives, since the country's 1997 election. The attacks referenced above occurred sixteen months after the country's last election, which unlike others before it, was not followed by violent unrest.

This book arises out of more than a decade of close engagement with ethno-politics in Guyana, mainly as an active participant in the public political debates on the subject. What started as a project intended to make the case for consociational power sharing as one solution to the country's ethnic divide evolved into a broader study of the country's ethno-political history and the discourse that accompanied it. It became difficult to discuss power sharing outside of this deeper examination of ethnicity and politics especially since there has never been an actual power sharing government. The book targets two audiences--the one that, because of age, is unfamiliar with the country's political history and the other, which is unfamiliar with the broader perspective that goes beyond the narrow government-opposition framework.

It is a book about ethnic conflict and the search for solutions to that conflict. It has a twin focus. First, it presents a historical account of ethno politics in Guyana from the late 1940s to the present. This account is premised on the following thesis: while other factors such as class, party politics, ideology, gender and political personality, have been prevalent in the political process, these have been manifested within the context of the ethnic competition and conflict between East Indians and African Guyanese. In the final analysis ethnicity has been the dominant factor in shaping the country's political evolution. An important aspect of this history has been the search for ways to bring about reconciliation. Hence power sharing. Second, the book provides an account of the discourses that accompanied the politics both as catalyst and outcome. If the history emphasizes the events—the splits, the riots, the elections, the demonstrations, the policies—the discourse emphasizes the debates, the interpretations of events and the ideological thrusts. This section examines the narratives of leading theoreticians, commentators, political leaders and ethnic gatekeepers. As is the case with the history, it is a discourse of both conflict and the need for reconciliation.

The book is meant primarily as a contribution to the literature on ethnically divided societies. It locates Guyana within the perspectives which explain such societies, but because there can be no single theory of ethnicity it also draws particular lessons from the Guyana experience. It is also meant to be a contribution to understanding the politics of the Anglophone Caribbean. While Guyana and Trinidad and Tobago, given their demographic profiles, are in some ways exceptions, they, nevertheless, share more similarities than differences with the other countries in the region.

The book builds on previous studies, which have not had the benefit of the developments since 1992. While those studies captured the country's ethnic politics within the context of an authoritarian political order, this one expands into the period of democratization. Another distinguishing feature is the broadening of the discourses beyond the standard examination of government and opposition action. In this regard alternative perspectives, which would ordinarily be marginalized, are situated as part of the discourse. Consequently, the book highlights the roles and perspectives of political actors such as Eusi Kwayana, Clive Thomas, Walter Rodney and Ravi Dev--all important but generally marginalized voices in political studies of the country. Similarly the book subjects more familiar voices such as Dr. Cheddi Jagan, one of the two foremost political leaders, to a fresh critique that, in some respects, runs against the grain of orthodox interpretations.

In the final analysis it is partly a work of historical revision. It challenges assumptions of Guyana's recent political history, which have conspired to create a history of ethnic aggression and victimhood, of heroes and villains, of ethnic saints and devils. Studies of racial and ethnic conflict are somewhat more subjective than other political studies, especially when the writer belongs to one of the contending groups or when one has been connected to the process. If there are any overt biases, they are not deliberate; I have tried to be as fair as the evidence allows me to. Obviously, coming as I do from a particular school of thought, the book reflects a distinct perspective.

Some of the perspectives in the book may be familiar to those who have followed my writings in the public media in Guyana. What I have tried to do here is to expand and, in many instances, refine those perspectives to reflect a broader approach to the issues. In the course of preparing this manuscript I have benefited from the insights of many colleagues and friends which I have found more than helpful. These came in the form of arguments, discussions, scolding and suggestions. But in the final analysis I am solely responsible for the finished work.

David Hinds
Arizona, USA
February 2010

1

Political History

Guyana's ethnic problems have arisen out of the evolution of the country's political economy in which power has always been ethno-racially determined. The Guyanese state emerged during the slavery era or what Thomas (1984) calls "the slave mode of production." During this period - which spans the years from the colonial conquest of the "New World" in the early sixteenth century to the end of slavery in the 1830s - the state functioned primarily as the medium of colonial control and regulation. The very nature of colonial activities-- the seizure of land from the indigenous population, the annihilation of their indigenous forms of government and the system of forced labor from the imported slaves-- necessitated the emergence of a coercive medium.

The abolition of slavery in 1838 led to the introduction of an indentureship scheme, which was meant to ensure the maintenance of the plantation as the engine of the economy. The ruling class justified indentureship through a narrative of the lazy African who abandoned the sugar plantation. The new immigrants, who came from China, India and Madeira, were introduced as saviors of the economy and as being more industrious than the ex-slaves. The latter, beginning in 1838, pooled their resources and bought what Kwayana and Kwayana (2002) call "cooperative villages." Soon an African Guyanese economy took root in these villages much to the chagrin of the plantation owners who used every power at their disposal to crush it. These included the denial of capital to the villagers, flooding of their lands and competition from the newly arrived immigrants, which was part of a deliberate "divide and rule" strategy.[1]

When plantation labor was deemed to be beneath the socio-racial status of the Portuguese immigrants, they were officially given a monopoly of commercial activity that was intended to push Africans out of this sector of the economy. This official assault on the desires of the Africans for self reliance and self emancipation had three major effects. It led to mistrust between Africans and the other ethnic groups which would greatly influence the country's social and political evolution. Second, it served to demarcate the political economy along ethno-racial lines. Third, the groups developed stereotypes of each other, which helped to shape ethnic relations.

According to Kwayana, an important factor was the levying of taxes on the freed Africans to finance indentureship. He argues that this "social injustice" was manifested, "but it has to be noted that oppression was the work of the plantocracy using the power of the purse to secure its profits." He also points out that "there was not a single Indian in the law-making machinery in those days, nor was there any African" (Kwayana 1988:2). The problem also has to do with the fact that two different ethnic groups were transplanted from their roots and placed in a hostile and alien environment. This view is supported by Premdas, who contends that "the foundations of inter-ethnic rivalry were forged in the anvil of the colonial policy of immigration and divide and rule." (Premdas 1993). These factors combined to create the deep suspicion and distrust which exist between the two groups. Kwayana (1988:15-17) refers to this development as the inter-racial dynamic:

> There has long existed an interracial dynamic in Guyanese society. In the absence of forward planning to contain racial rivalries, it could not be avoided. There are dynamics in social life in any case. And in areas where there are ethnic groups and where there is no forward planning or thinking for mutual security and for solving problems which arise, what can be called "the interracial dynamics" come into play. The fact that Guyana was becoming and had already become the home base of a population of inhabitants, most of whom were laborers or farmers, but who were defined

by time, right of occupation of time of arrival, and to a large extent by ethnic-type corresponding with these, gave rise to the need for management of the more important differences and conflicts of interest among these groups.

But as the plantation owners' drive for maximum profits intensified, the common suffering of the two groups became more evident. The working and living conditions of the Indians were no better than those of their African counterparts who had begun to move to the urban centers. The conditions of the "barrackyard" were similar to those in the "niggeryard." This common suffering precipitated united action between the two groups, despite their uneasy relationship. There were numerous instances of cooperation especially on the political and industrial fronts. One high point of this solidarity was the famous "1905 riots" when a strike against unbearable working conditions by African workers in Georgetown was joined by Indian sugar workers in the rural areas.[2]

Later, when strikes and demonstrations rocked the entire English speaking Caribbean during the 1930s, the protests in Guyana for the most part assumed a multiethnic character. The African based trade union, the British Guiana Labor Union (BGLU), and the Indian based union, the Manpower Citizens Association (MPCA), took a common stand against the poor working conditions and the excesses of the colonial state. This trend was manifested again in 1947, this time on the political front when at the elections of that year Cheddi Jagan, an Indian dentist, won a seat in the Legislative Assembly in a constituency that was evenly populated by Africans and Indians. Although he was Indian he won the support of the majority of poor, working class Africans who rallied to his call for workers' power.

But this show of unity was followed by ethnic distrust, which surfaced between African and Indian leaders. This dynamic was demonstrated during the 1945 debate on universal adult suffrage when most of the African legislators voted against the suffrage. There was an alleged fear of Indian domination in the political arena, given their majority status. However, Kwayana (1988:56) contends that this defensive position by the African middle class, and favored by the working class leader, Hubert Nathaniel Critchlow, who had earlier supported suffrage, was fueled in part by "the Indian revival movement, a section of which talked of making Guyana an Indian colony."

The Birth of the PPP

Dr. Jagan's election in 1947 was the forerunner to the formation of the People's Progressive Party (PPP), the country's first mass based political party, which was founded in 1950. Its leadership included Cheddi and Janet Jagan, Ashton Chase, HJM Hubbard, Forbes Burnham, Martin Carter, Eusi Kwayana (Sydney King), Rory Westmaas and Boysie Ramkarran. This leadership represented a departure from the old reformist type—they were committed to the total dismantling of colonialism, not afraid to use socialist rhetoric in their campaigns and fiercely pro-worker. Another significance of this leadership was its multiethnic composition, which enabled the party to speak to and on the behalf of members of both the major ethnic groups. This brought the party into conflict with the local elites, who felt threatened by the new movement.

Dr. Jagan, who was instrumental in the party's formation, was named leader and Forbes Burnham, an African who had recently returned from studies abroad, was appointed chairman or the de facto deputy leader. The multiethnic image of the party, however, masked the fragility of the coalition. The chief concern was the top spot. Some Africans in the leadership thought that Burnham was the better candidate and did not hide their feelings. At the party congress held before the crucial 1953 election, Burnham made a bid to wrest the leadership from Jagan. But he was thwarted by Eusi Kwayana, an African leader and ally of Jagan, who successfully defended Jagan against the no-confidence motion brought by Burnham's supporters.[3]

The party, therefore, entered the 1953 election as a coalition united mostly in its desire to win. Kwayana and Martin Carter proposed that instead of trying to gain a majority in the National Assembly, the party should aim to win just enough seats to give it a strong voice. The reasoning was that such an outcome would have given the party more time to strengthen the fragile multiethnic unity before eventually taking office. But the proposal was rejected by the executive including Burnham and Jagan. Kwayana and Carter were influenced not only by the ethnic division in the leadership but also by what was happening among the rank and file of the party. While most Indian supporters were satisfied with Jagan as the top leader, they had begun to express concern over the number of African candidates on the PPP's electoral slate, particularly those who were contesting predominantly Indian constituencies. African supporters were, on the other hand, unsatisfied that the maximum leader was not of their ethnic group.[4]

These attitudes were fueled in part by ethnic appeals mainly from parties and interests opposed to the PPP. Some Indian-centric parties in collusion with the British Guiana East Indian Association (BGEIA) accused Jagan of sacrificing Indian interests in his pursuit of socialism and unity with Africans. On the African side an African party, the National Democratic Party (NDP), with close links to the Africanist League of Colored People (LCP) argued that Burnham and other African PPP leaders were being manipulated by the Indian leadership, which sought Indian domination.[5]

The PPP, however, overcame these criticisms and not unexpectedly won the election with an overwhelming majority of the contested seats. The victory was understandably hailed as a triumph of class over ethnicity. But the euphoria was marred by another crisis over the position of maximum leader. As political leader of the party, it was thought that Jagan would become Head of Government. But Burnham had other ideas. He demanded the position of leader and refused to cooperate in appointing the cabinet. Some members attempted to break the deadlock by proposing Kwayana as the compromise leader. While Burnham expressed support for Kwayana's candidacy Jagan was noncommittal. Kwayana, however, declined the position and supported Jagan partly because he felt that Jagan had done nothing to warrant his ouster and partly because he did not want to be seen to be part of an African cabal that ousted the Indian leader.[6] Jagan eventually prevailed but the ethnic coalition was severely weakened.

The leadership crisis reflected the underlying ethnic tensions in the party and the society at large. Although the ethnic groups were united in the same party, both groups wanted its leader to be the maximum leader. The PPP's embrace of class politics based on multi-ethnic solidarity was both its strength and weakness. While it was correct in stressing the need for working class solidarity, it was mistaken in believing that class solidarity would be easily translated into ethnic unity. Its failure to directly address the ethnic question both at the level of the leadership and among the rank and file turned out to be a grave error. Further, the electoral success convinced the leadership that ethnic unity among the population was stronger than it actually was. They either did not realize or ignored the strong possibility that the results was less a reflection of ethnic cohesiveness and more a case of the two ethnic communities tying their separate interests to the party's victory-- both groups wanted independence and saw the PPP as the most potent vehicle for achieving that outcome.

The party's tenure in office was short lived. After a mere 133 days the British, at the urging of the US government, sent troops into the colony, deposed the elected government and suspended the constitution. In the context of the Cold War, the intervention was explained as an action aimed at putting down a communist conspiracy. The effect on the PPP was two-fold. First, the party was demobilized as several party leaders were detained while others were confined to their communities. Second, it created the context for the subsequent split in 1955.

The PPP Split and the Consolidation

A third challenge to Jagan's leadership occurred at the 1955 party congress, the first since the suspension of the constitution. Taking advantage of the fact that the congress was held in Georgetown where African Guyanese were the majority group, the Burnham faction packed the hall with its supporters. Sensing that it was being outmaneuvered the Jagan faction walked out, which effectively marked the end of the original PPP.[7] The ethnic nature of the split was not immediately obvious as most of the leading Africans stayed with the Jagan faction and two prominent Indians left with Burnham. While both maximum leaders publicly described the breach in ideological terms, they soon embraced ethnic mobilization as both tactic and strategy. Ironically it was a Jagan-Kwayana feud in 1956-57 that would elevate the ethnic consequences of the 1955 split and push the PPP and later the PNC into becoming full-fledged ethnic parties.

After attempts at reconciliation failed, the Jagan faction embarked on a strategy to woo hitherto hostile Indian support, particularly the Indian commercial and professional classes. This new attitude by the Jaganites was captured in Dr. Jagan's 1956 congress address in which he went to great lengths to portray these classes as patriotic. He, however, portrayed their African counterparts in unflattering terms. The address also tacitly endorsed a view among the Indian rank and file that the African leaders had not made much sacrifice during the period after the suspension of the constitution.[8] This accusation was unsubstantiated as African leaders were among those jailed upon the arrival of the British troops. Burnham was not detained largely due to a party directive which advised against further detentions; this directive was flouted by Dr. Jagan who broke the ban on his movements and was imprisoned.

Dr. Jagan also blamed the largely African "ultra left" of the PPP for the suspension of the constitution and made a strong case against Guyana's membership of the imminent West Indies Federation, a federation of the various Anglophone Caribbean colonies, partly on the grounds that Indians felt they would be a minority in such a federation. This caused Kwayana, who was thought by Dr. Jagan to be loyal to the ultra left, to declare that Dr. Jagan had lost confidence in the African executives of the party. He replied to Dr. Jagan by highlighting what he thought to be inaccuracies and inconsistencies in the address. But, most of all, he exposed the ethnic undertones and overtones. This exchange was followed by the exit of most of the African leaders from the party, leaving it solely in the hands of a mostly Indian leadership. By this time some prominent Indian businessmen, religious leaders and professionals had become part of the leadership.

Kwayana had delayed his departure because he did not want to exacerbate the ethnic problem. He had a strong following among rural Africans who looked to him for guidance; thus they did not immediately join the Burnhamite faction. He had also turned down Dr. Jagan's offer of the chairmanship of the Jaganite PPP, which would have made him the defacto deputy leader of the party. He also refused to be a candidate on the party's slate at the 1957 election and instead ran as an independent.[9] While the Jaganites fielded an Indian candidate, Balram Singh Rai, a recent recruit to the party, against him the PNC did not contest the seat, thus giving him its tact support. Rai narrowly won the contest, which turned out to be a dress rehearsal for the ethnic voting pattern that has since characterized the country's elections.

The Jaganite PPP won a majority of the seats at the election, a victory that proved to be the beginning of one of the most tumultuous period in the country's politics. The election was followed by two major developments. First, there was a closing of ranks on the African side. The conservative United Democratic Party (UDP) merged with the Burnhamite PPP to form the People's National Congress (PNC). This African consolidation was completed when Kwayana joined the PNC and became its General Secretary. As was the case with the Jaganite PPP, the early PNC came into being as an ethnic alliance that transcended ideology and class.

This ethnic consolidation was also manifested at the non-party level. Ethnic interest groups emerged in both communities. One such group was the African Society for Racial Equality (ASRE) whose leadership included Kwayana. While he had taken an interest in ethnic issues, Kwayana had not joined any of the African centered organizations up till the formation of ASRE. His movement towards an ethnic-centered politics has been described as an abandonment of his earlier Marxist and multi-ethnic orientation. However, such a reading is not consistent with his political actions. First, while he embraced Black Nationalism, his was a working class nationalism. Second, although he emphasized Black cultural empowerment, he eschewed Black superiority and saw ethnic unity as the ultimate solution to the country's problems. His embrace of the African cause was driven by what he perceived as a blanket Indian solidarity around the PPP. With the imminence of independence, he and others in ASRE felt that Africans were threatened with ethnic disenfranchisement. They also felt that while the PNC provided political representation and hope it did not engage the cultural question. ASRE, therefore, was primarily an organization concerned with both cultural empowerment and, as its name suggested, political equality.[10]

On the political front, ASRE proposed a joint-premiership of the leaders of the two major ethnic groups. It argued that since neither group was prepared to accept the leadership of the other, this was a just solution with partition as a last resort. The proposal was rejected by both the PPP and the PNC and Kwayana was accused of racism. The "partition as a last resort" aspect was treated as the proposal's "first resort." When the PNC leader pledged support for independence under a PPP government, Kwayana withdrew as a candidate for the party at the 1961 election and was later expelled for advocating racialism.

Kwayana's and ASRE's concerns arose in part from the growing restlessness among African Guyanese. The PPP's 1957-61 stewardship of the political economy had engendered a growing insecurity among them. Given their minority status, they not only felt the possibility of being shut out from government, but they also began to feel marginalized from the economic sector. Kwayana's stance, therefore, gave voice to this concern and in turn launched what would become a new movement in the African-Guyanese community. On the Indian side, the fact that the Indian party held political power and was perceived to be protecting and promoting Indian interests meant that Indian insecurity was less of a problem. In fact, there were signs of Indian triumphalism, which was first exhibited after the PPP's victory at the 1961 election. Although the leadership of the PPP utilized the rhetoric of ethnic unity, it did little to frustrate this development.

By rejecting ASRE's power sharing proposal, the PPP and the PNC had tacitly accepted domination as the solution. The 1961 election, therefore, became an ethnic zero-sum exercise. The PPP's predictably won the contest despite an increase in the PNC's share of the popular vote. This resulted from a higher voter turnout among Africans and the PPP loss of most of the African votes it got at the 1957 election. An interesting development was the relatively good showing of a new party, the United Force (UF), which captured the support of the Amerindian and Portuguese communities and some members of the Indian commercial class. The PPP tactically did not contest the Georgetown constituencies; thus allowing its supporters to vote for the UF.

The election results had immediate ethnic consequences. The PPP organized victory marches into the city, which turned ugly as marchers taunted Africans and poked fun at the PNC. This was followed by violent attacks against Africans in majority Indian villages. Kwayana, who had not been active on the national stage following his expulsion from the PNC, recorded these attacks and Dr. Jagan made reference to them in a radio broadcast.[11] But the national media generally reported them as isolated incidents. In 1962 Indians came under attack in Georgetown, which became the epicenter of the conflict. Opposition to the PPP's 1962 budget by the PNC, the UF and the Trade Union Congress (TUC) took the form of street demonstrations, which threatened to dislodge the government. Appeals by the PPP to the British authorities for help went unheeded.

The following year the government's attempt to pass a Labor Relations bill aimed at giving workers the right to be recognized by a union of their choice led to fresh eruption of violence. The opposition charged that the bill gave considerable power to the Minister of Labor. But of equal importance was the perception that it was a maneuver to get the PPP affiliated union, the Guyana Agricultural Workers Union (GAWU), to oust the anti-PPP Man Power Citizens Associations (MPCA) as the official representative of the mainly Indian sugar workers. When the government refused to withdraw the bill, the TUC called a general strike, which was supported by African workers while their Indian counterparts continued to show up for work. The strike, which lasted for eighty days, was accompanied by violent demonstrations that targeted Indian-owned businesses and PPP supporters.

Ethnic violence escalated in 1964 to war proportions. The opposition had convinced the British government to change the electoral system from first- past- the- post to proportional representation, much to the chagrin of the PPP. But the PPP contributed to its defeat on this issue by leaving the final decision entirely up to the Colonial Secretary. With the prospect of power slipping away, the PPP offered to form a coalition government with the PNC. But the PNC, buoyed by the PR victory, declined the offer. The PPP retaliated with a strike in the sugar industry. Attempts by African workers to break the strike resulted in violence, which quickly spread to the rest of the country. For six months the country experienced its worse period of ethnic conflict which resulted in widespread loss of life and property. The outcome was a de facto partitioned country as many people were forced to flee their homes for communities in which their group was in the majority.

The PNC's rise to Power and Indian disenfranchisement

The PNC's rise to power had immediate ethnic consequences. As was the case with African Guyanese during the tenure of the PPP, Indian Guyanese political instincts and actions were greatly influenced by the perception of disenfranchisement. The PPP's slogan, "Cheated, Not Defeated" reflected the feelings of the wider Indian community. The defeat of the PPP, therefore, served to further deepen Indian solidarity as several protest activities between 1964 and 1970 were widely and actively supported by the Indian community. In addition to the feeling of disenfranchisement, there was also fear of marginalization in the economic sector, which were somewhat justified as the new government sought to neutralize Indian control of the rice industry while facilitating more African involvement in the agricultural sector.

On the electoral front the PNC confirmed Indian suspicions by wresting control of the electoral machinery, a development that was crucial to the PNC's victory at the next election. The electoral changes, which provided the basis for the widespread malpractices that characterized the election, included the expansion of proxy voting, introduction of overseas voting and placing the Minister of Home Affairs in charge of the elections. The government also launched an expansion of the coercive arms of the state, which eventually transformed Guyana into the most militarized country in the Anglophone Caribbean. This expansion of the military and police had direct ethnic consequences. First, it became a major source of employment for Africans, especially the youth who were more willing than their Indian counterparts to join the forces. Second, in confrontations between the government and opposition the African dominated military was used against the largely Indian opposition.

With the PNC's rise to power the perception of African disenfranchisement dissipated. The government was fully in the control of African elites in the PNC. But the traditional African middle class, though supportive of the PNC government, gradually found itself at odds with the party which had begun to show authoritarian tendencies. Many of the former UDP leaders were either marginalized from the center of power within the party and government or sent overseas as ambassadors. This vacuum was filled with a new cadre of PNC activists whose positions were premised on their loyalty to Mr. Burnham. While he was able to neutralize the middle class leadership, Mr. Burnham was not as successful with Kwayana and ASCRIA. Attempts to appoint him as United Nations ambassador and to the cabinet were rebuffed by Kwayana who was able to influence government policy from outside of the formal structures of the party. But, more importantly, he influenced the party's ideological direction on both the ethnic and ideological fronts, ASCRIA, whose membership overlapped with the PNC's, pushed the PNC to the left and influenced its attentiveness to African empowerment.

The advent of the WPA

ASCRIA, however, fell out with the PNC in 1971 mainly on the issue of corruption in government, a development that had a defining impact on ethnic relations and ethnic politics in the country. The PNC was robbed of the cover ASCRIA provided on two fronts. ASCRIA's promotion of African culture in the community meant that the PNC did not have to be overtly Black Nationalist, thus allowing it to project itself as a national party. ASCRIA also provided class cover for the PNC inside the Black community where the party was seen as a political defense against Indian political hegemony but not as a champion of the African poor.

With Kwayana's departure from the fold the PNC became more overtly African as it competed with ASRCRIA for the loyalty of the African working class. Kwayana took with him some of the radical Black Nationalists whose ideological outlook was shaped by a combination of working class politics and Black cultural nationalism. The significance of this would be felt when this constituency became one of the initial bases of the Working People's Alliance (WPA). Kwayana's break with the PNC also ignited a new anti-government movement that, for the first time since the PNC came to power, cut across ethnic lines. ASCRIA's first action after the rupture was to initiate joint activities with a pan-Indian group led by PPP dissident, Moses Bhagwan, the Indian People's Revolutionary Associates (IPRA). These activities proved to be the building blocks of the multi-ethnic WPA and the wider multi-ethnic pro-democracy movement which emerged in the latter half of the 1970s.

Since the PPP drew its support mainly from the East Indian section of the population, its opposition to the PNC government was represented by the latter, and sometimes interpreted by the African masses, as ethnically motivated. Further, the Africans' participation in anti-government protests that included the PPP was viewed by the government as betrayal. This, therefore, hampered the development of a multiethnic resistance movement until the appearance of the WPA in 1974. Its platform of multi-ethnicity struck a chord among a population that had begun to show frustration with the politics of ethnic division and the rise of dictatorial rule. The WPA begun as an alliance of pressure groups consisting of ASCRIA, IPRA, RATOON, a university-based group led by Clive Thomas and Joshua Ramsammy and the Working People's Vanguard Party (WPVP) led by Brindley Benn, a former PPP chairman. It also attracted activists of the Movement against Oppression (MAO), an urban-based grassroots organization, a group of young University of Guyana students and individuals such as Rupert Roopnarine and Andaiye.

The birth of the WPA introduced a new chapter in ethnic relations and ethnic politics in Guyana. While ethnicity did not disappear, it was channeled into joint action by the two groups and this in turn opened up possibilities for a political solution. The central figure of this movement was Walter Rodney, an African Guyanese scholar who had developed an international reputation as a Marxist, Black Nationalist and Pan-Africanist. His message of multi-ethnic action based on working class solidarity struck a chord with sections of the African community already socialized by ASCRIA and among Indians frustrated with the PPP's lack of militancy.

While the WPA's thrust was similar to that of the PPP of the early 1950s, it differed in four significant ways. First, unlike the PPP, the WPA spent more time organizing in the two communities as it did not have the challenge of competing for office. Second, although the WPA stressed a class based message, it openly discussed ethnicity and race. Third, the WPA was not distracted by leadership problems; it adopted a joint leadership model whereby there was not a single leader even as Rodney emerged as the most forceful voice of the party. Finally, unlike the PPP, the WPA sought to build alliances with other parties and organizations in pursuit of a broad anti-dictatorial alliance. The growing popularity of the WPA put the PPP and the PNC on the defensive as the message of multi-ethnic solidarity threatened to undermine the overt and covert ethnic mobilization of both parties. The PNC fought back by projecting the WPA as a tool in an Indian bid to seize power from Africans while the PPP sought to portray it as an African party. The PPP protected its constituency from WPA's influence by suggesting that since the PPP was already organizing in the Indian community the WPA should concentrate on mobilizing the African community.

Soon Indians and Africans were jointly protesting the economic policies of the government and its human rights abuses. In 1977, for instance, African workers gave material and moral support to Indian sugar workers who went on strike for better wages. The strike, which threatened to shatter the growing ethnic solidarity, was partly motivated by the PPP's hurt over the PNC's rejection of its proposal for a power sharing arrangement between the two parties. However, the union, GAWU, officially called the strike over the sharing of profits accrued by the sugar industry. The PNC's message to the African community was that Indians wanted a disproportionate share of the nation's revenues. When ethnic tensions flared over the use of Africans as scabs it took the WPA's intervention, especially in the African community, to prevent the situation from exploding.[12]

Similarly, the trial of an Indian PPP activist for the murder of an African policeman was a source of ethnic tension. This shooting occurred against the backdrop of the Indian opposition to toll stations along the main highway on the Correntyne, a part of the country populated mainly by Indians. The government removed the trial from Correntyne to Georgetown on the grounds that it could not get an impartial jury in that part of the country. The Indian response was understandably hostile as it feared that a mostly African jury would convict Rampersaud. The politicization of the trial along ethnic lines by both sides of the political divide prompted the WPA to intervene. WPA leaders particularly Rodney, Kwayana and Bhagwan were in the forefront of the Arnold Rampersaud Defense Committee, which mounted a national and international campaign to draw attention to the case. Kwayana and Rodney spent a lot of time in the African communities explaining the dangers of cooperating with the government on this issue. Rodney described the situation as an affront to the dignity of Africans.[13] Rampersaud was eventually acquitted of the charges.

Earlier, the 1973 election turned out to be an ethnic flashpoint as elections usually are in Guyana. The PNC had announced its intention to seek a two-thirds majority, which required substantial crossover votes from the Indian community. Given the ethnic polarization of the country, this was almost impossible. The PPP and its Indian constituency understandably interpreted this to mean that the PNC planned to massively rig the elections. Their fears were realized on Election Day when the army hijacked the ballot boxes and transported them to its headquarters. When PPP activists on the Correntyne attempted to prevent the boxes from being removed, three of them were fatally shot by the soldiers. The PNC declared itself the winner with the predicted two-thirds majority, including "victories" in several PPP strongholds. The electoral fraud and the murder of the "Ballot Box Martyrs" infuriated the Indian community. The PPP retaliated with a civil disobedience and non-corporation campaign, including marches, strikes and sabotage of the economy in sectors dominated by Indians. The party also refused to return to parliament. Meanwhile the government's decision to introduce mandatory national service for university students was also opposed by the PPP; there was fear that Indian female students would be at risk at the camps, which were located in remote parts of the country.

The WPA and the PPP developed an alliance and joint protests by Indians and Africans became a regular feature of the politics of the period. This development was enhanced by the addition to the opposition movement of four dissident trade unions, The Four Unions, which openly opposed government policies, along with sections of the religious community, notably the leadership of the Roman Catholic and Anglican churches, and a group of right of center parties called the Vanguard for Liberation and Democracy (VLD).[14] Although this period was characterized by unity and coordinated protests, there were also instances of disunity within the opposition movement. These occurred whenever the issues of ideology and ethnicity either directly or indirectly entered the equation. Ideology tended to be the more direct of the two, as the PPP felt that there was a socialist element in the PNC that should be accommodated and that the real problem was imperialism. This view was counter to that of the WPA, which labeled the PNC pseudo-socialist and saw it as the principal source of the problems in the country. Ethnicity tended to manifest itself in a less direct manner--as an Indian-dominated party, the PPP was hostile to other groups seeking influence in the East Indian community, which created underlying tensions between itself and the WPA.

The first serious challenge to the PNC regime came in 1979 when the WPA, led by Walter Rodney, succeeded in bringing thousands of people on to the streets in what is popularly referred to as a Civil Rebellion. Rodney, who had remained in Guyana despite being denied a job at the University of Guyana, had emerged as the leading opposition figure. His message of multiethnic class solidarity, self-emancipation, and people's power had captured the imagination of the masses on both sides of the ethnic divide. In addition, he was able to expose the regime and its leaders and in the process removed the awe and fear that surrounded them. Untainted by the politics of the past and possessing a rare gift of being able to transmit complex ideas in simple terms, Rodney became the perfect voice for the WPA's thrust of a new politics. Unlike other leftist Caribbean groups, the WPA was not doctrinaire or pro-Moscow. It, for example, rejected the PPP's ideological litmus test for participation in the anti-dictatorial movement. Instead it advocated a broad multi-class and multi-ethnic alliance both for the struggle against the government and for a government to replace the PNC regime. Between 1974 and the beginning of 1979, the WPA had been engaged in popular education through public rallies, small bottom house meetings and its publication, *Dayclean*. Rodney, Clive Thomas, and Eusi Kwayana had also been engaged in teaching formal classes in labor economics and political economy to workers and the youth in Linden and Georgetown.

Several WPA leaders were arrested in July after the PNC's headquarters, which was merged with the Ministry of National Mobilization, was burned down. Three WPA members--Rodney, Roopnarine and Omowale-- were eventually charged with arson. Consequently, the WPA, which became a political party on July 27, 1979, held rallies across the country that attracted large crowds. The Four Unions supported the rebellion by staging a successful strike in August. But the government hit back by firing striking workers and harassing anyone suspected of being members and supporters of the WPA. Assassination and imprisonment also became part of the government's response. In July 1979, Catholic priest, Father Bernard Drake, was murdered by members of the House of Israel, a religious group that provided thugs for the PNC, as he photographed a WPA demonstration. In November 1979 and February 1980, two WPA members Ohene Koama and Edward Dublin were murdered by the Death Squad, an arm of the police force. Finally on June 13, 1980, Walter Rodney was assassinated when a bomb that was given to him in a walkie-talkie by an ex-army officer who befriended the WPA while working for the PNC exploded.

Rodney's murder was a serious blow to the WPA and the antidictatorial movement. Although the party and the movement continued to vigorously resist the government, Rodney's removal allowed the latter to regain the upper hand. The new constitution was enacted and Burnham became the new Executive President. In December 1980, elections were held which the PNC predictably rigged. These elections also caused a rupture of relations between the PPP, which participated in the polls, and the WPA, which boycotted.

As the economy continued to decline and scarcity of essential food items hit the country, the PNC relied on naked force to stay in power. In this regard, its control of almost eighty percent of the economy and the armed forces was pivotal. This, however, did not deter the opposition, in particular the WPA, which continued to be militant. In 1983, it spearheaded a series of food protests in the bauxite industry and the sugar belt. The WPA influenced the formation of the Sugar and Bauxite Unity Committee (SBUC), a coalition of sugar and bauxite workers, which called weekly strikes in the two industries to protest against a government ban on staple food items. The PPP, stung by the WPA's ability to successfully organize in the Indian community, encouraged its members to ignore the SBUC's strike effort. This led to tensions within the Indian communities where WPA members and supporters were harassed by PPP members. There were similar tensions in the African community, but it was generally between WPA members and the security forces. The PNC charged the WPA with sabotaging the economy and it fired several bauxite workers who had gone on strike.

So confident the opposition forces had become, they were able in 1984 to wrest control of the executive of the Trade Union Congress (TUC) from PNC. Shortly after this opposition victory, the PNC and the PPP began talks on the possibility of forming a joint government, a development that the PPP did not share with its allies in the opposition. When Mr. Burnham died suddenly in August 1985, those talks were discontinued by his successor, Mr. Desmond Hoyte. Burnham's death marked a turning point in the country's politics. Immediately, Hoyte agreed to some nominal changes in the electoral arrangements, even as he kept the rigging machinery in place. In fact, the election that followed in December 1985 was the most massively rigged. The scale of the rigging caused the opposition parties to drop their differences and on the initiative of the WPA they formed the Patriotic Coalition for Democracy (PCD) whose main objective was to agitate for the return to free and fair elections.

Between 1986 and 1992, a gradual breakdown of the authoritarian regime took place. It took persevering opposition both inside and outside of the country, a changed international environment following the end of the Cold War, and changes within the PNC regime, to push the situation to breaking point. Acting under the weight of mass opposition pressure for democratization and the dictates of the new international environment, the PNC regime initiated a transition period characterized by political reforms and economic liberalization. Although the thrust of the political reform was less aggressive than its economic counterpart, it nevertheless spawned a less repressive political order that proved to be conducive to the opposition's crusade for electoral democracy.

While the fundamental tenets of the authoritarian state remained intact, the reforms created a degree of political space for the opposition that was hitherto denied them. For example, opposition parties were able to organize and agitate without overt government sabotage; harassment of opposition leaders markedly decreased; and for the fist time during its tenure, the PNC granted a license for an independent newspaper. The latter was significant as the political opposition and Civil Society now had an independent medium through which to air their views.

After much campaigning and lobbying, both locally and internationally, the opposition, with the Carter Center, led by former US president Jimmy Carter, acting as mediator, was able to negotiate an agreement with the PNC for free and fair elections. Understandably this development did not sit well with the hardliners in the PNC who viewed free and fair elections as a sure recipe for the party's removal from office. Ferguson (1995:216) observes that once President Desmond Hoyte had agreed to free and fair elections, the hardliners were "traumatized" and "puzzled by its underlying political calculations." The electoral reforms included the appointment of a new Elections Commission headed by an independent chairman, provisions for the counting of the ballot at the place of polling and the admission of international observers to monitor the election.

But Hoyte, mindful of the changed global dispensation, in particular the changed stance of the US government, which had frozen all US aid to Guyana until electoral democracy was restored, and convinced that his economic liberalization program had set him apart from the repressive Burnham years, pressed on with the reforms. In fact, his decision to agree to all the demands of the opposition parties was taken above the head of the party. According to Ferguson (1995:216), "It is evident that Hoyte wished to marginalize the party in this area of decision making because he was not sanguine about his chances of getting support within Party councils."

Return to Overt Conflict

Despite attempts by the PNC to fan the flames of ethnicity, the multiethnic movement held together throughout the 1980s. The outcome was a decade devoid of any major ethnic conflicts. However, the return of free and fair elections in 1992 ignited a return of ethnic insecurities. Since fraudulent elections were the basis upon which the authoritarian regime rested, many observers felt free and fair elections would create the democratic opening for the country to restore itself to the family of democratic nations. But, given their minority status, Africans dreaded such an eventuality while Indians saw the opportunity to recapture control of the state. To diffuse the situation, the PCD parties attempted to field a single slate of candidates. However, this did not materialize as the WPA and the PPP could not agree on a consensus presidential candidate. The PPP insisted on its leader as the candidate while the WPA argued that the position should be filed by a neutral person. It objected to Dr. Jagan's candidacy on the grounds that his role in the ethnic politics of the past disqualified him from being a consensus candidate.

Apart from the PPP, PNC, and WPA, eight other parties contested the elections. New interest groups also emerged. These included the Elections Affairs Bureau (EAB), an elections watchdog group, and the Guyanese Union for Action and the Restoration of Democracy (GUARD), which had strong ties to the church and private sector. The election promised to be interesting from an ethnic standpoint, as for the first time in forty years a non-ethnic party was contesting a free election in Guyana. Given the unpopularity of the PNC, the PPP felt confident of winning. At the level of the masses, some sections of the Indian community had begun to express the view that since the Africans had held power for almost three decades, it was time for them to "get a chance". The PPP did not officially support this position, but one of its major campaign themes was the discrimination Indians suffered at the hands of the Black PNC government. The WPA reminded the nation of the consequences of the conflicts of the 1960s. One popular WPA slogan was "When the WPA wins, all races win." The party ran a strictly non-ethnic campaign, and sought to appeal to the need for ethnic unity as the prerequisite for national development. While not thought to win the most votes, observers expected the WPA to get enough votes to deny either major party a clear majority.

However, contrary to popular expectations, the electorate voted overwhelmingly for the two ethnic-based parties. The PPP got 52 percent of the votes and the PNC 44 percent. The WPA got a mere two percent. On Election Day, riots broke out in Georgetown when it became obvious that the PPP would emerge the winner. The rioting continued for four days and only stopped when the PNC leader conceded the election. Dr. Jagan was sworn in as President in a tense atmosphere that threatened to erupt any minute. The African community was split over the transfer of power. Some felt that the PNC leader should not have agreed to free and fair elections. This group followed the lead of the PNC's deputy leader, Hamilton Greene, who was eventually expelled from the party. Others blamed the defeat on the unreliability of the Indian community, which had benefited from Mr. Hoyte's free market economic policies.

Upon taking office, the PPP immediately embarked on a campaign that inflamed ethnic tensions. It initiated a program of witch hunting against top civil servants suspected of PNC sympathies. It also sought to shift the emphasis away from the activities around the country's annual carnival. The PPP argued that the celebrations did not reflect the sentiments of Indians and were more geared towards the birthday of the PNC's founder-leader. These moves reunited the African Guyanese who by the time of the next election closed ranks around the PNC.

Dr. Jagan's sudden death in March 1997 set in train a series of events that culminated in a prolonged period of ethnic violence. Fist, the PPP used Dr. Jagan's funeral as a demonstration of Indian strength. It in effect used the period of mourning to launch its election campaign. The procession began in Georgetown and ended at Dr. Jagan's birthplace more than one hundred miles away. Along the way there were scheduled stops in selected Indian communities but none in African communities. Second, the party nominated Dr. Jagan's wife, Janet Jagan, as its presidential candidate for the election. Ms. Jagan was long perceived by Africans as the most polarizing figure in the PPP's leadership. The fact that she was a naturalized Guyanese who was also white added fuel to the fire. The PNC immediately let it be known that it did not view her candidacy in positive terms. Ms. Jagan further inflamed the situation by announcing that she was asked by Dr. Jagan to assume the position and that if the PPP won the election and she became incapacitated her successor would be an Indian member of the PPP and not be the African Prime Minister.

The PNC's only hope of unseating the PPP lay in its ability to win a section of the Indian vote. Towards this end, the PNC established a REFORM wing, which included some prominent Indians. The election was held against the backdrop of a simmering ethnic situation. The opposition raised the usual questions regarding the voters' list and there was even a suggestion that the elections be postponed. A week-long delay in announcing the results in many

African communities proved to be fatal. But a decision by the chairman of the Elections Commission to swear in Ms. Jagan as president based on inconclusive results was the actual trigger. The PNC secured a restraining order from the courts but when it was served on Ms. Jagan at the swearing in ceremony she contemptuously threw it over her shoulders.[15]

The PNC leader vowed to make the country ungovernable and the party responded with daily marches and demonstrations in Georgetown, which eventually deteriorated into open attacks on Indians and Indian-owned property. Sensing that the situation was out of control, the PPP requested the assistance of the Caribbean Community and Common Market (CARICOM), which dispatched a team of mediators.[16] The two parties signed a ceasefire in the form of an accord-- The Herdmonston Accord-- which included the cessation of demonstrations by the PNC and its return to parliament in exchange for the PPP cutting its term in office by two years. It also mandated a forensic audit of the electoral results, the initiation of constitutional reform and dialogue between the two parties.

Some in the African community were angry with the PNC leader for not extracting more concessions from the PPP. The PPP, for its part, had great difficulty keeping its supporters from retaliating. They were severely criticized by a new Indian Rights party, Rise Organize and Rebuild (ROAR), for not being able to protect Indians.[17] Some prominent Indians released a report that documented the physical attacks on Indians by Africans. The general thrust of the report was that Africans had more often than not been the aggressors in the conflict between the two groups. The report, particularly a presentation by ROAR's leader, Ravi Dev, prompted a response from Eusi Kwayana who chided the authors for a biased presentation. He argued that since both ethnic groups were guilty of excesses it was unfair to label one the guilty party.[18]

Fresh demonstrations erupted six months after the signing of the Herdmonston Accord. Both parties charged the other with lack of cooperation. Eventually the two leaders met in St. Lucia where they signed an agreement, the St Lucia Accord, which reaffirmed their commitment to implementing the measures in the Herdmonston Accord. However, the hostility between the two parties persisted for the remainder of the PPP's term. Ms Jagan, who was the main object of African resentment, eventually stepped down from office in 1999 which the PNC perceived as a partial victory. Its African constituency was uncomfortable with a foreign-born white person as the head of state and government. This is a complex issue that has not been properly analyzed. After living in Guyana and being a major player on the political stage for almost six decades, it was unfair to portray her as an outsider. But on the other hand, her unabashed partisan positions on one side of the ethnic divide meant that she was viewed with contempt by many Africans. Further, for a community, which had for centuries endured the ignominy of white domination, the image of a white person as the face of perceived Indian domination was unacceptable. Hence Ms. Jagan's presidency embodied in the African mind a convergence of historical white domination and contemporary Indian domination.

The dialogue arising out of the Herdmonston Accord and supervised by a facilitator appointed by CARICOM never really got off the ground as the PPP insisted that it could not treat the PNC as an equal. The constitutional reform process was a bit more successful despite bitter wrangling between the two parties. The presence of smaller parties, in particular the WPA, was crucial in this regard.[19] As the constitutional reform process progressed, public service workers began to protest for higher wages. This industrial conflict quickly became part of the ethno-political conflict, as the public servants were mainly African Guyanese and supporters of the PNC. After a series of street demonstrations the government eventually set up a tribunal to arbitrate the matter.

As the deadline for the completion of the constitutional reform approached, the political temperature rose once again. When it became clear that the reform process would not be completed in time for the election, the question arose over whether the government should continue in office. The PPP insisted that it should stay in office but the PNC disagreed. The WPA then proposed a compromise in the form of an interim government made up of all the parliamentary parties that would remain in office for the two years that the PPP had given up. The proposal was rejected by the PPP, which accused the WPA of wanting to get into power through the backdoor. Though the PNC did not reject the proposal, it did not support it. To compound matters the court finally ruled on an election petition brought by the PNC; it found that the 1997 election was null and void because the use of identification cards was unconstitutional. This was a moral victory for the PNC. The PPP also claimed victory since the ruling did not uphold the claim of electoral fraud. It was in this atmosphere that the country went to the poll in March 2001.

Like previous elections the 2001 election was fiercely contested with each party appealing to its ethnic constituency. When the results were announced, not unexpectedly, the PPP was declared the winner. As was the case in 1997, this outcome led to demonstrations by the PNC. Unlike in 1997, however, the 2001 demonstrations were centered in Buxton, a PNC stronghold on the East Coast of Demerara. The village, which for a long time had been a center of WPA support, had voted overwhelmingly for the PNC since 1992. The demonstrations were initially supported by most village leaders but when PNC activists from outside of the village took over some withdrew. The peaceful demonstrations quickly became violent with demonstrators attacking Indians and damaging the highways. The situation reached a point where the leaders of the two parties decided to have a historic meeting, thus beginning a second round of dialogue. They came up with a menu of issues that needed immediate resolution and set up bi-partisan committees on each. However the dialogue quickly ran into problems as the government was either slow or refused to implement decisions taken by the leaders and committees.

In February 2002 a group of escaped prisoners encamped in Buxton and declared themselves freedom fighters for the African cause. In what turned out to be the worst period of violence since the 1960s, this group unleashed a reign of terror on nearby Indian communities. Indians were beaten, maimed and killed with impunity. The group also targeted law enforcement officers and villagers suspected of collaborating with the government and the police. The President's request for assistance from the army was initially rebuffed. When the soldiers eventually entered Buxton their presence did little to stop the violence, which also claimed the lives of a government minister and several members of his family.

The Indian business community retaliated with the formation of its own militia or "Phantom Group" comprising ex-police and military personnel. Dead bodies began turning up at various parts of the capital city, Georgetown with alarming frequency. A whistleblower was murdered a few weeks after he revealed that the squad was partly supervised by a government minister. Perhaps the most dramatic act was the murder of an African talk show host who was reportedly linked to the group in Buxton.[20]

Although the PPP and the PNC signed a communiqué and opened another round of dialogue the violence persisted until the next election in August 2006. The PPP was again victorious but there was no post election violence. However, after three months of relative peace, an attack on an Indian village claimed thirteen lives. This was followed by an attack on a police station which claimed another nine lives. Eventually the police captured or killed most of the leading "freedom fighters" while the head of the "phantom squad" was arrested and extradited to the USA where he was wanted for drug smuggling.

Shortly before the election a new party, the Alliance For Change (AFC), was formed by former members of the PPP, PNC and the WPA. Khemraj Ramjattan and Raphael Trotman, former executive members and parliamentarians of the PPP and PNC respectively, teamed up with Shelia Holder, the WPA's lone Member of Parliament, to form the new party. Ramjattan was expelled from the PPP while Trotman and Holder simply left their parties even though they continued to sit in parliament.

The PNC announced its intention to contest the election as part of a "Big Tent" with or without the PNC leader as presidential candidate. In the meantime the other opposition parties-- the WPA, ROAR, GAP-- and some prominent individuals formed a "Third Force," which was quickly disbanded over disagreements on an alliance with the PNC. The PPP, for its part, closed ranks even as some of its supporters expressed anger at the way the government handled the issue of safety. By the time of the election the PNC's "Big Tent" had floundered despite attempts to woo other parties. Except for the WPA none of the other established parties joined the platform. But on the eve of the election the WPA announced that it would not contest as part of a slate headed by PNC leader, Robert Corbin. In the end the PNC contested the election with a mainly PNC slate.[21]

The election led to some new developments. First, the PNC's support was markedly reduced. Second, the AFC, which captured the dissident PNC votes became the first "third" party since 1964 to win more than five percent of the popular votes. Third, despite positioning itself as a multi-ethnic party the AFC's vote came almost entirely from the African Guyanese community. Fourth, the PPP won the election despite its dismal stewardship of the government and its inability to guarantee the security of its constituency. Fifth, the WPA's non-participation in the election brought an end, at least for the time being, to that party's role as a major player on the national stage. Sixth, unlike the two previous elections, the PNC accepted the results and there were no post-election protests and violence. In the final analysis while the AFC could claim some satisfaction from its performance, the big winner was the PPP, which achieved its objective of staging the election despite attempts to derail it.

Having secured its objective, the PPP, as it did when presented with previous openings, pressed ahead with its agenda of dominance. Despite promises of national cooperation the party continued to ignore the opposition. It withdrew government advertisement from the independent newspaper, *Stabroek News*, and suspended the license of a popular television station owned by an opposition politician. Second, in its boldest move, it overlooked perceived anti-PPP military officers and promoted those it felt were less hostile to the PPP. It also confirmed as Commissioner of Police, an officer who many in the opposition felt was too compromised to hold the position. Third, allegations of torture by prisoners point to increase human right abuses. Fourth, the right to assembly also suffered as opposition protestors have been arrested ostensibly for illegal demonstrations. Finally, charges of corruption continued to surface with the auditor general revealing instances where government funds could not be accounted for.

On the opposition side, the PNC was not able to regroup. The main issue has been leadership. Party leader, Robert Corbin, was accused of being weak and uninspiring but he refused to demit office. Under his leadership the REFORM wing of the party peeled away and other so-called moderates also left. The party's 2007 congress saw a much publicized challenge to Corbin from party stalwart, Vincent Alexander but, amidst charges of irregularities, Corbin was returned as leader. The Alexander team walked out of the congress and disciplinary action was later brought against some members. This scenario was repeated at the next congress when Corbin was challenged by the party's Indian Chairman, Winston Murray. Although Murray secured the support of several African leaders he was eventually defeated by Corbin.

The AFC also had its problems. Despite its representation in parliament, the party has not been able to provide much representation or build on the optimism it engendered in the pre-election period. This was partly the result of the limited scope for the opposition in the political system and partly because the party put all its eggs in the formal political process. The AFC also had its internal fallout as one of its executives resigned in the wake of a dispute over who should occupy one of the parliamentary seats.

Conclusion

There are five major conclusions one can draw from the examination of ethnic politics in the post colonial period. First, both ethnic political parties adopted a model of inclusionary domination where the primary objective has been to capture power, defend it at all costs and use it to woo members of the opposite ethnic group. Although there was no ethnic cleansing, the out-group was systematically denied any meaningful participation in the governance of the country. Both major parties were supported by the wider ethnic communities, but the Indian support of the PPP has been more complete than African support for the PNC. Second, the emergence of the multi-ethnic WPA in the 1970s served as an obstacle to intense conflict and influenced the creation of a multi ethnic movement. One may conclude that the opportunity for multi-ethnic solidarity increases in situations where the contending groups are faced with a common threat and there is a multi-ethnic party to capture the moment.

Third, the return of democratic norms reintroduced ethnic conflict as the minority group felt threatened with permanent disenfranchisement and eventual dishonor. The group that retained power after a long period of disenfranchisement closed ranks in defense of its democratic right to govern while the aggrieved group made it difficult for the government to function. Fourth, in these circumstances elections became sites of conflict, which eventually spilled over into the post-election period. Fifth, ceasefires were used by both parties as tactical maneuvers rather than genuine avenues for peace. The governing parties usually resort to business as usual when relative stability returned.

2

Political Mobilization, Political Economy and Political Behavior

The two major ethnic groups in Guyana construct their realities and relationships in racial terms. In other words, although they have all the attributes of ethnic groups—distinct languages, religions, food etc—their relationship or lack thereof is defined by skin color. This is a critical element. African Guyanese, having been socialized in the institution of slavery, which was predicated on the ideology of racial superiority, place heavy emphasis on race or skin color as identity. Like other New World Africans they have given race a new meaning—whereas for white supremacists race has meant white superiority, privilege and power, for Black nationalists it has meant Black pride, dignity, liberation, self-love and empowerment. In effect race for the African Guyanese is an affirmation of Black humanity and rejection of white racism. African Guyanese identity, therefore, is driven by the need for respect and empowerment; hence an ethnicity that is deeply grounded in a larger Black racial identity. It follows, therefore, that they view the Indian reach for political power in terms of racial domination, disrespect and an affront to their honor.

East Indians to a large extent transcended their religious differences as a means of survival in Guyana. Although they maintained much of their religious identities, they have for the most part constructed an equally strong pan-Indian identity. While one may argue that the latter is more political than cultural, the fact is that from the Indian standpoint there is no conflict between the two identities. Differences based on skin color was part of the Hindu caste system, which the indentured laborers brought to the Caribbean. It was, therefore, not difficult for Indian Guyanese to conceive of the dark-skinned African Guyanese in caste or racial terms.

This racial conception by both groups has meant that their conflict has more often than not taken on a racial outlook. Although neither group has enslaved the other and both faced colonial domination, they have, since 1955, behaved as historical enemies. From the African Guyanese standpoint the perception and reality of Indian Guyanese domination have come to represent an extension of European domination. While not overtly advocating racial superiority, many African Guyanese feel that their longer experience of creolization better equips them for leadership. The notion of the Indian Guyanese as "coolie" is very strong in the African Guyanese community. Indian Guyanese, on the other hand, cite their strong religious roots as proof of a more stable cultural order. Many Indian Guyanese look down on African Guyanese as lacking in culture and, therefore, prone to violence and other forms of deviant behavior. In this regard Indians have incorporated some of the white conception of the inferior African.

While these stereotypes are not always overtly expressed they usually surface at moments of intense political competition and conflict. This suggests that they are generally not far below the surface. The defacto partition of Guyana both in terms of physical space and employment has not helped this "otherization" on the part of both groups. They define their successes and failures in relation to the other. In other words, they construct their collective realities based on their differences and then attach social and political meaning to these differences. For African Guyanese, Indian Guyanese are unfit for governance because they are clannish, miserly and would do anything to achieve wealth. It follows that when in government they are more prone to corruption. They are also perceived to be less likely to vote against their ethnic interests even if it means condoning bad governance. Indian Guyanese also perceive African Guyanese as unfit for governance given their propensity for hyper consumption, violence, mismanagement and the use of force to hold onto power.

The struggle between African and Indian Guyanese overshadows almost all other considerations in the public political sphere. Class-consciousness is obscured by ethnic solidarity leading to alliances between the working people and the elites of the two groups. Fear of domination by the other group has informed political decision-making both among the elites and the masses, leading to the promotion of ethnic solidarity as the first line of offence and defense. In other words, the mutual fear of domination is reflected in the choices the groups make both at the community and national levels. There has developed a culture where domination is seen as the best defense against bullying and then it becomes an end in itself. This is a critical aspect of the intra-group convergence of expectations. It is shared and promoted by the respective leaderships of the two parties, thus cementing a political culture that is resentful of co-operation, consensus, and notions of equivalence and shared governance. Kwayana sees this "ethnic insecurity" as a derivative or logical outgrowth of the inter-ethnic dynamic. (Kwayana 1988)

Ethnic Insecurity

While class-based political discourse has historically been an integral part of Guyanese politics it has not been the overriding factor in determining who governs. The consequence has been a primacy of ethnic solidarity whereby the Indian and African Guyanese working classes seek solidarity with their respective middle and ruling classes rather than with the working class of the other race. Ravi Dev (2004:26) observes:

> The competition for the same valued resources [high status jobs] might then explain conflict between the Indian and Africans elites, but cannot do so for the lower strata. Yet the latter have been most enthusiastic in support of their elites, contrary to their supposedly more rational and rewarding class interests, which would have dictated that they act in opposition to the elites' ambitions.

Despite sharp socio-economic differences between the working class African Guyanese and their upper class counterparts, both classes have most of the time been united in their support for the PNC, at least electorally. After the 1955 split, the Burnham faction merged with its former foes in an African middle class party, the United Democratic Party (UDP), to form the PNC. The PNC also attracted Eusi Kwayana, a working class leader and African nationalist, who had remained with the Jagan faction and who was a critic of the PNC's leader. Thus, the PNC came to include Blacks across the class and ideological spectrum. On the PPP side, members of the Indian commercial class and other anti-communist Indians were admitted into the upper ranks of the socialist oriented PPP and some became government ministers. Kwayana zeroes in on the objective reality and causes of ethnic insecurity in Guyana, which he locates in the country's colonial experience which placed the two groups in conditions of rivalry. As he argues:

> Time of arrival, as well as what can be described as social progress, like the village movement, kept them mainly separate, with the exception that minorities of Africans lived in the major estates and later a minority of Indians lived in the new villages. They lived separately but were visible to one another and within earshot of one another. It was to be expected then, that at least after a lapse of time, the action of one group would call forth consideration or response from other groups.

Ravi Dev concurs with the Kwayana thesis; he identifies what he calls the "ethnic security dilemma" as the major problem in Guyana:

> The Ethnic Security Dilemmas are inevitable consequences of the Guyanese demographic factors playing out in the Westminster-based procedural model of democracy. Africans could never capture the Executive and Legislature if they played by the rules of the game and the Indians could be checkmated from governing by the African-dominated incumbents of the state apparatus (Dev 2004:.21).

Indian Guyanese fear and insecurity result from the dilemma that although their party has won all free and fair elections, it has not been able to govern effectively given the African Guyanese control of the armed forces and the Public Service. African protests against

PPP governments have tended to target Indians and Indian-owned businesses; thus increasing Indian fear of physical attacks when the PPP has been in office. Dev (2004:22) puts it this way:

> Even though the latter are a majority under the Westminster system and can form the Executive after "free-and-fair" elections, that Executive cannot guarantee stability, especially for their supporters. Before taking any policy decision, the Indian-supported PPP executive has to always take into consideration, whether the opposition will initiate violence, under cover of their control of State institutions. At the same time their Indian supporters are under an omnipresent fear of being physically wiped out by their African political opponents, whenever the question of national power is contested. This is the Indian Ethnic Security Dilemma.

African Guyanese fear and insecurity spring from the knowledge that given their numerical minority status, their party has not been able to win free and fair elections. While they dominate the armed forces and the public service, given their smaller population size, they cannot in the context of ethnic voting patterns hope to control political power under the winner- take –all system. Since the administrative arm of government also wields legislative power and the power of resource allocation, African Guyanese in both the public service and the armed forces are ultimately at the mercy of the Indian government. The dilemma is completed by the Indian Guyanese dominance of the business sector in which the African presence is peripheral.

It follows that when the African Guyanese dominated PNC held power, Indian Guyanese fear and insecurity increased while the same is true for Africans wherever the Indian dominated PPP has been in power. To illustrate this point, it has been found that there is a relationship between confidence in the political process and which party holds of power. When the PNC governed, Indians expressed little confidence in the status quo. This was reflected in large part by the frequency of industrial actions by the Indian Guyanese workers and outward migration. Premdas (1995:119) captures this when he observes that "where communal malcontents did not strike and demonstrate, many migrated to Europe and North America." But with the return of the PPP to office, the situation has reversed.

While in opposition the PPP was critical of the political process, which it characterized as undemocratic. Most Indians felt the political process was stacked against them and they either migrated or participated in the opposition movement. However, the return of the PPP to power was accompanied by a reverse of this attitude – fifty three percent of Indian Guyanese are satisfied with the political process and forty percent registered dissatisfaction. On the other hand only sixteen percent of African Guyanese expressed any confidence in the process with seventy nine percent expressing dissatisfaction.

On the question of ethnic relations, African Guyanese were less optimistic than their Indian counterparts – 40 percent of Indians expressed optimism compared with 29 percent of Indians. Similarly 39 percent of Africans felt relations would get worse as opposed to 25 percent of Indians. To many observers this is most surprising given the fact that the poll was taken in the midst of ethnic violence, which was generally directed against Indian Guyanese. But it reflects the thesis that political attitudes are driven by the ethnic nature of the government in power. Indian Guyanese were clearly more confident that the PPP government would be able to bring the situation under control.

On a related issue--the vote--more Indian Guyanese (61 percent) attached significance to the relationship between their vote and electoral outcomes. On the other hand 47 percent of African Guyanese believed their vote was important. While 31 percent of Indian Guyanese doubt voting will lead to improvement 41 percent of African Guyanese expressed the same view. These numbers are interesting especially as it relates to Africans. While Indian optimism and African pessimism about the vote is expected the relatively high percentage of optimistic Africans is somewhat surprising. Given the ethnic voting patterns and the awareness that it will take a massive Indian cross over vote for the PPP to be voted out one can only explain African optimism either as a part of a larger national civic engagement or as the product of a consistent PNC propaganda that the previous election was rigged.

Poverty is one of the burning issues in the country regardless of ethnicity. A whopping 43.2 percent of the population lives below the poverty line. While African Guyanese record a higher percentage (43 percent), Indians are not very far behind (34 percent). Yet Indian perception of how much poverty has increased since the PPP came to power in 1992 is significantly different from that among Africans – while 60 percent of Africans feel poverty has increased only 35 percent of Indian share that view.

The ethnic difference is much starker on the issue of available opportunities for improvement of living standards. While 62 percent of Indians detected a positive environment a mere 26 percent of Africans felt the same way. Whether this reflects actual improvement or it is psychological on the part of the two groups, there is clearly a sense of optimism among Indians that is matched by an equal sense of pessimism among Africans. While 46 percent of the population is satisfied with the manner in which the PPP has managed the government, 66 percent of Indians and 18 percent of Africans feel the same. The same trend obtains when it comes to management of the economy. Whereas 38 percent of the population gives the government a rating of "good" or "very good" 57 percent of Indians and 14 percent of Africans answered in the positive. Equally significant is that only 24 percent of Indians gave the PPP a failing grade (poor or very poor) compared to 63 percent of Africans.

One of the major issues in ethically divided societies is the distribution of resources, particularly economic resources such as employment, government contracts and in the case of Guyana, land. In keeping with the ethnic trend, 63 percent of Indians and 18 percent of Africans feel the government has been fair in its distribution politics. Further 63 percent of African Guyanese accused the government of favoring Indian Guyanese compared to 15 percent of Indians who share the same view. Interestingly both ethnic groups argue that the government does not favor Africans—only 2 percent of both groups said that the government actually gives preferences to Africans. This statistic is also revealing in the relatively significant number of Indians (15 percent) who acknowledge the government's bias towards Indians—groups generally do not acknowledge the feeling of being the preferred section of the population. This could mean that, with an Indian government in power, there is a feeling of entitlement among Indians.

The evaluation of the president's handling of the political situation is consistent with attitudes to the government in general. Whereas only 29 percent of Africans gave him a "good" or "very good" grade, 67 percent of Indians said he deserved a passing grade. Conversely 37 percent of Africans assessed him poorly compared with 13 percent of Indians.

A large part of the problem in ethnic societies is that when groups are in opposition they do not trust the state to act in their interests even when some of those state organs are dominated by members of their own ethnic group. Significantly more Indian Guyanese trust the government (69 percent) as opposed to 28 percent of African Guyanese. A similar gap exists on the question of distrust of the government – 57 percent of Africans distrust the government, including 47 percent with "great distrust" while only 22 percent of Indians feels the same way. The same trend holds for the president, with an even higher sense of distrust among Africans. He is distrusted by 29 percent of Indians as opposed to 72 percent of Africans. On the other hand 62 percent of Indians expressed trust in him while 22 percent of Africans distrusted him.

The attitudes to the African Prime Minister makes interesting reading. Not surprisingly 84 percent of Africans distrusts him. That more Africans distrust him than the Indian president points to the betrayal syndrome that kicks in when a member of one ethnic group crosses over to the opposite party. Similarly his higher negative rating among Indians shows that while most Indians accept him as a member of the team, there is some skepticism which can only be attributed to his ethnicity.

The Judiciary in Guyana has always been the subject of controversy. Under the PNC, this branch of government was subordinated to the party as part of the paramountcy doctrine. The courts were used as a tool of persecution and prosecution of opposition activists and for the protection of the government from legal challenges. Given the lack of strict separation of powers, the judicial and legislative branches were open to manipulation by the executive. Indians in particular were suspicious of the courts, which in conjunction with the armed forces were seen as being anti-Indian. With the change in government in 1992, the judiciary has been less overt in its partisan stance but there have been opposition complaints over its ethnic composition. It is not surprising then that more African Guyanese (66 percent) are distrustful of the courts than Indian Guyanese (42 percent). Conversely Indian Guyanese have far more trust in the system (39 percent) than African Guyanese (23 percent).

In regards to the armed forces, Indians also expressed more trust in these institutions. Given the overwhelming African Guyanese dominance of the police force and the army this positive Indian attitude exposes the ethnic bias in favor of the government and state. The fact that the PPP has had great difficulty in securing the cooperation of these forces, one would think that Indians would have less confidence in them. But while Indian Guyanese expressed distrust of the police force is high (66 percent), it is even higher among Africans (80 percent). Similarly more Indian Guyanese (28 percent) expressed distrust in the lawmen then African Guyanese (17 percent). There is less of an ethnic gap in feelings towards the army—31percent of African Guyanese and 30 percent of Indian Guyanese distrust it. The same trend holds for those expressing trust – 56 percent of African Guyanese and 54 percent of Indian Guyanese. The more positive attitude to the army stems from the fact that, unlike during the PNC tenure, it has been less involved in day to day politics. The police have been much more visible particularly in quelling opposition protests. The PNC has complained about the hostile reception it got from the police former PNC leader, Desmond Hoyte, referred to as "kith and kin." This sense of betrayal, therefore, accounts for the high degree of distrust of the police among African Guyanese.. Quite apart from the automatic ethnic support for the status quo the more positive attitude among Indians is also explained by the willingness of the police to at least confront African Guyanese protestors. The more the police stand up to African Guyanese the less Indian Guyanese are distrustful of them.

Not surprisingly more Indian Guyanese (50 percent) than African Guyanese (37 percent) are optimistic that they will experience progress in the country. On the other hand (43 percent) of Indian

Guyanese expressed little or no hope that things will get better while a larger percentage of Africans (59 percent) were pessimistic. Indian Guyanese optimism is obviously predicated on the knowledge that unless there is a coup or massive desertion of the PPP by Indians, the PPP would control the government for a long time. African Guyanese, on the other hand, know that the likelihood of an African-controlled government in the foreseeable future is slimmer.

While the data analyzed here was collected a decade ago, the fact that the political conditions have not been altered, they are still relevant. If there is any change in attitude my sense is that there is likely to be a widening of the ethnic gap. The large lesson here is that the ethnic perception of power and powerlessness play a huge role in the construction of political attitudes. While these perceptions are not always consistent with the real situation, they provide the basis for the actions of the political parties. While the masses receive most of their information and perspectives from their party and other ethnic interest groups, their attitudes in turn inform the behavior of the parties.

Ethnicity, the Economy and the Armed Forces

After almost fifteen years of decline Guyana's economy begun to grow in the early 1990s thanks to an IMF/World Bank Economic Recovery Program instituted under the Desmond Hoyte-led PNC government. Between 1988, when the ERP started, and 1996 the GDP grew approximately 40 percent with an annual growth rate of 7.1 percent. However, by 1998 there was a rapid reversal. From 1998 to 2004, the average growth rate was 0.6 percent while there were moderate improvements from 2006. Like most Caribbean countries, Guyana's economy relies on a few major productive sectors-agriculture, mining, distributive services, forestry and government services. Employment in these sectors reflects the ethnic division in the wider society with Africans dominating the government and mining sectors and Indians dominating the agricultural, forestry distribution and service sectors. The outcome is that growth and decline in the individual sectors has ethnic consequences. Government policies, such as downsizing and diversification also have ethnic consequences. Updated data on the ethnic profile of the economy is scant but a survey carried out in 1992-1993 gave some insight in this regard. Thomas (1997) observed that while the data collected in the survey were important, they did not give an ethnic breakdown of ownership of productive assets or corporate decision making. He also pointed out that the data were inadequate as they gave a quantitative rather than qualitative ethnic profile.

The agricultural sector (sugar and rice), which has been the bedrock of the economy in the post-colonial era is heavily dominated by Indian Guyanese with 32.1 percent of its workforce located there as opposed to 13.1 percent of the African Guyanese workforce. This sector of the economy showed the highest growth between 1988 and 1996 with sugar and rice growing by 65 percent and 154 percent respectively. Fifty percent and 20 percent of the Indian and African workforce respectively are employed in the hunting and forestry and service sectors which grew by 186 percent and 42 percent respectively. By contrast the government sector, which employs approximately 20 percent and 6 percent of the African and Indian Guyanese workforce respectively, recorded zero growth. Of the sectors dominated by African Guyanese, only mining showed positive growth. But this was largely due to the very good performance of one company in the gold industry. The bauxite industry, which traditionally employed the bulk of the African Guyanese workforce has progressively declined over the last decade. Poverty and unemployment are also two areas which showed ethnic disparities. Forty three percent of African Guyanese live below the poverty line as opposed to 34 percent of Indian Guyanese. The national average is 43 percent. There is a similar trend in the area of unemployment. While the national rate is 11.7 percent, among African Guyanese and Indian Guyanese it stands at 13.6 percent and 11.5 percent respectively.[23]

One of the reasons for African insecurity is the perception and reality that Indians have an advantage in the ethnically demarcated economy. Given, the relative stability of the rice and sugar industries, thanks to government subsidies, Indian Guyanese have been able to withstand the economic downturn of the economy slightly better than African Guyanese. On the other hand, the steep decline of the bauxite industry, which has not received the same kind of government support, has had a devastating effect on the bauxite community. The IMF-induced structural adjustment policies in particular the downsizing of government has had a similar effect on African Guyanese. Most of these displaced African Guyanese workers have either migrated to neighboring Caribbean countries, joined the ranks of the unemployed and underemployed or have opted for service jobs such as the security services. While Indian Guyanese have not suffered the same fate as African Guyanese they nevertheless earn similar low incomes. Hence the poverty levels of the two groups are similar. But the seeming stability of the sugar industry leads African Guyanese to perceive their fate as worse than Indian Guyanese.

Perhaps the most compelling reason for this perception is the Indian dominance of the commercial sector. The African marginalization in this sector can be traced back to the immediate post-emancipation period when the colonizers did everything in their power to frustrate African entrepreneurship. Indians, on the other hand, did not have the same kinds of obstacles. Although the African PNC government encouraged some degree of African Guyanese entrepreneurship this did not bear much fruit partly because the government was apprehensive of the emergence of an independent African Guyanese middle class and partly because the limited local space was already monopolized by Indians, Portuguese and Chinese. Attempts by the PNC to contain or undermine the Indian commercial class did not prove successful as Indians shifted their operations to the parallel economy. When the Hoyte government scaled back the state-centered economy in the late 1980s and encouraged private investment, Indians were better able to take advantage of the opportunities. The PPP's continued embrace of the Hoyte policies has meant that this trend continued, with the commercial sector now having easier access to the government.

Similarly, Indian insecurity is predicated largely on the perception and reality of African dominance of the coercive arm of the state, which like the economy tend to reflect the ethnic divide. Despite recommendations by a Commission of Inquiry in 1964 and recruitment efforts by the current PPP government, Indians have not joined these forces in significant numbers. Initially they were frustrated from joining by the physical requirements imposed by the colonial authorities. Although these restrictions were removed, other factors such as the perception of the armed forces as African institutions served to alienate Indians. African Guyanese, on the other hand, gravitated towards the forces out of economic necessity. From as early as the late 1800s when they were marginalized from the commercial sector, Africans moved to the cities and joined the civil service and the armed forces. Further, during the reign of the PNC and the attendant militarization of the society many Africans joined the military both as a means of employment and a form of ethnic control of an important sector of the state.

During the PNC's tenure the military served two major functions. First, it carried out its traditional function as the coercive arm of the state. Second, it served as a form of employment for Africans who comprised almost 90 percent of both the membership and leadership ranks. The implication was that the coercive apparatus of the state, under the control of African Guyanese, functioned as a tool of African ethnic domination. Moreover, in a society that was conditioned to view employment by the state as a favor rather than a right, the Africans in the military carried out the repressive dictates of the government, convinced in part that they were being good public servants.

An important point is that although African Guyanese dominate the army and police force, they have been critical of them especially under PPP governments. In the context of a civilian-led army, the military does not function as an autonomous entity as in Latin America and Africa. Despite rumors of coups over the years, especially under PPP governments, these have not materialized, as the upper echelons of the forces have remained loyal to the government of the day.

The army and police were much more pro-active in crushing opposition protests during the PNC reign than under the PPP governments. They were engaged not only in physical attacks on the opposition but participated in the removal of ballot boxes during elections. Under the PPP government the army refused to move against African opponents of the government who launched paramilitary attacks on known PPP supporters. The police on the other hand have taken some action against opposition protestors under the PPP government, but whenever this has occurred the police ranks have been described by African leaders as "sell outs" and have in some instances been targeted for physical attacks.

A second observation is the PPP's suspicion of the army and police when in power. During its first tenure, 1957-1964, the PPP government complained of non cooperation by the police with the Home Affairs Minister resigning in protest. Since its return to power in 1992, it has had mixed relations with these forces. While the government has attempted to develop close relations with the top brass of both forces, this has not translated into political loyalty. Because the government is forced to choose the leadership from within the ranks, it often has to appoint officers with known sympathies to the PNC. In the end, it has resorted to a divide and rule tactic whereby some senior officers have been overlooked for promotion to top positions.

Ethnicity and Party Affiliation

Despite general support for the PNC, African solidarity around the party has not been as strong as the Indian solidarity around the PPP. This is due largely to the fact that despite a strong ethnic identification the rural working class was initially suspicious of the mainly urban middle class whose members had emerged as the national political and cultural leaders of the group. These middle class leaders who were organized around the Black Nationalist League of Colored Peoples (LCP) had adopted a social democratic political outlook along the lines of the British Labor Party. While they were generally anti-colonial and pro-Black, they did not advocate a fundamental transformation of the colonial order. In that regard they were not as invested in a program of socio-economic change whose objective was to achieve more social equality in the society.

The African Guyanese left, as represented by many of the African Guyanese in the leadership of the early PPP, were more revolutionary in their outlook. In fact Dr. Jagan dubbed them the ultra left of the party. Unlike the middle class, which was organized around the LCP, these leaders were generally Marxists who did not stress their ethnic identification. The unofficial leader of this group was Kwayana who Jagan (1972) called a "Simon pure Marxist." As a leader with rural roots he was more in tune with the needs and aspirations of the working poor than some of his colleagues. By the end of the 1950s he had carved out his own national niche as an independent thinker and activist. He had supported Dr. Jagan in the struggle for the leadership of the PPP but when Jagan moved in an Indian ethnic direction he broke with him. His movement into the PNC was driven less by his agreement with Mr. Burnham and more by the developing ethnic divide.

Burnham, who upon his return to the country was shunned by the traditional middle class mainly because of his association with the PPP, was not a part of the ultra left. Although he had engaged in left wing activism as a student in England he was not an ideologue. His approach to politics was driven by a pragmatism that would more often than not manifest itself as opportunism. He was similarly pragmatic on the ethnic question. He did not overtly identify himself with ethnic nationalism as Jagan and later Kwayana did. If Kwayana and the LCP leaders represented a working class and elite Black nationalism respectively, Burnham represented a more pragmatic nationalism. The LCP's tendency aimed to preserve the central elements of the social order which characterized colonialism while Kwayana championed a change of that order. Burnham's ethnic pragmatism was centered on the achievement of political power as an end in itself while Kwayana's class based ethnic nationalism viewed political power as a means towards the breaking down of social inequality in the African Guyanese community and between the ethnic groups. The Burnham tendency, therefore, was not averse to opportunistically embracing ethnicity and ideology in pursuit of political power.

Burnham had to share leadership of the community with Eusi Kwayana and Walter Rodney in the 1960s and the 1970s. During the 1960s, Kwayana's ASCRIA was both an ally and competitor of the PNC. Although ASCRIA supported the PNC, it remained independent of the party. ASCRIA was urged to contest the 1964 election by some sections of the African community, but partly at the urging of Burnham and partly because of Kwayana's reluctance to split the African vote, it declined to do so. In the late 1960s the ASCRIA branch in the bauxite community, Linden, called several strikes in the industry, some of which were opposed by the PNC. One of those strikes actually brought the two groups in direct confrontation. Relations between the two were finally ruptured in 1971 over the issue of government corruption. But leading members of the PNC were long suspicious of Kwayana's influence and there were even rumors of a planned Kwayana-led coup. While these rumors were unfounded there was no doubt that Kwayana enjoyed as much influence in the community as Burnham.

Even after the 1971 break, ASCRIA in partnership with IPRA, an Indian organization, was able to mount a successful campaign that urged citizens to occupy lands vacated by the sugar companies. Unlike Indian Guyanese leaders who parted with the PPP, when Kwayana broke with the PNC he took some mass support with him, which became the base of the early Working People's Alliance (WPA). Walter Rodney expanded that base when he returned in 1974. By 1979 the WPA, like ASCRIA before it, was an almost equal force to the PNC in the African Guyanese community. This would last until 1992 when with the return of free and fair elections, Africans returned to the PNC fold. In 1994 the Good and Green Guyana (GGG) formed by the expelled PNC deputy leader, Hamilton Green, actually defeated the PNC in municipal elections in Georgetown, a PNC stronghold. Later in 2006, another party led by dissident PNC leader, the Alliance for Change (AFC) gained eight percent of the popular vote, almost all of which came from the African Guyanese community.

This shared loyalty and vote splitting among Africans have not been replicated among Indian Guyanese. East Indians in Guyana have developed an Indian nationalism that transcends religious and ideological differences. Although there are low-level tensions between Muslims and Hindus those have not been an obstacle to Indian political solidarity. This solidarity arose initially out of the need to survive in a new environment and evolved as part of the struggle against disenfranchisement. Further the more Indian Guyanese begun to define themselves in relationship to African Guyanese the more they developed a pan Indian consciousness. The more African Guyanese became the "other," the more Indian Guyanese, regardless of religious difference, became the "same."

A vivid reflection of this strong East Indian solidarity was the embrace of the communist Cheddi Jagan as the undisputed Indian leader. Although Jagan never embraced any of the Indian religions he assumed a god-like standing in the community, which became even more pronounced after his death. The PPP has used the Jagan factor with great effect to ensure continued Indian loyalty. Despite charges of nepotism and corruption Indian support for the PPP has remained steadfast.

Dr. Jagan was never seriously challenged as the ultimate Indian leader. Several dissidents, including some with religious grounding in the community and others with strong Indianist positions, have been rejected by the Indian electorate, which has remained loyal to the PPP. None of the dissident Indian leaders or their parties has made any significant inroads into the PPP's support base. In 1964 two Indian parties, grounded in the two major Indian religions, received negligible electoral support although one leader was a former PPP cabinet member. In the 1980s, Paul Tennasee's Democratic Labor Movement mounted the most spirited challenge to the PPP from a pro-Indian party but it was unable to sustain it beyond 1992. Later in the 1990s the most openly pro-Indian party, ROAR, challenged the PPP on the grounds that it did not protect Indian security. While this message resonated with sections of the community, it did not translate into a mass base or electoral success. Ironically, the greatest challenge to the PPP's influence in the Indian community came from the WPA during the period of authoritarian rule. Many Indians who had become impatient with the PPP's lack of militancy joined or supported the WPA, which had emerged as the most consistent opposition to the regime. However, with the imminent return of free and fair elections, like their African counterparts, they returned to the PPP's fold.

In the pre-1955 period, when the leadership was united under the same banner, the major mobilization strategy was directed towards harnessing the anti-colonial sentiment of the people which cut across ethnicity—a strategy the proved successful at the 1953 election. After the split in the movement in 1955, the mobilization strategy of the two factions reflected to a large extent the ethnic rupture. Though not abandoning the anti-colonial appeal, both parties sought to consolidate their respective bases among the two ethnic groups. As Desperes (1967:221-222) argues:

> By 1958 the East Indian and Afro-Guianese cultural sections appeared to represent the only bases of mass power accessible, respectively to the People's Progressive Party

and the People's National Congress. In order to integrate these cultural sections politically, however, adjustments in organizational strategies were needed. Specifically, particularistic appeals had to be made to the groups contained within each cultural section. Accordingly, the two major political parties devised and implemented plans to achieve this effect.

Both parties adopted the strategy of "Apanjat" -- a Hindi word that means "vote for your kind." A key part of this strategy has been the enlisting of religious and cultural organizations. Initially, the Dharmic Maha Sabba and the United Sad'r Islamic Anjuman, the main Hindu and Muslim associations respectively, were connected to the PPP. The President of the Maha Sabba, Sase Narain, had close ties to the PPP, the Secretary Repu Damam Persaud was a PPP member of Parliament and the Anjuman's president, Yacob Ali, was also a PPP parliamentarian. Desperes found that these officials used their influence in the temples and mosques to steer their followers to the PPP.

According to Desperes, "reverse racialism" was a central component of the PNC's strategy. While not openly calling for an African vote, the PNC mounted a campaign to "inform the African people of how the PPP was practicing Apanjat politics in order to mobilize the Indian community for the purpose of bringing Guyana under communist rule." African Guyanese farmers were told that the PPP planned to settle Indian Guyanese on African Guyanese "ancestral" land. This strategy was successful among the Africans since Indian Guyanese were indeed squatting on lands historically occupied by African Guyanese, and some "African land" was merged into the agricultural development schemes (Desperes1967:261- 262).

Another aspect of the mobilization strategy has been ethnic double-speak, whereby leaders have had two separate messages, one for the nation and another for their supporters. The PPP, for example, insists that it is a national party and projects a multi-ethnic outlook. However, when it speaks directly to the Indian Guyanese constituency it resorts to a message aimed at ethnic solidarity. Similarly, the PNC denies that it is an African party, but to a purely African Guyanese audience it refers to them as "kith and kin." The

PPP and PNC describe other parties attempting to break into their respective bases as "fringe parties" and "small parties," but, when speaking to the faithful, these parties are accused of "splitting the vote" and being agents of the opposite group. The WPA has been a prime victim of this tactic. Though multi-ethnic in membership and ideology, it has been projected to both the Indian and African Guyanese constituencies as an African Guyanese party. The PNC accused the WPA of wanting to seize power for Indian Guyanese, while the PPP, despite its alliance with the WPA during the 1970s and 1980s, branded the WPA an African Guyanese party concerned solely with African Guyanese interests.

Other victims have been the Indian rights party, ROAR, and the country's newest party, the Alliance for Change (AFC), which challenged the two parties in the 2006 elections. After its initial appeal to some sections of the Indian Guyanese community, the PPP labeled ROAR members extremists who were bent on creating racial division in the society. However, when speaking directly to its Indian Guyanese constituency, the PPP accused ROAR of "splitting the vote" and wanting to join the African PNC. This mode of mobilization has had the effect of consolidating ethnic solidarity along party lines and stifling the emergence of a viable multiethnic "Third Party."

Despite their ethnic bases and leaderships, both major parties have historically refuted claims that they are ethnic-based. They have used "ethnic window-dressing"—the device whereby individuals from the opposite group are brought into the party at the leadership level as a means of projecting a multi-ethnic image. Thus it was not uncommon to find Indian government ministers and parliamentarians in successive PNC governments. Prior to assuming office in 1992, the PPP entered into a partnership with a loose group of Indian Guyanese PPP supporters and African Guyanese professionals called CIVIC. The leader of the group, an African Guyanese, was named Prime Minister. But, having assumed the presidency in 1997 when President Cheddi Jagan died in office, he was forced to cede the presidential candidacy to Dr. Jagan's wife at the next general election. Similarly, the PNC formed an alliance on the eve of the 2001 election with a group of PNC supporters and Indian Guyanese professionals called REFORM, thus renaming the party PNC/REFORM. However, contrary to popular expectations the leader of the REFORM was not named as the party's Prime Ministerial candidate. Although neither the CIVIC nor the REFORM has been able to garner any cross over support, the parties have not abandoned the idea.

Ethnic Clientelism

Upon assuming power, the ethnic parties have used state power to channel tangible benefits to their respective groups which generally take the form of top positions in the government and other state sectors. But they also include economic programs that are beneficial to the particular ethnic group. During its 1957-1964 term in office, the PPP implemented extensive programs in the agricultural sector ostensibly to improve the conditions of the working class. However, because Indian Guyanese dominated agriculture, the party was able to steer benefits to its base in the name of national development. In the PPP's 1959 five-year development plan, for example, 52.5 percent of the funds were allocated to agriculture while 3.6 percent was allocated to industrial development -a sector dominated by Africans. Most of the funds allocated to agriculture went towards the extension of the existing rice acreage, an area in which African participation was almost non-existent (Desperes 1967:246).

Similarly, the major plank of the PPP's 1961 election campaign platform was its agricultural thrust of which a land development scheme located in the heart of the PPP's stronghold was central. Of 150 families settled on the site of the project, 147 were Indian Guyanese. While the three African Guyanese families were all PPP members (Desperes 1967:248). Rice farmers, most of whom were Indian Guyanese, benefited from a generous deal the government struck with Cuba. In addition the government undertook extensive drainage and irrigation projects in the rice producing areas.

These developments caused great concern among African Guyanese who felt shut out of power. Those who hitherto had not supported the African Guyanese party now rallied to its call for ethnic solidarity. African Guyanese began to overtly sabotage the government by using their strategic location within the Civil Service to initiate political strikes which continuously crippled the economy. Finally, with the collusion of British-US imperialism and a small capitalist party, the African-dominated PNC rose to power in 1964. The situation was quickly reversed. Under the PNC, African Guyanese dominated the top echelons of the three branches of the government as ethnicity and party affiliation were the criteria for employment in the state sector. The PNC also sought to woo support from PPP cadres with promises of jobs and other prestigious appointments. Many of the PPP's programs were either scrapped or "reformed" and most of the political appointees were relieved of their positions.

The PNC did a better job at ensuring symbolic representation of the opposite group in the top echelons of government. The cabinet was more ethnically diverse than the PPP's even after the PNC took over the reins of government on its own in 1968. For example, the PNC appointed a Muslim to the cabinet, something the PPP had not done during its tenure. The government also introduced public holidays for significant Hindu and Muslim observances. Ironically it did not introduce a similar holiday for African observances. The PNC's actions yielded some results as it lured a small section of the Indian middle class over to its side.

Non Accountability

Ethnic insecurity and competition engender an almost religious faith in the power of the political party as the mechanism through which security is secured and maintained. The party is the symbol of ethnic power and security. While many Guyanese do not actually join the parties, they nevertheless defer to their authority and look to them for their political cues. While, criticism of and resistance to the omnipotence of the party by its supporters are sometimes demonstrated between elections, these are often muted or confined to a small section of the population.

In a country where state institutions are relatively weak, the political party assumes the role of official and unofficial mobilizer and enforcer. In fact the PNC in 1974 introduced the concept of "Paramountcy of the Party" whereby the ruling party was deemed to be paramount to all organs of the state. Although the current PPP government has disavowed this idea in theory, it has, however, governed in much the same manner. One clear example of this is the use of the public media in an openly partisan manner.

As was the case during the PNC's tenure, the state-owned media gives the ruling party and government a disproportionate amount of coverage. For example, during the 1997 election campaign one monitoring agency found a 78, 60 and 88 percent bias in favor of the ruling party by the state-owned radio, television and newspaper respectively (EAB, 1997).

The parties, therefore, have taken their ethnic support for granted. For example, although the PNC has provided weak representation on behalf of African Guyanese since it became the opposition in 1992, they have generally remained loyal to the party. One PNC official revealed to this writer that the PNC had refused to press the government to improve services in African Guyanese communities because it feared the government would take the credit and the party will be robbed of an electoral issue. When asked if the PNC does not fear losing the support of African Guyanese he said, "They have nowhere else to go." (Personal Interview, December 2000). Although the PNC lost some votes at the 2006 election, those went to a party led by an ex-PNC executive member. Even when the PNC supports the policies of the PPP, African Guyanese wrath is targeted only at the PPP. A glaring example of this phenomenon surrounded the issue of relocating a group of mainly African Guyanese vendors from the popular shopping center to a less accessible location. Although the PNC City Councilors supported the move, the vendors concentrated their venom on the PPP-led central government while ignoring the PNC's complicity in their removal.

If the political party enjoys pride of place, the leader is larger than life. He or she is the "Messiah," "Liberator," "The Greatest" and "Comrade Leader." The convergence of the people's expectations of the leader and his perception of their meaning has resulted in the institutionalization of an authoritarian form of leadership that begins at the level of the party and is transferred to the state when the party assumes office. This authoritarian attitude to leadership is endemic in Guyana's elite political culture. Both the PPP and PNC founder-leaders, Dr. Cheddi Jagan and Mr. Forbes Burnham, ruled the parties with iron fists. Both were unchallenged and consequently dictated who gained ascendancy or fell out of favor within the party. Despite rhetoric of collective leadership by both parties the concept of "one-man" leadership or "leaderism" is entrenched. The WPA's concept of collective leadership--rotating leaders and co-leaders--has been ridiculed by both major parties as a quaint concept.

The leaders of the PPP and the PNC function less as "first among equals" and more as generals and commanders-in-chief. This unlimited authority is both formal and informal. The PNC's constitution, for example, gives the leader power over all organs of the party. He has the power to appoint and fire senior officers and to dissolve organs if he so desires. Although the PPP's constitution is less explicit about the unlimited power of the leader, its historical adherence to democratic centralization ensures that the actual power is concentrated at the top. Former PNC leader, Desmond Hoyte, captured the awesome power of the leader when he explained his summary dismissal of a rebellious General Secretary in the following terms: "The General Secretary is the creature of the leader" (Stabroek News: October 15, 1999). Hoyte also engineered the expulsion of his deputy and rival for the top spot from the party despite the latter's popularity both in the party and among its supporters. Although many executives and rank and file members questioned his actions in both instances, very little could be done as the leader had acted well within the powers granted to him by the party's constitution.

The same culture exists in the PPP. In 1997 Mrs. Janet Jagan, widow and successor of Dr. Jagan, demoted a popular cabinet member when the latter rebuked the President's son in the media. Mrs. Jagan was also instrumental in catapulting the present holder of the presidency, Mr. Bharrat Jagdeo, over more senior party members. According to party insiders, Mr. Jagdeo was preferred to the more popular and senior Mr. Moses Nagamootoo because of the leader's dislike of the latter, and the fact that Mr. Jagdeo was her protégé. Mrs. Jagan's power within the party has been the subject of much scrutiny as she is known to be one of those leaders who prefer to wield power behind the scenes. In assessing her leadership role in the party Kissoon (2001) argues:

> She doesn't seek the leadership of her party, but the party knows she owns it, and she is in control, so they know she

must have her decisions implemented...Once you play up to her, you will inherit her kingdom. Everyone who rose through the PPP leadership thinks that she lacks humanism and that she has a motto that either you are for me or you are against me.

The leaders' authoritarianism is buttressed by the sycophantic attitude of the senior party members who routinely defer to the maximum leader, even when they disagree with him [24] or her. A case in point was a June 2000 move by some senior PNC members to get Mr. Hoyte to step down. Mr. Hoyte refused to step aside and contrary to popular expectation, the matter was promptly dropped. Similarly, in 2004 when a senior member of the PPP accused the leader of smearing him, all but one of the executive members sided with the leader. The accuser was eventually expelled while his supporter was ostracized.[25]

Multi Ethnic Parties

The two major ethnic groups construct their realities based on their differences. In the process, class and gender have been subordinated to ethnicity. Insofar as class solidarity has been manifested both groups have used it as a means to secure ethnic ends. The rise of ethnic parties since the 1955 split of the original PPP has made it almost impossible for multi-ethnic parties to survive. The most prominent multi-ethnic party, the WPA, managed to inspire a multi-ethnic movement against the ethnically based authoritarian PNC government. But the return of free and fair elections prompted the collapse of the movement and the subsequent decline of the WPA as a major political force. This confirms Horowitz thesis that in ethnic party systems left wing parties eventually "wither and die" (1989:338).

On of the peculiar characteristics of the Guyana case is the extent to which both parties employ non-ethnic and class-based rhetoric while jealously guarding the ethnic constituencies. Both parties have refused to publicly admit that they are ethnic in composition and appeal and when in power they have denied that there is an ethnic problem. The PPP, given the Indian Guyanese majority, has been more guilty than the PNC on this score; it has played on the more resilient Indian Guyanese solidarity along with their insecurities which was reinforced by almost three decades of PNC authoritarian rule. The PNC, while not always able to count on complete African Guyanese solidarity, has benefited from the PPP's crude manipulation of the democratic process when in power—a motivating factor in the return to the fold of its various break away factions.

Clive Thomas (1993) attributes the partial success of the WPA to what he calls the "universalizing tendency" of political democracy which is a central aspect of the Caribbean political culture. This, according to Thomas, is what motivated the multi-ethnic resistance to PNC's authoritarianism. While I agree with Thomas' thesis, it is worth pointing out that Indian Guyanese objection to the PNC government was also grounded in its ethnic fear of African Guyanese domination. On the other hand, the African Guyanese rejection was more class-based. ASCRIA, through its class-based Black Nationalism, had distinguished itself from the middle class nationalism represented by the PNC. The break between the two organizations in 1971 created a rupture in African Guyanese solidarity, which was exacerbated by Rodney and the WPA and was crucial to the survival of the multi-ethnic movement. Experience in ethnic party systems have shown that while it is difficult to woo support from ethnic parties it is much more difficult to woo the supporters of the governing party.

The current situation bears this out. Although the PPP's performance in office since 1992 has been dismal and its misuse of state power has not been significantly different from its predecessor, its Indian Guyanese supporters have shown little sign of deserting the party. While some Indian Guyanese joined the WPA when the PPP was in opposition, there has not been a similar movement to the AFC. Appeals by Indian Guyanese commentators critical of the PPP have had little effect; such commentators have been portrayed by the PPP as anti-government, which is the code for anti-Indian. Similarly Indian-based parties and interest groups, while appealing to the Indian Guyanese sense of victimhood, have not been able to translate sympathy into electoral support or an anti-PPP movement.

The WPA maintained its momentum for eighteen years due largely to the existence of the authoritarian government, which engendered united action between dissident Africans and sections of the Indian community. The longer life of the WPA as a multi-ethnic party made it difficult for it to become an ethnic party after 1992. But the rapid decline of its Indian membership at all levels left the party with a mostly African membership, some of whom became associated with African-centered organizations or began to speak out on African grievances. While the party has remained committed to its multi-ethnic roots, it has had to fend off charges, especially from the PPP, of being an African party. These charges are part of the PPP's strategy of tying opposition parties to the PNC, which remains discredited among Indian Guyanese. But it points to the difficulty of sustaining multi-ethnic parties in conditions of intense ethnic conflict. In addition to the democratic ethos observed by Dr. Thomas, the WPA's earlier success was due in part to its capacity to undermine ethnic conflict even when these were encouraged by the two ethnic parties. In the final analysis a multi-ethnic party is powerless to affect the ethnic environment where there is no significant multi-ethnic constituency.

There was not much the WPA could have done to prevent its own decline and that of the multi-ethnic movement. Because the PPP's quest for dominance has always been premised on free and fair elections, the prospect of the return of electoral democracy invariably reignited the party's instinct for dominance. As was the case with the PNC in 1964, the PPP's first instinct was to capture power on its own with a coalition in which it played the dominant role. Whether presenting its PCD allies with the inflexible demand for the all-powerful executive presidency was intended as a tactic or not, it had the desired effect--it broke up the alliance and freed the PPP to assume power on it own. This was almost a repeat of the pre-1955 scenario in the original PPP when both factions were inflexible about the top spot. The WPA's inflexibility about Dr. Jagan's candidacy arose from its multi-ethnic logic whereby it could not support a symbol of the old divisive politics as the embodiment of a new multi ethnic beginning. The PPP's inflexibility also arose from its own culture of domination in which it could not envisage itself as part of a coalition that it did not dominate especially in conditions where it had an ethnic advantage.

The WPA's only hope of achieving its full objective lay in a power sharing government in which both ethnic groups felt secure. While the PPP read the ethnic situation correctly, especially as it related to Indian Guyanese, the WPA miscalculated the electoral impact of its multi-ethnic work and standing. Just as the early PPP underestimated the depth of ethnic identification in the political realm, the WPA overestimated the resilience of multi ethnic solidarity in the face of ethnic insecurity. To be fair, the WPA had more reason for optimism given the longer period and the intensity of its mobilization. In the end the WPA has had to live with the reality of having played the major role in deposing an African Guyanese government, which was replaced by an Indian-dominated one. This is compounded by the fact that the PPP has totally marginalized the WPA and has sought to write its role out of the history of the anti-dictatorial movement.

Like the WPA, the AFC, which was formed as a multi-ethnic alliance of PPP, PNC and the WPA dissidents, has a multi-ethnic leadership and employs a similar rhetoric. But unlike the WPA, the AFC opted for a traditional leadership structure with a maximum leader. After some hesitation the party named Raphael Trotman, an African Guyanese, as leader and Khemraj Ramjattan, an Indian Guyanese as deputy leader. Immediately the PPP mounted a concerted attack on Ramjattan who was portrayed as a betrayer linking up with a former oppressor of Indian Guyanese. The PNC, sensing the drift towards the AFC by many in the African Guyanese middle class, adopted a different strategy--it ignored the AFC. The AFC garnered eight percent of the vote, but almost all of its support came from the African Guyanese community. Understandably, the party named four Africans as part of its six-person parliamentary team. This, however, led to the acrimonious resignation of an Indian member who claimed she was promised a seat. Invariably charges of anti-Indianism were leveled at the leader and the party.

The all-African support base of the AFC has been its greatest nightmare. Since the elections it has been unable to carry out its promised multi-ethnic mobilization as the Indian community has shown little interest in the party. Some African spokespersons have accused the AFC of not representing the interests of its African supporters. Further, because of its sensitivity to Indian concerns, the party has also not been able to develop an effective relationship with other opposition parties, in particular the PNC. Even when it eventually joined an all-opposition alliance in the wake of revelations of possible government involvement in extra-judicial killings, it took great care not to appear too cozy with PNC leaders.

With Indian Guyanese voters off limits to the AFC and the party's inability or reluctance to pander to its African Guyanese support base, the future of the party as a viable third force is in doubt. Whether it retains the same level of support at the next election will depend on the internal situation of the PNC. If the instability within the PNC persists, the AFC stands a better chance of retaining at least some of its support, if not all. But should the PNC settle its differences and present a united front, the AFC's portion of the vote could significantly decline.

3

The Discourse on Race and Ethnicity 1955-92

Eversince the ethnic split of Guyana's nationalist movement in 1955 there has been a vigorous discourse on the root causes of the problem, the extent of its consequences and possible solutions. The discourse has been characterized by four tendencies—a denial that there is an ethnic problem, ethnic narratives based on victimhood and accusation, separate ethnic organization grounded in mutual respect and ethnic unity or multi-ethnicity. Often the nature and tone of the discourse have been determined by which ethnic party has been in power or which ethnic group feels more insecure. For the most part the discourse has been driven by politicians of the major parties, leaders of ethnic interest groups and radical scholar activists. Interestingly, academics have not been as central to the discourse as one would have expected.

The discourse on race and ethnicity in post colonial Guyana can be placed in two broad phases—the post and pre 1992 phases. There were two tendencies during the first phase. On the one hand there was reluctance by political figures, scholars and other opinion shapers to directly address the issue—the public debate was conducted in ideological rather than ethnic terms. However, both Eusi Kwayana and Cheddi Jagan in different ways expressed some of the ethnic fears of their respective communities. The second tendency occurred during the multi-ethnic phase from the 1970s to 1992 when the discourse was dominated by those who sought to move the conversation beyond ethnic victimhood and accusation.

This discourse was dominated by leaders of the WPA, in particular Walter Rodney and Eusi Kwayana. The second phase of the discourse from 1992 to the present has been characterized by both a narrative of victimhood and a counter narrative that has sought to transcend those narratives.

Ethnic Discourse 1955-1974

The 1955 split and the concomitant rise of ethnic political competition ushered in an ethnic discourse that has mirrored both the political divide and the desire to transcend it. Despite evidence to the contrary, both factions of the PPP played down the ethnic nature of the split; they preferred to explain the rupture in ideological terms. But beneath that rhetoric was an acknowledgement of the ethnic consequences. The Jaganite faction was the first to admit these consequences and quickly moved to transform itself into an Indian Guyanese party. The defining moment in this process was Dr. Jagan's address to the party congress in 1956. Although the address was presented as an ideological statement that sought to separate Dr. Jagan and his faction from the Burnhamite faction, it was also a treatise on ethnicity and race from an Indian Guyanese standpoint. The address also began what became an important aspect of Dr. Jagan's praxis- the articulation of ethnic narrative in the guise of class discourse.

The discourse has been dominated by a combination of ethnic narratives and counter-narratives whereby each group has highlighted its perceived sufferings at the hands of the other and in the process constructed a narrative of guilt and innocence. The PPP's grand narrative was one of justification; it sought to explain Dr. Jagan and the PPP's decision to abandon the class praxis, which they had hitherto championed and embraced, and their embrace of an ethnic form of mobilization. This narrative was articulated in his 1956 congress address, which introduced three important sub-narratives. First, it introduced a Pan Indian narrative, which was premised on Indian solidarity across class lines. This was accompanied by the narrative of the reactionary African opposition represented by the ultra left, the African Guyanese middle class and the break away Burnhamite PPP faction. The third sub-narrative was that of the oppressed Indian, which highlighted Indian Guyanese class and racial suffering but was silent on the suffering of other ethnic groups.

Although Jagan accepted the primacy of class, he was one of the chief contributors to the narrative of Indian Guyanese victimhood. He described state violence against Indian Guyanese during the colonial period as "African policemen shooting Indian workers" (Jagan1954: 51). Kwayana observes that apart from the fact that policemen of other ethnicities were also involved in some of these incidents, notably in Leonora, Ruimveldt and Enmore, Dr. Jagan ignored the chain of command in the police force during the colonial period. This statement according to Kwayana had an effect on the Indian Guyanese consciousness of (Personal Interview November 2008).

In his 1956 address to the PPP congress Dr. Jagan explained Indian opposition to the West Indies Federation as part of their "sense of national oppression." He argued that this opposition cut across class lines with the Indian Guyanese capitalist class taking a position in opposition to its class interests. According to Jagan:

> The Indians feeling as they do feel a sense of national oppression are almost 100% opposed to Federation. This is why the Indian native capitalist who predominate in the Junior Chamber of Commerce go against their class interests and oppose Federation. The Indian capitalist up to this stage puts his "national" interests before his "class" interests. Consequently he can be a resolute ally against imperialism within these considerations (1956:16).

Although Dr. Jagan expressed opposition to the federation in anti-imperialist terms, it is clear from the above quotation that ethnicity was also a pivotal, if not the most important factor, that drove his opposition. His characterization of the Indian Guyanese commercial class as patriotic and anti-imperialist was in contrast to that of the African and Portuguese middle class, which he described as reactionary. Jagan's embrace of the Indian commercial class in 1956 accompanied his decision to opt for an ethnic strategy following the 1955 split of the PPP. This led to the second split in 1956-57, which was in effect a purge of the remaining African leadership in the Jaganite PPP.

While Dr. Jagan painted the Indian Guyanese commercial class in glowing terms and articulated the fears of the Indian Guyanese working class, he was harsh on those leaders who he accused of "left deviationism and adventurism." He charged these "ultra leftists" with alienating "native capital support for the party" (1956:5). Though this may not have been his objective he in effect blamed the mainly African Guyanese "ultra leftists" for alienating Indian Guyanese capital for the party. A close reading of the 1956 congress paper, therefore, gave the party a clear choice between "patriotic Indian capitalists" and "African ultra leftists."

From an ethno-racial standpoint, the 1956 congress address did four critical things. First, it characterized the Indian Guyanese commercial class as patriotic and progressive while labeling the African Guyanese middle class as reactionary. Second, the mainly African Burnhamite faction was blamed for the 1955 split. Third, the mainly African Guyanese ultra-left was blamed for the suspension of the constitution and the alienation of the Indian Guyanese commercial class from the party. Fourth, the address used the Indian Guyanese sense of victimhood as justification for Dr. Jagan's opposition to the West Indian Federation.

Eusi Kwayana's reply to Jagan's address began an exchange between the two that would dominate the discourse for the next decade. Kwayana is the country's political leader who in the popular psyche is most associated with race and ethnicity. He was integrally involved in the conflict by the early 1960s when he emerged as the leading voice articulating African Guyanese fears of domination. Later he was an equally vigorous proponent of ethnic unity between the two groups. There are four major reasons why Kwayana has been central to the discourse. First, he was the first major political leader of the independence generation to publicly engage the issue. Second, he became the foremost Black Nationalist leader beginning in the 1960s and in the process emerged as the most visible African Guyanese cultural leader. Third, as one of the most outspoken African Guyanese leader during the ethnic riots of the 1960s he became most associated with anti-Indian sentiment during the period. Finally, he more than any other Guyanese political activist or intellectual, has consistently engaged race and ethnicity in the public sphere. When Kwayana first engaged race in the early 1960s he did so in opposition of what he saw as the threat of African Guyanese disenfranchisement and in pursuit of African cultural and political empowerment. He viewed the PPP government of the day as tending towards Indian Guyanese domination and became one of its harshest critics. After his proposal for a joint-premiership of the two ethnic leaders was rejected he spent the next few years chronicling and speaking out against this tendency.

Kwayana (1956:4) observed that the conclusions in Dr. Jagan's 1956 address raised "great doubts" about whether his analysis was driven by class or race. He described Dr. Jagan's treatment of the issues surrounding the split as a "disgrace" and suggested that it opened "the door of racism and confusion." Particular reference was made to Jagan's refusal to criticize Indian Guyanese members for wrongly concluding that African Guyanese executives refused to make sacrifices. He was also critical of Dr. Jagan's tendency to treat Indian Guyanese as a monolithic progressive group while dividing Africans Guyanese between those who were politically aware and those who were not.

There were three related outcomes of the 1956 address. The immediate effect was the ethnic purging of the party of most of its senior African Guyanese members. Though they were not officially expelled from the party, Dr. Jagan's denouncement and his embrace of the Indian Guyanese commercial class left them no alternative. Had they remained they would have been doing so on Dr. Jagan's terms. The related consequence was the emergence of an Indian party in which socialists, capitalists, and religious leaders co-existed. Finally, this Indian Guyanese solidarity was reciprocated on the African Guyanese side with the merging of the Burnhamite PPP, the middle class United Democratic Party (UDP) and Kwayana into the PNC. It was, therefore, not surprising that the African Guyanese who remained in the PPP were all voted out of the party's Central Committee in 1959. While Ms. Jagan publicly spoke out against these racist tendencies in the party at the time, Dr. Jagan was not as forthcoming. During the ethnic riots 1961-64 he was also less vocal when there were attacks against African Guyanese.

The conflict of the 1960s gave rise to a second grand narrative—one of "the guilty race," which was projected by both sides of the ethnic divide. This was manifested on the Indian Guyanese side as the narrative of ethnic siege whereby the Indian government and its supporters perceived a conspiracy to rob them of power.

Dr. Jagan was the major Indian Guyanese voice in this regard. On the African side, the consolidation of the parties and the lopsided victories of the PPP at the 1957 and 1961 elections led to an African Guyanese narrative of fear--fear of disrespect, disenfranchisement and domination. Consequently both sides located their narratives in the context of self-defense. The African fears were articulated by Kwayana who, beginning in 1961, became the leading advocate of African self-love and self-defense against what he saw as Dr. Jagan and the PPP's quest for Indian domination and a deliberate campaign to portray Indians as victims of African oppression.

Kwayana's narrative was two-fold: exposure of the PPP's racial agenda and providing an African counter-narrative. He cited as evidence of the PPP's ethnic agenda an independence petition sent by Dr. Jagan to the United Nations. The tenor of the petition, sent in November 1960, was similar to that of the 1956 congress address. Africans were portrayed as privileged while Indians were described as "nationally oppressed" and their "misery," deplorable working conditions, "starvation" wages and non-education were highlighted. The petition also made reference to Portuguese and African Guyanese wealth and African dominance of the public service respectively, but no reference was made of similar Indian Guyanese successes. While the PPP did not release the petition to the public, it did not deny its existence.

In his account of the ethnic conflicts of the 1960s Dr. Jagan dates the beginning of the violence in 1962 when the PPP came under attack in Georgetown. He, therefore, ignores the attacks on African Guyanese following the 1961 election. He chronicles in great detail the events in 1962 and 1963 in which African Guyanese were the aggressors and the PPP and Indians were the victims. His account of the 1964 conflict included incidents in which both Africans and Indians were victims but he emphasized the fact that the strike breakers were "mostly Africans" who were also used as vigilantes "terrorizing the Indian workers who had started a passive resistance campaign." (1972: 306) He also highlighted the cooperation of the police, who were "mostly African", with the vigilantes on the West Demerara where "the African police mostly taking sides with the African rioters" (1972: 307).

Kwayana accused Dr. Jagan of using the petition to paint "black tar on the non-Indian races and pinning medals of martyrdom on the East Indian race" (1999: 2). Kwayana's counter narrative emphasized the threat of domination and disenfranchisement. He charged the PPP with genocide against African Guyanese and accused the colonial establishment of collusion. Towards this end he opposed independence under a PPP government; a position that ran against the grain of his own anti-colonial agitation. He was critical of the PNC leader for his willingness to support independence with the PPP in power – a reversal of positions by Burnham who had previously opposed that approach. As Kwayana observed "the leader who had warned the people of the dangers of independence under the PPP- "if we lose, we done, we dead" – is now speaking as if we did not live in British Guiana… Our position is peculiar. This is not a land of one race…" (1961:2). He also argued that independence under the PPP would "strangle the breath of the African people and the minorities to create here an East Indian state to plant the East Indies in the West Indies" (1961:3).

Kwayana's *Next Witness* (1962) and *Genocide in Guyana* (1964) chronicled the African – Guyanese "suffering" during the ethnic conflict 1961-64. *Next Witness* listed a series of attacks on African Guyanese in 1961, which Kwayana referred to as "evidence of events" meant as "a protest against Jagan's democracy". The booklet also published letters from African Guyanese citizens to Kwayana detailing attacks in their communities. Kwayana contends that he chronicled the events because the media refused to do so; he accused the "white" media and the colonial establishment of being "up to their old tricks" of trying to stifle African Guyanese. Similarly *Genocide in Guyana* gave an account of African victimhood in 1964. It chronicled attacks on African Guyanese by Indian Guyanese and the failure of the police to provide them with protection. It charged the PPP with having a "cold blooded plot" to "wipe out thousands of African voters" before the pending elections. He warned that the "worst is yet to come" and of "two potential nations in collision" (1964:18).

The exchanges between Jagan and Kwayana cut to the heart of the problem during the first decade after the split. It is clear that Dr. Jagan's ethnic narrative was a logical extension of his decision to pursue an ethnic mobilization strategy after the split. His use of

Marxist class analysis did not hide the suggestion that Indians were victimized while Africans more often than not were the aggressors. Dr. Jagan's refusal to project the problem as part of a larger breakdown of ethnic relations in which both groups were victims meant that he could not be critical of Indian excesses. Further, having constructed an enemy list that included the Burnhamite rightwing and the ultra leftists who were mostly African Guyanese, his criticisms of those groups and their supporters logically took on an ethnic tone. Dr. Jagan also clearly underestimated the difficulty of one-race rule in a multi-ethnic society. His seeming surprise at African resistance to PPP rule was either a function of political naiveté or miscalculation.

It is difficult in situations of conflict to determine exactly which event or political actor initiated a process. But if the 1955 split provided the opening for the subsequent ethnic polarization, Dr. Jagan's 1956 congress address was critical in speeding up its consolidation. In this regard the 1956-1957 split has to be given as much weight as the one in 1955; the former for all intents and purposes closed the door to ethnic reconciliation. By disregarding the significance of the African Guyanese leaders' refusal to join the Burnhamite faction, Dr. Jagan left no doubt about his political priorities. In reducing his choice to one between his African executives and the Indian community he boxed himself into an ethnic corner from which he was never able to free himself and the PPP.

A critical factor was Kwayana who had hitherto been Dr. Jagan's staunchest supporter. A committed Marxist, his only venture into ethnic politics before 1957 was support of the local Indian Guyanese independence movement. He endured severe criticism from the African Guyanese political class for his support of Jagan against an African candidate in the 1947 election. His sense of political fairness was central to his refusal to accept nomination to replace Jagan as leader of the PPP during the leadership crisis in 1953. It is in the context of the above that Kwayana's extreme criticism of Jagan's descent into the politics of ethnic polarization has to be largely seen. He was obviously disappointed at this development, but his own embrace of African Guyanese self-defense was gradual. His response to Dr. Jagan's congress speech drew attention to the ethnic direction in which Dr. Jagan was headed rather than the construction of an

African Guyanese counter-narrative. It is interesting to note that Kwayana's ethnic narrative did not fit in with the PNC's agenda, which like the PPP's was driven by a public downplay of the ethnic problem even as it pursued an ethnic mobilization strategy. In other words both parties engaged ethnicity not as the root of the problem but as a consequence.

The rejection of Kwayana's multi-ethnic solution in 1961, his subsequent expulsion from the PNC, Dr. Jagan's overt and covert construction of an Indian Guyanese narrative of suffering, and his perception of a deliberate conspiracy to hide African Guyanese suffering combined to shape Kwayana's construction of an African narrative of suffering. This narrative served two functions. First, it served to deepen the isolation the PPP and Dr. Jagan in the African community. Second, it introduced a new African Guyanese nationalism that would prove critical in the PNC's early years in office and also the rise of the WPA in the 1970s.

Kwayana's later self-criticism of his 1960s narrative stressed his overgeneralization of race and ethnicity, which led to sweeping critiques of the entire group without regards to class differences. This raises the question of whether ethnic narratives even when they are counter narratives can avoid ethnic generalizations. Because ethnic solidarity across class lines is an essential ingredient of ethnic conflict, the intra group differences and contradictions are less obvious. What is worth noting, however, is that Kwayana's self criticism was not reciprocated by Dr. Jagan who never revisited his early ethnic narratives.

The Multi Ethnic Discourse: Kwayana, Rodney and the WPA

The PNC's rise to office and subsequent consolidation of power led to a change of the political discourse. Initially the Indian narrative of victimhood continued as exemplified by the slogan "cheated not defeated." The African narrative became less anti-Indian and more Black Nationalist along the lines of the Black Power movement. As the PNC moved towards a more authoritarian form of governance these ethnic narratives were overtaken by a multi-ethnic narrative that eschewed the guilty race thesis and stressed ethnic unity and equality, class solidarity across ethnic lines and power sharing. The WPA was the chief purveyor of this narrative which ignited a new multi-ethnic movement.

Although Kwayana supported the PNC after it assumed office, he remained politically independent of the party. With the formation of ASCRIA in 1964 his discourse on race became more in line with the Black Power movement that emerged in the second half of the 1960s. But his was a class-based nationalism that centered the empowerment of the Black working class as an integral part of national cohesion. State power then for Kwayana was a means to an end—a medium of ethno-racial democratization and national reconciliation. This was at variance with the PNC's nationalism which was premised on Black control of state power as an end in itself. It, therefore, was not surprising when he openly broke with the PNC. By 1971 ASCRIA had concluded that it had mistakenly led Africans to believe that their salvation lay with an African government. They also concluded that socialism which they supported could not be built with one ethnic group:

> ASCRIA's mistake was to lead the African people to believe that, once the problem of African solidarity was solved, a people's political line would be followed. Again, we, especially our leadership, trusted too much in the platform declarations of the elite and our leadership was slow to believe rumors of corruption among ministers. It did not exercise the vigilance necessary always, and especially when dealing with opportunists. ASCRIA therefore, unwilling to risk a 'split', remained silent at the PNC's doings and accepted rather weak excuses for the failures of the Government to develop a mass line, to inspire the people and give them the right to govern (ASCRIA Bulletin: April 1973).

Kwayana and ASCRIA developed ties with other radical leftist groups, an alliance that became the foundation for the emergence of the WPA. The birth of the WPA was accompanied by a new discourse on race and ethnicity that stressed multi-ethnic solidarity as opposed to the narrative of suffering that characterized the one in the 1950s and 1960s. Walter Rodney was a critical voice in this new discourse, but Kwayana, and to a lesser extent Dr. Jagan, were also part of it.

In 1978 Kwayana delivered what I consider to be his most important statement on race and ethnicity in Guyana. He argued that the ethnic problem in Guyana is the result of "racial insecurity" which he locates in the historical evolution of the country's political economy. He defines racial insecurity as a group's collective sense of its condition in relation to another group:

> What we mean by racial insecurity is the collective sense of uncertainty, sometimes amounting to fear, felt by large sections of a given group in a society of more than one group about its future welfare, its future status or its future safety as compared to other groups, or to its own present or past condition (Kwayana 1978:2).

Like most Marxists, Kwayana contends that race and ethnicity are integrally linked to class, but unlike many Marxists he does not dismiss race as irrelevant. Having acknowledged race as a "material factor," he argues that racial differences become a political problem when they are linked to the pursuit of political power. He locates this in the development of mass ethnic/racial consciousness and ideas which according to him "cannot be separated historically from the general productive activity of the given population" (1978:2).

In this regard he traces Guyana's ethnic problems back to the post emancipation political economy and the social relations it spawned among the various ethnic groups. He identifies the development of ethno-racial stereotypes as one of the consequences of the social relations of production which he contends has its roots in both the divide and rule tactics of the local colonizers and international slavery. Kwayana does not take the impact of these stereotypes lightly; he sees them in contemporary society and suggests that they must be confronted by those who seek social change:

> It is possible that the development of racial stereotypes, took their origin mainly out of the productive process and the social relations of production. Certain factors were taken from real life by the propagandists of colonialism and made into general truths calculated to sow the seeds of division among the working people. Certain other stereotypes were internationally fostered by the slave owners. Africans, Indians, Chinese, Portuguese all were at various times

in terms of which haunted them wherever they were discharged. The stereotype is perhaps the unwritten literature of the process of racial and political polarization. It is one area in which conscious efforts will have to be made by revolutionaries, artists and other workers at the level of images and ideas to destroy the stereotypes of race, which affect not only the consciousness of people about others, but also the concept of people about themselves (1978:2-3).

Regarding his own attitude to race and ethnicity in Guyana in the 1960s, Kwayana claims that class analysis was not always sufficiently transparent in his assessment of the situation; he tended to lump the Indian Guyanese leaders and followers together without sufficient regard for the class differences. But according to him this "imperfect behavior" was prompted by the fact that race and ethnicity rather than class were much more developed among Indian Guyanese than among African Guyanese. This self-criticism by Kwayana is an important aspect of the discourse on ethnicity/race in Guyana. As the only public figure to publicly engage in self-criticism his testimony assumes much more credibility which allows him more than his political peers, to venture beyond mere partisan accounts.

Kwayana does not accept the thesis that external intervention was solely responsible for the split in the PPP in 1955 and the later ethnic polarization. He points to ethnic considerations and "cultural pride" as important factors. As he contends,

> The actual birth of the Peoples Progressive Party and the choice of what came to be known as a Leader brought some noticeable pause and suspicion among important sections of Afro-Guyanese on a mixture of racial-ideological grounds. The more astute of these elements organized within the party around their own Leader and laid the foundation for later developments. Some East Indian strata also felt insecure at the development of the PPP. The petty overseeing stratum, like drivers and pandits and some other strata, had their own racial objections to the composition of the PPP leadership and membership, as it conflicted with their own social

doctrine in the estate ghettoes. However, elements of these also were to find their way into the party after 1955 and they too were to lay the foundation for later developments. A cultural factor also had some influence on the situation. The Indian independence movement had not only shaken up the whole colonial empire, but had imparted much dignity and pride to Indians in the Caribbean (1978:3).

Unlike other PPP leaders of the period he views Mr. Burnham's bid for the top position within the context of the fears of sections of the African Guyanese community. He puts the responsibility for the split partly on the inability of the PPP to devise approaches to leadership and party organization consistent with the challenges it faced.

With our comparatively narrow vision of mass struggle, we did not organize the masses for self-defence or for self-emancipation. We put ourselves forward, with the noblest intentions, as champions of the people, with all that this implied to the people. We must therefore share the blame for the type of political structure that still persists in Guyana in which the masses tend to search for and look to leaders, at the expense of efforts of self-emancipation (1978:5).

Kwayana believes that the country's ethnic problems are not intractable. He thinks the solution lies not in evasion of the problem but in addressing the root causes. Towards this end he advocated a political solution, which guarantees security to all ethnic groups by addressing the mutual fear of domination. His 1961 joint-premiership proposal addressed the problem at the level of leadership and forty years later he supported a broader power sharing that include other sectors.

In many respects Walter Rodney is a political descendant of Kwayana. Like Kwayana he engaged multi-ethnicity, not by ignoring ethnicity, but by acknowledging its reality. Unlike Kwayana, Rodney was not part of the conflicts of the 1960s; he returned to Guyana in 1974 and joined the WPA which was still in its infancy. Prior to his return, he had developed an international reputation as a leading proponent of Black Nationalism. As the leading intellectual voice of Caribbean Black Power he was banned from Jamaica in 1968; an act that became the catalyst for the region's Black Power movement.

Rodney spent the next six years in Tanzania where he wrote his seminal *How Europe Underdeveloped Africa* and became a leading theoretician of Black and Third World radicalism. His ideological outlook was a blend of Black Nationalism and Marxism but his political positions were guided by concrete situations rather than ideological dogma.

While the ideas he developed during the Guyana years were part of his larger political praxis, the fact that Guyana was a peculiar society riveted by ethnic conflict between two non-white peoples, his emphasis was not the same as when he dealt with conflict between Blacks and Whites. Rodney's call for unity between African and East Indian Guyanese along class lines was not an abandonment of Black Nationalism; he did not find it a necessary tool in Guyana. During the Jamaica years he had advocated the inclusion of East Indians in his articulation of Caribbean Black Power. His, therefore, was always a class-based Black Power. Hence his Black Power was racially-oriented as it related to the Black/White question and class-oriented in relation to the ethnic conditions in Guyana and Trinidad.

Rodney viewed African liberation in Guyana as being tied to working class liberation. He rejected the notion that African Guyanese should not oppose an African Guyanese government and contended that unity between the African and Indian Guyanese working classes was essential. He was adamant that any advance in Guyana had to be premised on unity across ethnic lines. Towards this end, he argued that although external influence and the machinations of the political parties were responsible for ethnic polarization, Guyanese, in the final analysis, must rise above the division. He further contended that the soci-economic problems faced by the Guyanese people had very little to do with race and more to do with class. As he observed:

> No ordinary Afro- Guyanese, no ordinary Indo-Guyanese can afford to be misled by the myth of race. Time and time again it has been our undoing. Does it have anything to do with race that the cost of living far out-strips the increase in wages? Does it have anything to do with race that there are no goods in the shops? Does it have anything to do with race when the original lack of democracy as exemplified in

the national elections is reproduced at the level of local government elections? Does it have anything to do with race when the bauxite workers cannot elect their own union leadership? Does it have anything to do with race when, day after day, whether one is Indian or African, without the appropriate party credentials, one either gets no employment, loses one's employment or is subject to lack of promotion? (Rodney 1981:6)

But unlike other Marxists, he did not dismiss race and ethnicity as irrelevant; he accepted their salience in Guyanese politics. He argued that ethnicity was institutionalized in the socio-political and economic system and was critical of those who interpreted the absence of ethnic violence as a reflection of harmony. He drew attention to the linkage between white subjugation of non-white peoples and ethnic polarization between non white communities and observed that non-white groups tended to view each other through the lens of the dominant culture. As he stated after a visit to Guyana in 1970:

...my belief is that, while, ultimately socialism is an ideology which takes no cognizance of color and so on, our recent situation is one in which we have to admit to the reality of racial divisions, not just the oppression of the White World over the non-White world, but also of the forms of division within the non-White world, itself, as in our own Guyanese society...there is a single dominant culture to which each sub-group relates, so that when I as an African, in Guyanese society, speak of an Indian, I really am speaking of the European's Indian. I see that Indian through the eyes of the European, and the other way round. (Rodney, 1970:1)

As I observed earlier, Rodney had advocated a multi-ethnic position as far back as 1968 when he argued then that Caribbean Black Power must include East Indians. He posited the view that and unity between Indians and Africans was pivotal to Caribbean liberation. He contended that the problem should be tackled at two levels. First, he called for the development of separate ethnic consciousness as a prerequisite for ethnic unity. Second, he advocated the simultaneous development of "integrative" or multiethnic consciousness and political mechanisms based on the socialist principle of social equality. Rodney's multi-ethnicity, therefore, was premised on the acceptance rather than the rejection of ethnic identity. He saw no contradiction between the two; for him one was necessary for the success of the other.

> What we must try and understand (and this is a point I'm always trying to make very clearly) is that there is no contradiction between saying that, at this particular point in time, a man needs to assert his given identity, so that, at another point in time, he won't he wouldn't have to assert it... And I think that within our community of Guyana, different ethnic groups need to assert their identity, need to put themselves together, to pull themselves together, and when they have and when they can operate on the basis of mutual respect, which they are not doing, now, then I think that the way will be clear for building a new society, a society of a mixed unity (Rodney 1970:3)

Rodney accused both major parties of exploiting ethnic insecurity to further political ends. He pointed to the fact that although the PNC regime discriminated against Indian Guyanese, Indian merchants and other sections of the Indian Guyanese middle class supported the PNC. He particularly chided African Guyanese for allowing the PNC regime to manipulate their fears to further its political agenda. Although he seldom invoked Black Nationalism in his public discourse on ethnicity, he linked Black dignity to the African Guyanese need to avoid ethnic animosity towards Indian Guyanese. He, however, did not think that cross-ethnic solidarity was impossible. Towards this end he urged both groups to draw on their common history of struggle against colonialism. Rodney viewed cross-ethnic solidarity as crucial to ethnic peace and the overall development of Guyana. But he was opposed to a "hypothetical" unity; he preferred an active unity or "unity in struggle." Rodney, therefore, rejected the superficial unity embraced by the PPP and the PNC such as ethnic tokenism and multi-ethnic rhetoric (Rodney 1981).

While Kwayana and Rodney saw class unity as the answer to the ethnic problem they were careful not to downgrade the importance of ethnicity both as a cultural factor and as a destructive force when linked to the struggle for power. Coming out of the Black Power movement they were conscious of the need for cultural pride and regeneration among Africans, which they viewed as a necessary precondition for African liberation. Rodney's work in Jamaica and Africa and Kwayana's in Guyana during the 1960s bear this out. Unlike Rodney's, Kwayana's Black Nationalism was played out against the backdrop of African-Indian conflict. Hence it was viewed by some as anti-Indian. The issue of the relationship between race and class, which Walter Rodney also confronted, has been a difficult one for most analysts of class conflict, particularly Marxists. While the tension between race and class is never fully resolved, Kwayana and Rodney, because of their lack of fidelity to orthodoxy and dogma, managed to take the discourse further than most without sacrificing the centrality of either construct.

4

Post-1992 Discourse on Race and Ethnicity

This chapter examines political discourse in Guyana since the return of electoral democracy in 1992. It argues that the discourse has been driven on the one hand by the need to construct the notion of a guilty and an innocent race, project the suffering of one group as greater than the other (ethnic suffering), justify the political actions of the ethnic parties (ethnic justification) and elevate the ethnic party as the vanguard of the freedom struggle (ethnic vanguardism) and its leader as visionary, revolutionary and above reproach (ethnic heroism). On the other hand there has been an alternative narrative, which is premised on the rejection of the notion of a guilty race (no guilty race). It privileges instead the idea of collective suffering and aggression and holds the ethnic parties and their leaders as equally responsible for the continued ethnic hostilities.

Crucial to the discourse was the emergence of new organizations on both sides of the ethnic divide. The Africanist African Cultural and Development Association (ACDA) was formed by a group of Africans led by a re-migrant, Violet Jean-Baptiste and initially included Kwayana, other WPA members who belonged to ASCRIA and some leading PNC members. As the name suggests, the organization aimed at continuing the work started by ASCRIA three decades before. Towards this end it did not take a leading role in the political arena; concentrating instead on educational and cultural activities, especially in the capital city. The other major ethnic organizations were the Indianist Rise Organize and Rebuild (ROAR) and the Guyana Indian Heritage Association (GIHA).

The forerunner of ROAR and GIHA was the Jaguar Committee for Democracy (JCD). Ravi Dev, the leading figure in these organizations, returned to Guyana in the late 1980s after being part of the anti-PNC movement in the USA. He injected into the discourse an Indianist narrative that combined ethnic victimhood and African Guyanese guilt but with the PPP's rise to power in 1992, the JCD toned down its rhetoric.

Ethnic Suffering

Ethnic Suffering characterizes the experiences of the group as one of victimhood and innocence while the rival group is portrayed as the guilty race and its narrative of victimhood is dismissed as a myth. The Indian Guyanese Narrative of Suffering is steeped in its perception and experience of violence and disenfranchisement perpetrated by African Guyanese. The experience of indentureship is projected as victimhood and resilience and is sometimes articulated as comparable to slavery. In this regard Indians are credited with saving the Guyanese economy after emancipation which gives them a claim to an equal, if not greater entitlement. Another important aspect of Indian Guyanese victimhood is the narrative of singular suffering under PNC rule, which argues that it was Indian Guyanese who bore the brunt of the oppression under the dictatorship. In the process, African Guyanese suffering is either minimized or silenced. This aspect of the narrative dismisses charges of African Guyanese marginalization as a myth and stresses African Guyanese domination of the military, the Public Service and the professions as evidence of African Guyanese power.

The African Guyanese Narrative of Suffering centers both African Guyanese historical victimhood dating back to slavery and its sense of victimhood since the PPP's return to power in 1992. Prior arrival and extreme suffering during slavery are projected as a form of patrimony. Second, it accuses the PPP of an Indian Guyanese conspiracy of domination and ethnic cleansing, which leads to African Guyanese marginalization. Third, it locates this PPP's quest for dominance in an Indian cultural hierarchy in which blackness is at the bottom of the ladder. In this regard the Indian need to dominate is viewed as absolute. Fourth, it dismisses the post 1992 violence against Indian Guyanese as a function of PPP's racial governance and the Indian Guyanese refusal to condemn it or disassociate from it.

Ethnic Justification

Ethnic Justification is the narrative that accompanies a major political action by an ethnic party that results in perceptions of domination and exclusion by the rival group. The narrative is aimed at satisfying the security concerns of the party's constituency and inspiring feelings of guilt by the rival group. The first Indian Guyanese Narrative of Justification arose out of the PPP's decision in 1956 to move towards an ethnic based mobilization, which was in contradiction to its rhetoric of class and multi-ethnicity. The second narrative, which followed the party's return to office in 1992, was meant to justify the abandonment of its promise to eschew a winner-take-all form of governance even if it won a free and fair election. Central to this narrative is the notion that given the illegal African Guyanese monopoly of power, Indian assumption of power is just and morally correct. Towards this end democracy is constructed in majoritarian terms and consociational power sharing is viewed as a device to rob the PPP of power. It instead embraces inclusionary domination whereby others are included in the government on the PPP's terms and Africans and other minorities are urged to join or vote for the PPP. The African Narrative of Justification, which sought to justify the PNC's tenure in office, is two-fold--it minimizes the severity of the regime's actions and policies and locates those actions within the context of African fear of Indian domination. This narrative fluctuates between a majoritarian definition of democracy and an embrace of "shared governance" along consociational lines.

Ethnic Vanguardism

Ethnic vanguardism places the ethnic party as the most progressive and revolutionary force in the country and the principal fighter for independence. The Indian Narrative of Vanguardism identifies the PPP and Indians as the leading political actors in the fight against the PNC regime. In the process the contributions of other parties, organizations and ethnic groups are silenced, minimized or cast in negative light. This narrative describes the PNC as anti-democratic, racist and violent while the WPA is portrayed as a minor force which was more preoccupied with violence and romantic Black Nationalism. The African-Guyanese narrative of Vanguardism locates the PNC as the party that brought peace and stability after the ethnic conflicts of the 1960's.

Ethnic Heroism

This aspect of the narrative elevates the leader of the ethnic group to Hero-Saint status whereby he becomes the leader of the nation and the embodiment of peace, integrity, inclusion and moderation. On the other hand leaders of the rival groups are characterized as violent, evil, naïve and lacking in vision. In this regard the Indian narrative elevates Dr. Jagan to sainthood, portrays other major Indian leaders as traitors and vilifies or derides African leaders. The Indian Guyanese leader is characterized as peaceful, visionary, humane, democratic conciliatory and pragmatic while the opposite leaders are viewed as violent, inhumane, undemocratic, inflexible, cunning and devoid of vision. Similarly, the African Guyanese narrative elevates Forbes Burnham as the father of the nation whose vision surpasses all others.

There has been a counter-narrative to the Ethnic Counter Narratives which contends that because both the PPP and the PNC and by extension Indian and African Guyanese have been guilty of ethnic aggression, it is wrong to identify one side as guilty. Second, it argues that during the period of PNC rule both Indian and African Guyanese were subjected to unfair treatment. It also rejects the Ethnic Vanguardism of the Indian Guyanese narrative by emphasizing the multi-ethnic and multi-party nature of the opposition to the PNC regime. In this regard it centers the role of the WPA and projects Walter Rodney as the visionary of multi-ethnicity. Third, this narrative contends that although class and gender are significant factors, ethnicity is the primary problem that must be overcome if the country is to move forward. Finally, it contends that since the root cause of the problem is ethnic insecurity, any solution must be premised on ethnic equality and the guarantee of mutual security. Towards this end, it argues that a democratic political system and process that goes beyond winner-take-all is the most desirable form

of government.
Dr. Jagan and the construction of Indian Victimhood

With the prospect of free and fair elections in the late 1980s Dr. Jagan returned to the ethnic narrative which he first expounded in the 1950s. In a 1988 address to a Pan Indian conference in New York he observed that under PNC rule Indians were treated as "second class" citizens and compared the Indian Guyanese condition to that of African Americans. According to him they were discriminated both on account of their ethnicity and the fact that they were mainly of the working class. The following quotation captured his sentiments in this regard.

> Racial discrimination and "second-class" status have been the lot of Indians. Like Blacks in the USA, they suffer doubly: from discrimination because of their race and culture; from exploitation as members of the working class and peasantry. In Guyana, after more than two decades of rule by the petty-bourgeois Black-dominated People's National Congress (PNC), the vast majority of Indians feel "left out." Through electoral fraud and military intervention in elections, they have been virtually disenfranchised. And through political racial discrimination under the doctrine of "PNC paramountcy," equality of opportunity is denied. Consequently, many Indo-Guyanese see their salvation in emigration, mainly to North America (1988:23).

Dr. Jagan defended Indians against charges of disloyalty. He argued that Indian Guyanese support of Indian and Pakistani cricket teams over the West Indies team should be seen in the context of "the social psychology of Indians; their second class status; the discrimination meted out to them" and "as compensation for a sense of persecution, an inferiority complex which has been forced into their psyche over the years" (1988:25-26).

He also acknowledged that ethnic polarization was a major problem in Guyana, but he explicitly privileges class. He contended that "class is more fundamental than race" and that race must be "neither underestimated nor overestimated" (Jagan 1988:29). This privileging of class by Jagan led him to argue that Indian support for him was based not on ethnicity but on his advocacy and defense of their working class interests. While he is correct that ideology influenced Indian support of his party, he is incorrect in believing that it was the only or primary factor. How does he account for the fact that Indian Guyanese did not support other non-Indian working class leaders except for Rodney? Further, how does he explain Indian Guyanese middle class support and membership of the PPP after the 1955 split?

For Dr. Jagan the solution to the country's ethnic problem lay in a combination of "constitutional guarantees" and other reforms including affirmative action. Unfortunately upon his return to office in 1992 he became a victim of the imperatives of political office and failed to implement any of these reforms. While he abhorred racism, he became a prisoner of the ethnic politics he helped to usher in after 1955. Although he never acknowledged his role in shaping the country's ethnic politics, he was a pivotal actor both as political leader and opinion shaper.

During a speech in Toronto, Canada in November 1996, Dr. Jagan declared that Blacks were generally located at the bottom of the social ladder. The statement was made in the context of explaining that race was not the criterion used by the British and Americans to remove the PPP from office in 1964:

> And the British and Americans did not remove me and put Burnham in because of race. In fact, if they were using race, I should have been kept there and Burnham should have been kept out forever because, as we know, Black People are generally at the lowest scale of the social ladder (Jagan 1996:10).

The PNC condemned the statement as the "height of irresponsibility, divisive and fraught with danger" and wrote to the Reverend Jesse Jackson, former US president Jimmy Carter and other US civil rights organizations calling on them to condemn Dr. Jagan. Other African and opposition commentators also called the statement inexcusable and urged the President to apologize. Dr. Jagan retorted that the statement was taken out of context. According to him, "anyone who has listened to my entire address and has an iota of commonsense would have noted that the sentence could not have referred to Afro-Guyanese but to Blacks in the United States of America" (Jagan 1996:4).

While he did not specifically refer to Guyana it was clear that he meant Blacks in general and not just in the USA. But Dr. Jagan missed the larger point. In ethnic discourses statements such as the one in question are more often than not subjected to ethnic specific interpretations. Journalist Rickey Singh agreed that the statement reflected a poor choice of words but was not racist. He accused the PNC of playing "the race card" and reminded the party that the social neglect of African communities is a "legacy of PNC rule" (Singh: November 24, 1996). The independent Catholic Standard, organ of the Catholic Church, referred to the matter as a "little storm" and also exonerated Dr. Jagan of charges of racism (Catholic Standard: November 24, 1996).

A closer reading of the statement in the context of the entire speech shows that Dr. Jagan did not intend it as an ethnic or racial slur. Apart from the fact that he stated an established truth he was making the point that the white racial logic should have meant a preference for the Indian over the African. But in the context of ethnic suspicion many Africans perceived it as disrespectful.

Ravi Dev's Ethnic Suffering and Guilt and Kwayana's No Guilty Race

When ethnic violence erupted in the wake of the 1997 election as African mobs in Georgetown assaulted Indians after the court validated the PPP's electoral victory, Ravi Dev took up the challenge on behalf of Indians. Pointing to the ethnic nature of the violence he observed that "all the attackers were of African origin and all those attacked were either Indians or looked like Indians" (Dev 1998:1). He insisted that the attacks were part of a larger historical phenomenon, which is grounded in African Guyanese sense of greater legitimacy. He cited the African Guyanese suffering during slavery and their prior arrival in the country as the basis of their feeling of greater entitlement and that Guyana is essentially an African nation. This, he argues, is part of a larger Caribbean manifestation: "The Caribbean as a whole, including Guyana, has been defined by its African section as an African nation and other groups are expected to assimilate into the prevalent Creole culture" (Dev 1998:14).

According to Dev the African Guyanese experience of slavery resulted in an inherent frustration and anger, which in turn predispose them to the use of violence as the solution to socio-political problems. He argued that Indian Guyanese, on the other hand, are less disposed to this type of violence on others; they tend to inflict violence on themselves. As he puts it:

> In addition to the nurtured tradition of revolt, African socialization patterns predispose them into aggressive habits and frustrating situations elicit aggressive responses even against authority figures i.e. there is normative support for violence in the African community. The Indian on the other hand, is conditioned to repress his anger especially when the frustrating situation involves authority figures. Thus unlike the African who is predisposed toward externalising his anger, the Indian internalises his, into a retroflexive anger pattern that is eventually unleashed upon himself (Dev 1998:19).

Dev took his narrative a step further by describing Africans as bullies which he claimed is part of the African belief system that finds resonance in the frequency with which Indians were shot by the African-dominated police force. He contends that:

> In addition to the African tradition of rebellion, which the educational system fosters, there is also a more diffused, generalised belief amongst Africans that they can bully the Indian and get away with it...That Indians were shot and killed in 1870,1896,1903,1913,1924,1939,1948, and 1973, which would have demonstrated a great history of violent struggle for justice in Guyana is assiduously kept from the general population. As a point of fact almost every painful step out of colonialism into independence has been earned at the expense of Indian blood (Dev 1998:20).

Dev's narrative was part of a coordinated response to the riots by the Guyanese Indian Foundation Trust (GIFT), which compiled a report on the attacks including testimonies from victims. The report drew several conclusions. It concluded that the attacks were "explicitly racist" as the victims were attacked "not for anything else but that they were seen to be Indians". GIFT also concluded that the attacks were "unprovoked" and "well orchestrated". The report rebuked African Guyanese women for condoning the attacks on Indian women and children but commended six African Guyanese for helping victims.[26]

Kwayana responded to Dev in the form of a booklet, *No Guilty Race*. While acknowledging his own role in calling for retaliation to the violence in the 1960s, he expressed his strong opposition to African initiation of aggression against others (Kwayana 1999:3).

Kwayana described the violence against Indians on January 12 as the handiwork of Africans he was not proud of and who were "selfish people and not of people who care about their own race" (1999:5-6). He recounted an incident involving an African woman who was rescued at sea by Indian fishermen to argue that kindness across ethnic lines did not deserve violence against those who extended a helping hand. Without naming Dev he cautioned against establishing ethnic "right" and "wrong" and labeled such history "false alarm:"

> My challenge to writers of history, or of the story of the peoples is this--an African writer or Indian writer should not try to pretend that his or her race is always right and the others always wrong. This cry:" My race (Indian or African) is always right, my race suffered the most, my race is the most wronged in the country, all the violence done in history was against my race"--is a false alarm. This kind of history, so far as Guyana is concerned, can be seen as war propaganda. It has no basis in the facts of our experience and will condemn later generations to endless conflict. (1999:2)

Kwayana then reached for his central thesis: while all wrongs are not equal, the Guyanese ethnic experience does not reveal a guilty race.

> We can arrive at a conclusion of a guilty race, only by twisting facts, missing facts and treating readers or listeners with disrespect. This does not mean that in every department of wrong the scores are equal. It means that there has been to date no ground at all for the idea of a guilty race of Guyanese.

He also rejected the thesis of the inherently violent African:

> I know also that the present public image of violence is an African one. Few people regret more than I do the degeneration of sections of Africans in Guyana but to say that it is natural or that it was always so or that all are downhill must be due to ignorance or mischief. My present mission includes waging jihad against the doctrine, not the person, of anyone who claims that there is a guilty race in Guyana (1999:37).

He recounted the ethnic violence of the 1960s and contended that contrary to the popular narrative on the Indian side, both ethnic groups initiated violence--African Guyanese were the aggressors in 1962 and 1963 and Indian Guyanese in 1961 and 1964. This intervention by Kwayana is important because most accounts of the conflict place its beginnings in 1962. He, however, had documented violence against African Guyanese in 1961 in a booklet *Next Witness*, which he re-released at the same time as *No Guilty Race*. Kwayana also addressed the issue of whether there is a place for ethnic organizations in multi-ethnic societies. According to him such organizations inevitably attract the attention of the opposite group, but urged them to have a public message of "reconciliation" and a "people's peace" (1999:55).

In 1999 ROAR was transformed into a political party, thus becoming the country's first party to openly describe itself as ethnic. Despite Dev's direct appeal to the Indian Guyanese community, he was only able to gain one seat at the 2001 election. By then he had begun a wave of criticism of the PPP for not adequately protecting Indian Guyanese. Unlike previous criticisms, which were meant to push the PPP to act, the objective of this new criticism was to present Dev and ROAR as an Indian Guyanese alternative to the PPP. This invariably made him fair game for the PPP's machinery, which accused him of trying to split the Indian vote. Dev's entry into parliament as ROAR's lone representative presented a dilemma for him. He had to determine how to oppose the PPP without offending the East Indian community and as a member of the parliamentary opposition he had to decide the extent to which he would associate with the African Guyanese parliamentary leadership of the PNC.

ROAR's entry into electoral politics was accompanied by the rise of the Guyana Indian Heritage Association (GIHA), which also took up the Indian Guyanese cause with much enthusiasm. Like Dev, GIHA focused on violence against Indians; it effectively used the public media to highlight the problem. Its leader, Rhyaan Shah, took a no-nonsense approach to the issues. It advocated for Indian Arrival Day to be named a public holiday and in 2003 organized an all-Indian cricket match, which was boycotted by some cricketers. GIHA's criticism of these players was condemned by the PPP, which accused the organization of having an "extremist agenda" and with trying to divide the country's youth (Guyana Chronicle: September 13, 2003). The PPP, which created its own Indian organization, the Indian Arrival Committee (IAC), also pushed back against GIHA's criticism of the government for not correcting the imbalance in the security forces. It described the charge as inaccurate and accused GIHA of "looking for attention" (Stabroek News October 3, 2003).

Indian Justification and Vanguardism

The major target of the Indian Narrative of Justification and Vanguardism has been the WPA whose achievements are viewed as miniscule and its multi-ethnic claims are questioned. It is reduced to a fringe Black Power organization that flirted with revolutionary violence and whose rhetoric was not matched by its ability to attract lasting support. While Dr. Jagan had described the WPA as a group of Black intellectuals in 1979 it was Ravi Dev's JCD who first popularized the view of the WPA as Black Nationalist. He did so in the context of his argument that while African Guyanese of all political persuasions have promoted Black interests, Indian Guyanese activists and politicians have not similarly promoted Indian interests. The JCD described the WPA's multi-ethnic image as a myth by arguing that the African WPA leaders "never lost sight of the Black interests in their national struggles" (Ramharack October 1992). On the other hand it charged the Indian WPA leaders with not identifying with Indian interests. The JCD also argued that the claim of Indian dominance of the economy was another myth aimed at weakening the Indian community and that Indian economic power should not be used as an excuse to prevent an Indian government as Africans would still control the army, police and government bureaucracy. According to the JCD:

> Economic and political powers are not equivalent. People who claim that Indians control the economy should remember that political leaders can fashion the economy in their interest as the Burnham era clearly demonstrated when the regime controlled more than 80% of the economy. No one cared or raised similar concerns for Indian lack of political power under the Burnham Regime (JCD: August-September 1992).

Despite its criticisms of Dr. Jagan for not taking an Indianist position, JCD aggressively supported the PPP at the 1992 election. It defended the PPP against charges that it was an Indian party and charged the WPA with having a "conspiracy" against the PPP. In the process it overtly and covertly linked the WPA with the PNC as representative of African Guyanese interests, a charge that the PPP would later use against the WPA.

Randy Persaud, an Indian university lecturer based in the US who later became an employee in the Office of the President, located this PNC-WPA alliance in the Black Nationalist tradition, which he contended was always part of the WPA's "intellectual pillars"- the other being Marxism (Persaud: July 1, 2006). Persaud argues that the WPA was founded on two intellectual pillars Black Power and Marxism-but in the post 1992 period it abandoned Marxism and embraced what he calls a "narrow and dehistoricised form of Black Nationalism." This Black Nationalism according to Persaud is in "contradiction to Rodney's Fanonian critique of European cultural supremacy over non-Europeans, the WPA now intimates that Africans in Guyana are being dominated by Indians."

He identifies David Hinds, a WPA member based in the USA, as the "intellectual architect" of this WPA tendency. He charges Hinds with incorrectly advocating that the PPP represents Indian interests and for being silent on Indian marginalization and African domination of the Armed Forces and the Civil Service. Persaud further accused the WPA and Hinds of promoting violence by suggesting that if there is no political solution violence could erupt. For Persaud the WPA has always had a predisposition towards Black Nationalism: "The multiracial façade has now crash landed and the Black Nationalism that has always underpinned the movement is now there for all to see, only this time without apologies" (Persaud: July 1, 2006).

Persaud cited as evidence of the WPA's Black Nationalism, its work with the PNC in all-opposition initiatives, which he dubbed a PNC-WPA alliance. As he puts it "the WPA is like a Minibus Tout Man for the PNC" (Persaud: July 2006). He also criticized Hinds and the WPA for equating the PPP with the PNC. According to him:

> To equate the PNC record of misrule (to put it politely) with the record of the PPP/C is nothing short of another form of everyday bullyism. The PNC ran a National Security State. In such a state, most of the resources were spent on bolstering the armed forces, police, and militias etc. Command of the disciplined forces is paramount, and that is something the PNC had "under full control." They apparently still have the confidence of the military and police force. I'll leave others to talk about the Guyana National Service. The PPP government is the diametric opposite of that. Most of their resources go into housing, education, healthcare, water supply etc. The current government does not enjoy the confidence of the military or police (Persaud: July 1, 2006).

Finally, Persaud dismisses Hinds' call for a peaceful settlement as destabilization of the government. He argued that since the WPA did not have electoral following and that the PNC was violent, the government should have no settlement with them:

> The notion of a "peaceful settlement" is actually conducive to the destabilization of the current government. Why in the world should a government elected by the people of this country enter into a "settlement" with the WPA which is made up or no more than a dozen individuals? Go out and win some votes first! Why should the government enter into a so-called settlement with the PNC who has brought violence to this country at every election? (Persaud: July 1, 2006).

Persaud's thesis on Hinds and the WPA was challenged by other commentators. Alissa Trotz and Freddie Kissoon accused him of being guilty of committing the same errors he accused Hinds of.

> His was not a letter inviting a conversation, seeking to build a culture of mutual respect. By rushing to tar (the pun here is deliberate) all Black people with the same brush – Gibson, Hinds, Corbin, who else one wonders? I suppose me, after this letter - Randy Persaud has demonstrated the very thing that he accuses David Hinds of. We all know how this works; we all know that the beneficiaries of this race baiting are the two political parties; we all know that the outcome of this stereotyping is the kind of fear and division that leads to votes along racial lines, rather than votes on principles (Trotz: June 21, 2006).

Evan Thomas zeroed in on what he saw as the significance of Persaud's thesis, which he describes as "intellectual dishonesty and linked to the larger PPP narrative:

> Dr. Jagan had failed to grasp the olive branch for consolidating national unity as offered him by the WPA and instead, showed that the PPP was only using other progressive forces to get their hands on power, so to speak; the reason today for such extreme Afro-centric expressions coming from leading members/supporters of ACDA (once WPA activists). Dr. Persaud in criticizing Dr. Hinds is trying to give legitimacy to the PPP's current political interest, even if by employing his notion of Trouillot's concept (Thomas: June 20, 2006)

Leading columnist "Peeping Tom" countered Persaud's claim that the WPA had abandoned Marxism by pointing out that all the major parties, including the PPP, had retreated from left wing politics (Peeping Tom: July 22, 2006). Peeping Tom also contested Persaud's charges that Hinds and the WPA advocated violence. As he argued:
> David Hinds has not called for Africans to take up arms against the government. In fact in the midst of the Buxton

criminal uprising of 2001- 2003, Hinds, Andaiye and Kwayana were some of the voices of reason, opposing the christening of murder, rape and robbery as a resistance struggle…All that David Hinds has been advocating is that if a government, widely perceived to represent Indian interests, is unwilling or resistant to meet the demands of another grouping within society, then it may force that grouping to opt for other measures. All this says is what is likely to happen should one group that feels that it is being dominated sees not the possibility of its concerns being addressed. This is not advocacy; it is analysis, bringing to the attention of the ruling elite the risks that it runs by ignoring certain things. Hinds, in fact, has made it clear that he does not believe that Guyana has reached that stage where armed struggle can be justified. Kwayana had also insisted that there were non-violent means open for redress by those in Buxton. How therefore can Hinds be accused of advocating violence, when in fact he is on record as saying that Guyana has not reached that stage where violence can be justified? (Peeping Tom, July 25, 2006).

Another exponent of this aspect of the Indian narrative is Annan Boodram, a former PPP activist also based in the USA. Like the JCD and Persaud he sought to demolish the WPA's multiethnic image and accused the WPA and Rodney of embracing violence. While acknowledging Rodney as a great scholar he describes him as a "political novice of the first order" who had left no lasting legacy or strong political organization. On the other hand he characterized Dr. Jagan as a visionary who eschewed violence as a political solution. Further, according to Boodram:

Rodney did not build any political entity that endured with viability; did not lay down any policy/program that was visionary or impactful; did not establish a cadre of leaders that forged ahead with any degree of political success. His appeal was transient and personality-centered rather than premised on the potency and message of the political entity – the WPA (Boodram: December 31, 2009).

Finally, Boodram dismisses the crowds at Rodney's meetings as the result of "Rodney's rhetoric, the novelty factor, curiosity, an opportunity to anonymously express their frustrations without being targets, crowd-pull factors, attendance encouragement from many quarters, et al." He suggested that the WPA all but declined with the death of Rodney who was a "one man show" (Boodram: December 31, 2009). Boodram describes Dr. Jagan on the other hand was "neither radical nor extremist;" he was "Bapu, the father figure a la Mahatma Gandhi" and his "embrace of Marxism was not dogmatic and deterministic." Dr. Jagan and the PPP faced "paradoxes" while the WPA "flailed, floundered and flapped." For Boodram, Jagan was not "naïve" not to realize that "he was insulated from the daily maneuverings and manipulations of the party and that he was fed only what those with regular access to him." According to Boodram:

> Dr. Jagan was a human being who was warm, caring, honest, approachable, humble, moral, and ethical, a man for whom ostentatious displays of wealth had little attraction. That same person will be the first to also admit that Cheddi had his imperfections, but that these flaws did not detract from a man who lived the conviction of his beliefs – an unwavering belief in the capacity of Guyana to be a successful nation and an abiding interest in the welfare of the Guyanese people (Boodram: December 31, 2009).

David Hinds pointed out that Boodram's views fit into the larger Indian "ethnic vanguardism" narrative which is meant to project the PPP as the most authentic medium of freedom. Describing Boodram's criticism of Rodney as "ridicule" and "war propaganda" he argued that such a narrative is unhelpful to ethnic relations:

> The larger implication of this narrative on Jagan-PPP and Rodney-WPA for ethnicity and race in Guyana is instructive. If the PPP were the leaders of the resistance to the PNC then Indians are the ones responsible for freedom…The African becomes the obstacle to freedom. They are written out of positive history. Their history is a history of guilt and

violence, never a history of freedom struggle... Boodram's treatise is not about the examination of political events and actors but about the construction of truisms in pursuit of that vanguardism. It is what Kwayana once called "war propaganda" (Hinds: January 5, 2010).

Nigel Westmaas, a WPA activist, observed that while Rodney was an important leader, he was not the only influence on the WPA. He also drew attention to the fact that the WPA actually expanded in membership and activity after Rodney's murder:

> It is highly inaccurate to suggest that the WPA floundered or collapsed after Rodney's assassination in 1980. This view is understandable in one sense because the record of WPA activity between 1980 and 1992 is insufficiently recorded and there is always a tendency in discussion of the broad opposition in the period to ignore or downplay the veritable siege conditions the WPA, unlike the PPP as the formal parliamentary opposition, had to endure. The fact is that the WPA grew strikingly in terms of grassroots work in African, Indian and Amerindian communities after 1980, and held an impressive multi-racial membership from Georgetown extending all the way to the Corentyne, and Amerindian communities in the interior. (Westmaas: January 3, 2010).

Joey Jagan, son of Dr. Jagan also took issue with Boodram's thesis on Dr. Rodney:

> Walter Rodney was a true patriot, defender of the peoples' rights, and he brought new political ideas and praxis to Guyana when he was alive. Rodney galvanized huge gatherings on the streets, crowds with Indian and African Guyanese and this was significant at that point in our history; the fact that the WPA went into decline after his death is instructive in understanding the power Walter held in his hands, and Mr. Boodram's comments on this point represent baiting, because in infancy (like the WPA), if the PPP or the PNC had lost Jagan or Burnham respectively,

those parties would also have declined. A statue should be built of Walter Rodney and placed in the most prominent place we can find in this country; he deserved such a tribute (Jagan: January 8, 2010).

Like Hinds, Abu Bakr places Boodram's analysis in the larger context of the ethnic discourse. He also cites the favorable treatment of Dr. Jagan as part of the "us" versus "them" which Boodram suggested that he was against. He views the different treatment given to Jagan and Burnham as the crux of the problem.

It is through a reading of the treatment of these two figures in the literature, including the letter columns, that the core of the 'us' versus 'them' conflict is revealed. Dr. Jagan, as historical figure and effigy, is most often insulated from the sins and wickedness of his successors. Mr. Boodram is careful to insulate Dr. Jagan "warm, caring… honest ethical" personage, from the "immoral, unethical and criminal" character of those who now lay claim to his heritage. On the other hand, Mr. Burnham is generally, in the 'us' versus 'them' schema, portrayed laden with all the sins and wickedness of those who surrounded him during the 28 years. Dr. Jagan is a character above the impurity and the fray. Mr. Burnham is 'collectivity,' both a man and a system, standing accused of responsibility for choke and rob, kick down the door, multiple murder and all the immoralities that marked his time… While Cheddi marches unsullied in the national consciousness, the figure emblematic of the Afro-Guyanese political leadership, Burnham, decked out in his usual demonisms is unceasingly flayed and flung on the fire. But neither man was without a share of the responsibility (Bakr: January 3, 2010).

Bakr also pushed back against the notion that the WPA's importance was exaggerated. He contended that the WPA "offered hope" as the country began to decline in the 1970s; it removed the "veil of invincibility" from the PNC; and it "brought new ideas and a new praxis to our politics" and an "alternative model of party organization" that was fresh. He also contended that while the WPA did not do well electorally it played a leading role in "defining the post 1992 arrangements for the sharing of power." For Bakr new parties such as the AFC could benefit from emulating the WPA's praxis and explains the WPA's legacy in this manner:

> The WPA's lasting legacy is the example of all of those courageous people who lost lives, careers, time…to insist on a change from which many now benefit. The truth is that the PPP at the time, while active on many fronts and still organised, would not have been able, alone, to bring the internal and external pressure that led before the change in the cold war geo-politics, to the PNC having to humble itself. We cannot forget the WPA; neither can the PNC or the PPP. The role or lasting influence of a movement cannot be measured only in the number of votes it commands or the seats it occupies. It may also be measured by the power of its example and the ideas it has left in the national consciousness. Much political writing and thought and activism on an international scale has had the effect of planting new ideas in a society. And often the electoral results are neither immediate nor measurable (Bakr: January 6, 2010)

Eusi Kwayana also weighed in on the debate. He called Boodram's negative assessment of Rodney "self serving:" He also pointed out that Dr. Jagan and Mr. Burnham had both advocated for violence and accused Boodram of "quoting words and ignoring them at the same time." He claims that while Boodram puts Dr. Jagan's politics in context he does not afford Rodney the same:

> Although he is at pains not to reveal his own political culture, except in broad national and patriotic terms, Mr. Boodram indirectly tells a lot about his preference. Although Rodney is no longer here, he can find not a single positive quality to speak of the dead. Everything he says has a touch of disdain and he does not hide it. (Kwayana: January 13, 2010)

The criticism of the WPA in the Indian narrative is meant to erase the PPP's main competitor as hero of the anti-dictatorial struggle. This erasure of the WPA from settled history and the popular consciousness does several things. First, it leaves the PPP with a monopoly of the freedom space in modern Guyanese politics. Second, the PPP would not have to contend with a period in its history when significant sections of its supporters gravitated to the WPA. Third, the stress on the WPA's electoral returns is part of the PPP's elevation of electoral performance as the ultimate test of a party's worth. As a party generally guaranteed of the majority ethnic vote, it would always be the major star. Fourth, the location of the WPA within the context of Black Nationalism achieves two things for the larger narrative. It removes the WPA from the mainstream of Guyana's political tradition and places it within the violent African tradition that is central to the Indian narrative of the guilty race. Further, it places the WPA in the same box as the PNC, which is severely discredited in the Indian Guyanese community. Fifth, the critique of Rodney is meant to remove Dr. Jagan's competition as the leader with the highest multiethnic standing. Rodney's accomplishments are, therefore, acknowledged in the context of his overseas activities while there is either silence on or ridicule of his activities in Guyana. Sixth, the minimizing of the WPA's role means that it could not lay claim to a share of the democratic dividends after 1992. As I observed elsewhere:

> Political history is in part about contestation for historical space. The absolute role of the vanguard PPP and its leader during the period in question is challenged by the existence of other significant forces such as the WPA and Rodney. Since it is foolhardy to deny that Rodney and the WPA existed, the alternative is to minimize their roles. It is in this context that Boodram's forthright pronouncement of the death of Rodney and the WPA in 1980 must be understood. If the WPA was born in 1974, came of age in 1979 and died in 1980 then logically it was the PPP that carried the struggle for most of the period in question (Hinds: January 5, 2010).

African Marginalization and Indian Guilt

The PNC's loss of power was accompanied by division in the African community that led to a temporary split in the party. Some members and supporters rebuked party leader, Desmond Hoyte, for giving up political power while others welcomed the return to democratic elections. This group also blamed Africans in the WPA for leading the charge to remove the PNC and in the process saddling the country with an Indian government. While this charge is unjustified, as the WPA fought for a power sharing government to replace the PNC, in the context of ethnic politics and given the PPP's abandonment of a multi-ethnic solution, such a charge was inevitable.

Between 1992 and 1997 the PNC accused the PPP of marginalizing African Guyanese by engaging in ethnic witch hunting in the public sector and discrimination in land distribution. It also charged the PPP with "ethnic cleansing" and the pursuit of Indian domination. A conflict between two farmers' cooperative societies in 1995 over the ownership of 750 acres of land on the West Coast of Demerara became the first ethnic flashpoint during the PPP's first term. The PNC, which represented the interests of the African based Rosiante society charged the Indian-based Boerasierie society with ethnic aggression. Party leader, Desmond Hoyte advised the members of the Rosiante group that in the face of aggression they had a right to use "deadly force" to protect themselves and their property. The independent Stabroek News deemed Mr. Hoyte's statements to be "excessive," "intemperate" and "inflammatory." (Stabroek News: January 30, 1996). Hoyte replied to the Stabroek News in the form of a letter which, much like Kwayana's *Next Witness* in 1962, itemized instances of PPP's victimization of Africans. He accused the PPP of ethnic cleansing including "ruthless purges" in the Public Service and "systematic and ruthless" harassment and marginalization of Africans. Hoyte charged the PPP with a "three-fold...interlocking program."

> First the PPP regime's pervasive disregard for the rule of the law. Second its methodical victimization of the Public Sector of citizens of African descent and other citizens deemed to be non-supporters of the PPP, and third its policy of discrimination against these persons in respect of state land tenure and leases (Hoyte: March 7, 1996).

Hoyte also drew attention to the PPP's description of Mashramani as an African celebration and viewed Ms Jagan's writings as arousing "latent fears and suspicions and strengthened the conviction that the PPP is hell-bent on pursuing a racist agenda." He also accused the PPP of arming its supporters under the guise of vigilante groups and left no doubt about where he stood on the issue of "ethnic self-defense:"

> I repeat what I said at Farm on January 17. The PPP seems bent on monopolizing all political, economic and cultural space in Guyana. If citizens of African descent and other members of the target group are deliberately denied employment opportunities and evicted from land, they will be relegated to the status of trespassers in their own country. But they are not trespassers, they have a right, as much as anybody else, to live in peace, to enjoy all the opportunities for making a living which this country offers, and not to be discriminated against. If these opportunities are absent, then they will rightly conclude that they have no stake in the country and its destruction will be a matter of no consequence to them (Hoyte: March 7, 1996).

While the PNC's rhetoric was extreme and there was no evidence of ethnic cleansing, the PPP did very little to allay African fears. In fact, it played into the PNC's hands by moving to dismantle the country's largest cultural festival which it claimed did not cater to Indian Guyanese. The African Marginalization thesis found another voice in a university lecturer, Kean Gibson. Her book *The Cycle of Racial Oppression in Guyana* caused much controversy. It characterized the PPP as being intent on pushing Africans to the periphery of the political and economic processes. Gibson's central argument was that Hindu East Indians consider Africans to be an inferior race who are un fit to govern. She invoked what she saw as the Hindu duality of good and evil in which the Indian is "virtuous" and the African is "evil" (2003:61). She locates PPP's governance in this Hindu conspiracy to dominate Africans. Hence the execution of African youth, and African marginalization in general arose out of this desire to dominate. For Gibson Indians and the PPP were less concerned about the nation and more with the preservation of their caste. As she observed:

An ideology that has no moral obligation to the nation and which gives free rein to our instinct of self-preservation means the change is not feasible as long as the PPP remains in power. The break down of law and order is necessary to facilitate and maintain the creation of a racial state based on racial criteria (2003:64).

There were virulent responses to Gibson's book especially from Indian Guyanese who viewed it as incendiary. Many Africans rose to her defense and hailed the book as an important document. In the final analysis the debate was less about the content, which was not vigorously argued, but about the context in which it was taking place. While Gibson's scholarship was faulted by some commentators her advocacy was not different from others like Ravi Dev who sought to highlight the ethnic suffering of their ethnic groups. One commentator who took Gibson to task was university lecturer and columnist, Frederick Kissoon. He labeled the book "propagandistic" and a "pamphlet, whether willfully or not, designed to encourage feelings of hate". He observed that rather than utilize credible sources, the book relied on calls to and comments on television talk-shows. He rejected Gibson's charges of ethnic discrimination and oppression against African Guyanese as part of her "imagination" (guyanaundersiege.com: 2003).

Prem Misir also deemed the charges of African marginalization a myth. He contended that the socio-economic status of Africans were similar to those of Indians. He instead argued that the PPP had to confront the PNC's legacy of institutionalized racism. Further, instead of favoring East Indians, the PPP is perceived by its supporters to pander to Africans. Misir referred to this as "de Indianization":

The current administration inherited a legacy of institutionalized racism and discrimination from the Burnham/Hoyte dictatorship. While the PPP- Civic attempts to govern predominantly through the process of 'de- Indianization', the Burnham/ Hoyte administration essentially created policies and programs, aimed at sustaining the power base of the African elite.

Ethnicity and the Economy

In 1997 ACDA held a symposium on Africans and the Guyanese economy. The panelists included WPA members Clive Thomas and Andaiye, PNC executives Haslyn Parris and Kenneth King and an ACDA activist, Dennis Wiggins. The composition of the panel was significant as it brought together on the same platform members of two parties who had been bitter enemies for two decades. Thomas' participation was particularly revealing; unlike other African WPA leaders he was never viewed in ethno-racial terms. His academic and public education work were noted for their strong Marxist orientation. But he had since 1992 begun to grapple with race and ethnicity as evidenced in his call for a revisiting of theories of race and ethnicity in the Caribbean in a paper that essentially rejected the notion that race and ethnicity are social myths.[27]

His presentation at the ACDA symposium found that Indians dominated those sectors that showed the most growth between 1988 and 1996 and the top levels of a thriving clandestine economy, which had linkages to the formal economy. On the other hand there was little or no growth in those sectors of the economy dominated by Africans namely mining and the public sector. He contended that the African Guyanese problem could not be corrected solely by "community self help" and "the market mechanism" and instead called for "focused and targeted action by the government that should prioritize the youth and policies such as education, the promotion of small business, land reform, affirmative action in employment and housing and multicultural policies, including cultural education." In addition to government policy he urged the African Guyanese community to engage in "the promotion of our culture in enhancing self identity, group cohesiveness and non-conflictual mode of behavior among African Guyanese and between African Guyanese and other ethnic groups." He also called for the formation of NGOs and cooperatives in the community and for African Guyanese organizations to participate in the economy. Towards this end he suggested the promotion of an ACDA development bank (1997:14).

Thomas' presentation drew a terse response from Ravi Dev who described the presentation as "misconceived" and "dangerous." According to Dev, Thomas' correlation of high unemployment among

Africans with high employment among Indians suggested "causation" between the two, which he suggested was untrue. He contended that African non-employment in the rice and sugar sectors was due to their shunning of these sectors. He criticized Thomas for suggesting that salaried African Guyanese workers were more vulnerable than self-employed Indian Guyanese who he claimed were at the mercy of nature and the market. Accusing Thomas of "libeling" the Indian community by relying on media reports, Dev argued that even if his data were correct the differences between the two ethnic groups were insignificant. Finally, Dev predicted that Thomas' presentation would "widen the arena of possible conflicts between African and Indians." (Dev, April 6, 1997)

In his reply, Thomas observed that Dev had relied on media reports of the presentation rather than reading the manuscript. He correctly pointed out that the paper looked at the economic condition of all ethnic groups (Thomas May 7, 1997). Dev responded that Dr. Thomas did not address his substantive concerns and accused him of hiding his true position behind "jargon-filled academic papers" (Dev May 8, 1998). Eusi Kwayana was not surprised at Dev's response to Thomas' presentation: "when I read the paper by CY Thomas days after he delivered it at an ACDA conference, I knew what to expect." (Kwayana 1999:54). Kwayana had had a similar experience in the 1960s when he was labeled a racist for among other things highlighting African suffering. Kwayana chided Dev for bringing Indian grievances into the public sphere but denying that right to those who seek to highlight African grievances and observed that in Guyana both groups measure their suffering and progress in relation to the other. Hence Dr. Thomas' citing of data which shows greater unemployment among Africans is not the problem. As Kwayana states, "the unemployed do not need Clive Thomas' data to tell them that they are unemployed" (1999:54).

In a later interview on ethnicity and the economy Thomas linked the performance or non-performance of the Guyanese economy to the ethnic struggle for power.[28] As he observed "It has absorbed our energies and it has marginalized our talents and led to migration of people." This migration has had a negative impact on population growth which between 1992 and 1999 grew by 0.61 percent. Thomas cited waste of resources by both PPP and PNC governments and continuing opposition protests as an important factor in influencing the economy. He also contends that lack of serious debates on the economic and social policies has hurt the country. He blames this on the loss of talents arising from migration. Finally, he points to the fact that Guyana has become "an important experimenting ground" for the IMF and the World Bank rather than a space for "creative response" to the economic problems. In this regard he expressed disappointment at the PPP which given its history of progressive politics, was well placed to introduce an alternative approach to the economy.

Thomas shares Dr. Jagan's views that African Guyanese are at the bottom of the social ladder. He drew attention to the linkage between their condition and their lack of political power. As he put it, "they don't control the levers of decision making and wealth. They don't control the state so they don't control the distribution of public income." This observation, according to him, is important because most studies tend to focus on private income and not as much on public expenditures, which account for 30-40 percent of making households. Thomas also draws attention to African Guyanese lack of control over land as a second important problem. He points out that because in "pressure" situations people tend to use the land for "survival" the lack of land limits the African community. Thomas also draws attention to the decline of educational excellence in the African Guyanese community and the concomitant rise in other ethnic communities. He blames this on low wages and salaries in the public sector and the weight of poverty. As he argues:

> Education has lost some of its initial appeal as a way out of your condition. I think maybe because wage payment and salaried payment in the public sector is so low and unrewarding, people don't find the benefits from education to be as attractive as it used to be. Poverty has been weighing down so long on the society; people are looking for faster ways to make a buck (Thomas: July 14, 2005).

Thomas disagreed with the view that African Guyanese feared better under the PNC. According to him the fact that the PNC did not have an electoral majority it had to appease Indian Guyanese community in order "to maintain a situation of quiet." On the other hand the present PPP government because of the Indian majority does not have to pander much to African Guyanese. Instead they are forced to do everything to maintain Indian support.

> I think there is a lot of pressure on the PPP to maintain the support of their base than it was for the PNC who in similar circumstances was particularly concerned about trying to maintain or pacify through economic bribery the racial group that is in the majority (Thomas: July 14, 2005).

African Self-Criticism

As the debate raged over which ethnic group was more victimized and as relations deteriorated, commentators on both sides of the ethnic divide closed ranks. Fresh violence after the 2001 election escalated the following year when a group of African prison escapees set up camp in the African village of Buxton from where they built a militia that launched attacks on Indian communities and businesses, the police and African Guyanese suspected of cooperation with the government. This development was accompanied by a vocal group of television talk-show hosts who used their programs to give voice to the extreme anti-Indian and anti-government sentiments that had developed in sections of the African Guyanese community. They charged the government with pursuing a program of Indian domination and African marginalization in every sphere of the political economy.[29] They also expressed overt and covert support for the "Freedom Fighters" in Buxton who they viewed as a necessary component of the African resistance.[30]

Kwayana, David Hinds and Andaiye, three African Guyanese members of the WPA, countered the argument that African-Guyanese plight resulted from Indian oppression and separately and together condemned violence against Indians. Hinds contended that African marginalization was part of the historical development of the country's political economy, which has systematically placed Africans at the margins of the political and economic processes. He argued that both African and Indian Guyanese are marginalized, but Indians feel less insecure given the dominance of the economy and the government by their counterparts. He condemned those Indians who deny African marginalization and observed that while the PPP did not introduce African marginalization it had done nothing to alter the structured which have facilitated marginalization[31]

When the Buxton-based violence erupted, Kwayana, Hinds and Andaiye declared that Buxton had become a "terror camp" and condemned the violence against Indian Guyanese while observing that there were also African Guyanese victims.

> In the past, each of us has made statements condemning African Guyanese atrocities against Indian Guyanese, and we condemn them even more strongly now, as the violence becomes more brutal. A similar though less brutal violence has begun to spread to African Guyanese victims. We warned before that in the end, crime and violence know no race. This is coming to pass. In recent weeks the violence has taken on added proportions as African Guyanese are being targeted. While it is difficult to distinguish naked crime from political violence, we think that there is a political element in all of this. Today, African families and communities are also becoming victims of the madness that is consuming Guyana. And according to news reports and eyewitnesses, a few Indian Guyanese criminals are operating out of Buxton under the leadership of their African Guyanese counterparts (Andaiye, Hinds and Kwayana October 19, 2002).

They concluded that there was a "political element" to the violence and urged the government to take action to stop the flow of illegal weapons. They also called for "an expert voice from the law enforcement agencies" to speak to the offenders and offer options, "including the option of a fair trial under international observation," a suggestion that was previously made by Kwayana when the violence first begun. Finally, they urged the government to consult opposition parties and civil society in a bid to "apply standard coercive regulations necessary to prevent the country from sliding knowingly into the abyss" (Andaiye, Hinds and Kwayana

October 19. 2002).

The PNC and the PPP were equally blamed for the state of affairs:

> Both the PPP and the PNC must take full responsibility for that deterioration, for it is their zero sum political behavior that paved the way for the boldness of the criminal and other extreme elements who now run things there. We warn that if the situation is not brought under control, more Buxtons will emerge overnight (Andaiye, Hinds and Kwayana October 19. 2002)

They criticized the government for its failure to act on the instances of police violence against African Guyanese which "fueled the claim of an Indian Guyanese conspiracy against African Guyanese". While reiterating their belief that "power sharing" is the solution to the ethnic problem, they distanced themselves from any power sharing arrangement that resulted from "the calculated escalation of violence." The PNC were also criticized for not "publicly breaking" with "those who have been using Black Supremacy and violence and excusing murder, rape and mayhem as revolution". Speaking directly to African Guyanese they urged the following:

> As African Guyanese we urge Black People who are supporting the violence to stop confusing naked terror with our historical quest for freedom; and we urge Black people who mutter quietly that they oppose the violence to say so in a loud voice, because your public silence is encouraging the perpetrators of the violence and adding insult to the injury caused to the victims of the violence. Any freedom that any group seeks through the rape and murder of its fellow citizens, including some of its own race, can never be real freedom (Andaiye, Hinds and Kwayana October 19. 2002).

Thakur (2008: 114-115) contends that the Kwayana et al statement checked the dissent of the discourse into one focused on the "guilty black community" which he claimed was being pushed by GIHA which had criticized African Guyanese for not being "forthright: in their condemnation of the violence against Indians. Thakur believes that the statement also "emboldened" some Indians who begun to question the helplessness of the PPP in the face of the attacks on the Indian community.

Andaiye had earlier expressed outrage at the ethnic responses to the violence whereby Indians dismissed police violence against Africans as "a legitimate attack on crimes against them," Africans explained violence against Indians as the result of drug wars while both sides highlighted their losses as examples of victimhood. Turning her attention to the "Freedom Fighters" she declared:

> I have not seen the two leaflets distributed by men describing themselves as "freedom fighters", but friends I trust have seen them and tell me it's true that they describe themselves as freedom fighters on behalf of the African Guyanese nation. To this my answer is, as one African Guyanese: "No. Not in my name" (Andaiye 2004)

Andaiye also addressed violence against women within the context of the larger ethno-political violence. She took issue with a statement by then president Janet Jagan that since women enjoy the same rights as men, "if women want to agitate and cause problems, they have to face the same police the men face." According to Andaiye, Ms Jagan was "equalizing downwards, equality at the lowest common denominator and accused the PPP of double standards in relation to female "agitators." She also suggested that the PNC should acknowledge police brutality of women during its tenure in office.

Finally, while acknowledging that most Guyanese women privilege their ethno-racial identity, Andaiye argued that women are "incapable of being as cavalier as men about "collateral damage- perhaps because we give birth to and raise and care for the persons who constitute this collateral damage." She also posited that if women see themselves as independent thinkers "without party blinders" they would view sexual subjugation as unacceptable regardless of the perpetrators (Andaiye 2004).

The collateral damage Andaiye referred to were the victims of the violence, including women and children. Many supporters of the "freedom fighters" viewed the victims of their violence, Africans and Indians, as a necessary by-product of the "struggle". The PPP also suggested to Indians that their retaliation would escalate the violence which in turn would depose the government. For the PPP, therefore, Indian victims of violence were necessary to keep the party in office.

A week after the statement by Andaiye, Hinds and Kwayana, the latter in an impassioned appeal to the gunmen to return the guns to the "donors," declared "Indians were not responsible for the enslavement of Africans." He denounced the "donors" as having no knowledge about "race relations in Guyana and its rights and wrongs. They pick one thing here and another thing there. They are one sided and dangerous". Recalling the events of the 1960s, he observed that Buxtonians "never attacked." He also claimed that "the Indian Guyanese, whether they have guns or not have shown better behavior, yes better civilization than we have shown." Invoking his well known history of promoting African pride and dignity he declared: "And I am jealous of African civilization and its values". (Kwayana: September 8, 2002).

Kwayana eventually wrote a book *The Morning After* that chronicled the evolution of the violence in Buxton. As is the case with his writings in contemporary politics he locates the violence in the larger political conflict arising out of the historic ethnic competition. He contended that the "freedom fighters" were led by "masterminds" who have made Buxton a "cemetery". He questioned the argument that poverty was the cause of the violence: If poverty was the cause, why did the masterminds not deliver fifty, seventy computers and get teachers to train the youth in the skills needed to use them (Kwayana 2005: 2).

Kwayana located the problem in a combination of the opportunism of the masterminds and the reluctance of the PPP to respond positively to constitutional methods of struggle by the WPA and others. As he puts it:

> The standing of the WPA in Buxton-Friendship and in many other places had gone down not for lack of interest or because of any failure of the WPA to render the usual, small political social and business services. Our standing went down because people looked on to see the response of the state to our methods of struggle. In every case they saw our

constitutional moves as fruitless. Rebuffs from the ruling party and the state officials who look to the ruling party for approval and sometimes for orders (Kwayana 2005: 67).

Despite his criticism of the government and the police Kwayana argued against "militarism" as a solution. He opined that "we cannot include the right to kill and injure among the civil rights of a people claiming to be oppressed and deprived or actually depressed and deprived" and that "the problem with a coup is the morning after" (2005: 96). According to Kwayana "coups give power only to the coup leaders." Although he understood the fear of permanent African Guyanese exclusion from political power he felt that such a possibility "could be reversed at less human cost and less squandering of survival possibility than a coup would" (2005: 95). He also criticized African Guyanese for putting too much emphasis on voting and marching in preference to "planning, documentation, political organization, training in self-representation and advocacy". As he argued:

> They pin their hopes on elections and if that fails to give them victory, they are ready to move without any sense of the political process, even to the point of having hope in an armed solution which leads to major social shattering (2005: 95).

African Justification

The Kwayana, Hinds and Andaiye statement drew fire from some African leaders. PNC leader, Desmond Hoyte, who expressed "total solidarity" with Buxtonians denied that they were harboring criminals. In announcing a $250 million scheme he told the villagers that their cause was "just" and that "it was fashionable for some idiots to say that Buxton is a criminal village, Buxtonians are criminals, Buxtonians are violent people. The People's National Congress (PNC) and I reject this gross definition of the character of the people of Buxton- Friendship." Hoyte invoked the history of resistance in the village and urged the villagers not to be pacified by "guns and force." In an obvious reference to Kwayana, Hinds and Andaiye he warned that letters to the press should not deter the villagers.

It doesn't matter who writes long letters in the newspapers, it doesn't matter who writes long editorials, these people can't even find Buxton on the map but they want to analyze your problems and make prescriptions and the prescriptions usually are as follows: pacify Buxton, send in soldiers and police to kill you" (Stabroek News October 12, 2002).

The government-owned *Guyana Chronicle* in an editorial accused Mr. Hoyte of "political opportunism" and took him to task for speaking about "guns and force" only in relation to those killed by the police and not those beaten, robbed and killed by the gunmen. The newspaper also questioned the merit of 250 million revival plan for Buxton when many other villages were similarly depressed. Speaking directly to his denial of criminals in Buxton the newspaper asked:

If indeed Buxton has not been a sanctuary for criminals, then the PNC leader has a responsibility to tell the nation who are the ones who have been engaging in criminal activities that have occupied so much of the resources and time of the security forces. Where was he when the Chester family was forced to flee Buxton Village? Where was he when those better informed such as Eusi Kwayana, were openly and specifically condemning criminal acts and urging that the way forward could not by use of guns, violence or generally making life a nightmare for innocent people? (Guyana Chronicle October 13, 2002).

The independent daily Stabroek News also condemned Hoyte. It bemoaned his failure to impress upon the villagers the need for law and order and opined that his denial of criminals in the village was "not grounded in reality". The speech was described as "full of harsh invective and uncompromising demands," but unlike the Chronicle, Stabroek News did not dismiss the revival plan. It argued that the plan offered an opening and slammed the government for its equally uncompromising response. (Stabroek News October 14, 2002). Both the president and his Local Government Minister dismissed the Hoyte plan as extortion. The minister suggested that the government's endorsement of the plan could materialize if the PNC "pledge unequivocal support for the fight against crime... such a pledge would be warmly welcomed." The president said he would not be blackmailed and pointed to the fact that the government had spent $227 million in five years in Buxton (*Guyana Chronicle* October 21, 2002).

There was reluctance by most African Guyanese leaders and commentators to condemn the violence against Indians largely because they felt that Indians were oblivious to the plight of African Guyanese. They suggested that the unwavering Indian support of the PPP, was responsible for the African marginalization. One of the charges against Kwayana, Hinds and Andaiye was that while they condemned African excesses they did not similarly condemn police violence against Africans. While this was not an entirely accurate assessment it was in the context of polarized discourse, not unexpected. Although the PNC made general statements, it stopped short of condemning the gunmen or commenting on the ethnic nature of attacks. It instead blamed the PPP for the violence.

African commentators viewed the extra judicial killing of mainly African Guyanese youth as a deliberate attack on the African Guyanese community. Although police brutality of African Guyanese was prevalent under the PNC government, the fact that it was happening under the watch of an Indian government meant that it was seen in ethnic terms. There were also charges of ethnic preference in relation to the economy whereby the government was charged with steering contracts towards Indian- owned companies and spending more on the Indian dominated sugar industry than on the African Guyanese dominated bauxite sector. Trade Unionist, Lincoln Lewis, called this "economic genocide" and accused the government of racism. Tacuma Ogunseye, who characterized the gunmen as the "African Guyanese Armed Resistance," was also reluctant to roundly condemn them. While he did not condone the violence against Indians. He deflected the anti-Indian emphasis of others by pointing out that "the evidence will show that African Guyanese armed resistance has killed policemen, phantom mercenaries, informers and persons in the wrong place at the wrong time" (Ogunseye: March 22, 2003). The following statement by the then PNC Vice-Chairman captured the feeling of many Africans:

We have had some unfortunate incidents but I don't know that social development is ever without price. Whilst I do not look forward to paying a high price the fact is in the long term these things add up to the general good of the society…You must also bear in mind that you might go to the doctor and you might not want to take an injection because it is painful. Certainly when it is taken there is that moment of pain but then there is that period of happiness thereafter. What I find is that even though these instances may be painful and costly, the accumulation of all these interactions and conflicts may result in a state of affairs, which is far better than that which existed before (Alexander August 14, 2002).

Alexander's statement was labeled insensitive and roundly condemned by one of his Indian colleagues in the PNC, Jerome Khan.

I am therefore at wits end to understand why a senior ranking person would rationalize when asked about crime that appears to be directed at persons of East Indian descent, that such conduct is 'interactions' that even though 'painful' could lead to some positive outcomes. No amount of intellectualizing or academic gymnastics can mask the fact that such statements have served to raise questions amongst persons associated with the PNC on whether a justification is being made for the vicious and violent attacks on East Indians in the current spate of criminal activity. That is how the ordinary Joe, Abdul or Jailall Public would have read it, would have interpreted it and internalized it. So have I. If those statements have affected me, as they did my family and my colleagues and people who support the PNC/R, then I can expect that it has affected hundreds of thousands of Guyanese of all ancestry (Khan September 6, 2002).

This exchange between Alexander and Khan reflects the dilemma of minorities in majority ethnic parties, especially when one's ethnic group is under attack. Khan, who joined the PNC as part of its REFORM wing, was one of the most visible PNC spokespersons.

A few months before he offered this explanation of the PNC's position on the violence:

> The phenomenon of persons abandoning their homes on the East Coast is chilling and warns of a much more serious consequence which must be averted. We empathise and sympathise with all those who continue to suffer the loss of loved ones, whether at the hands of policeman gone mad or by a bandit, without care or consideration for the value of human life (Khan June 2002)

Calling the violence, the Buxton Conspiracy, columnist Freddie Kissoon viewed it as part of a plot to overthrow the government by an extremist alliance of elements in the PNC, WPA and ACDA and dissidents of the army. He characterized it as a "conspiracy" of crime and violence that was not motivated by high ideals and that had no parallel in the world. According to him "it is a desecration of political theory and revolutionist philosophy to classify the Buxton conspiracy as an armed resistance" As proof he argued that of the many acts of violence carried out by the group only two could be classified as "political violence" directly aimed at the PPP and the government (Kissoon June 14, 2003). He had earlier claimed that the PNC's tacit support for the violence was a "survival" tactic.

> There can hardly be any question as to the fragility of the PNC at this moment. The sadistic impulses that find an outlet in village confrontations with the state, the ubiquity of anti-police attack, the unstoppable criminal savagery with an anti-Indian prejudice are not manifestations of PNC's dynamism which makes it an indispensible factor in the political equation. On the contrary, however unpalatable it must be for PNC cadres, its supporters, and its voters to accept it, the PNC has found in these perversities, a hand of survival. This explains the descent into the politics of the unimaginable by some leaders of the PNC whose textures was a refined one before the question of viability presented itself (Kissoon August 6, 2002).

Ravi Dev explained the violence against Indian Guyanese in the context of their larger security, both physical and economic. He returned to his earlier thesis of Indians being vulnerable to African Guyanese violence largely because they do not retaliate and because their government is incapable of protecting them. As he wondered: "why are Indians crying all over the country? It is because they themselves have put the PPP in office ... they have created a monster that looks after only its own needs and is totally contemptuous of those who have suffered for many years to return it to office." (Dev July 15, 2002). He painted a bleak picture whereby Indians were "beaten like dogs and their women molested" and "they work all day and then keep vigilante at nights." He described the violence as a culture of "Indian beatings" in which whole communities are brutalized. He drew attention to the Indian economic situation which was burdened with huge debt by Indian rice farmers, the declining condition of the sugar workers and the closing of businesses. Without overtly calling for violent retaliation he observed that "something will snap soon" and called on Indian Guyanese to stand up and make decisions for their own good." These include breaking their loyalty to the PPP:

> Indians cannot retain their mentality of the logies which encouraged them to give their undying loyalty to the big ones; never mind the big ones only had their own interests at heart. Indians have to stand up for themselves and do the right thing. Even God only helps those who help themselves (Dev July 15, 2002).

Indian Self-Criticism

Moses Bhagwan, an Indian member of the WPA, viewed the return to ethnic voting as a "momentous act of self-betrayal" by the two groups which had found ways in the previous two decades to unite around a common cause. While expressing understanding of the Indian voters return to "communalism" given their experiences under the PNC regime, he nevertheless blames the PPP leadership for not recognizing that a similar return to communalism had occurred among Africans. Recounting his own experiences in the PPP in the 1960s he revealed that by

1964 he had arrived at the "settled view" that there was need for constitutional arrangements aimed at ethnic peace:

> From 1963 I began to feel quite uncomfortable "being in office" and in a party objectively fighting to keep Black people out and treating them as an enemy. By 1964 I had had become settled in my view that nothing short of a new constitutional arrangement will be enough to make peace between the two major ethnic groups (Bhagwan 2006).

He argued that as the majority ethnic group, Indians had an "obligation" to relieve other groups of "fear of ethnic oppression and security."

> Indians are the majority ethnic group. I am of the view that it is a fundamental obligation of a majority ethnic group in a multi-ethnic society to relieve other ethnic groups in the society of the fear of ethnic oppression and insecurity. Indians are not now culturally oppressed under a colonial power. They have become a power and are in a position now to reverse or reorder the ethnic hierarchical status in the spirit as a colonial power would. Or they could abolish ethnic hierarchies as a liberated revolutionary force would. Indians, who have been magnificent in their historic contributions to the making of Guyana, should not occupy any inferior position in guarding the integrity of the state and acting patriotically to prevent the dismantling and diminishing of the nation (Bhagwan 2006).

He was critical of Indians being "paralyzed" by communalism. Describing their condition as "pitiable," he lamented what he viewed as an unfortunate "compromise" with the worst in the society.

> They have lost much of their dignity and self assurance and have placed themselves in great peril by remaining silent and tolerant in the face of rampant corruption in the ruling political directorate, the compromise with organised criminality and a resurgence of authoritarianism in governance (evidence of insecurity and moral and political crisis in the leadership)

As the political directorate has grown more powerful in the state, the Indian collective has lost the capacity and will to control the leadership (Bhagwan 2006).

After initially giving the PPP the benefit of the doubt, Kissoon became one of its most bitter critics, a stance that earned him the wrath of many Indians. His criticism of the PPP is twofold. First, he accepts the African Guyanese marginalization thesis which charges the government with discrimination of Africans. Second, he contends that the government has become an "elected dictatorship" whose political excesses outstrip those of the PNC. Like most of the government's critics he cites official corruption as the central problem. Kissoon has also been critical of the Indian political culture, which he argues is built around Indian political solidarity and the superiority of the PPP and Dr. Jagan. Towards this end he has been critical of Dr. Jagan who he describes as "flawed." He views Dr. Jagan's dogmatic embrace of communism as a fatal error that is at the center of the country's problems. He also charges the PPP with committing violence and other destabilizing acts during the 1960s and 1970s and locates Dr. Jagan's book, *The West on Trial*, in the larger Indian – PPP narrative of victimhood, which has sought to exonerate Dr. Jagan and the PPP from any blame.

Finally, like Bhagwan, he has been extremely critical of the continued Indian support of the PPP despite expressions of dissatisfaction with the government. He cites the 2006 election as evidence of this behavior, whereas Africans split their votes between the PNC and the AFC, Indians voted overwhelmingly for the PPP. According to Kissoon the presence of the AFC meant that the Indian excuse that the alternative to the PPP is the discredited PNC was no longer viable. He declared that this ethnic vote by Indians made him "ashamed" to be Indian. He repeatedly pointed to the fact that many Africans opposed the PNC government and played a major role in its downfall, an observation also made by Bhagwan. Kissoon's displeasure with the PPP also led him to reassess the PNC and its leader Forbes Burnham. While remaining critical of Burnham and his party he has called for a revisiting of their role in the larger politics. He has also been less critical of what he earlier regarded as "African extremism." [32]

Ravi Dev objected to Kissoon's characterization of the government as a dictatorship on the grounds that it encourages extra parliamentary opposition. While Dev agrees that the government has committed excesses, the fact that it was democratically elected means it cannot be a dictatorship. He contends that the opposition has not done enough to woo Indian Guyanese votes, a position also advanced by PPP leaders and supporters such as Ralph Ramkarran, Randy Persaud and Prem Misir. This convergence has led Kissoon to place Dev as part of what he calls the "Indian mindset."

> The particular nuance of this mind-set is its racist emblem. It has moved from its initial mundane paradigm of "Indian time has come" to shameless apology of Indian domination. At this point the infamy of oxymoron emerged. Many in this mindset don't care for the PPP but the PPP rule is nevertheless apologized for and protected because the PPP is the only Indian game in town. A love/hate process now characterizes this mind-set. Some people hate the absolute miasma in which the PPP is swimming but the PPP government must not be confronted because Indian power could be lost (Kissoon December 22, 2009).

Conclusion

There are some general observations one can make about the discourse discussed in this chapter. The first is its ultra-defensiveness, which is rooted in the feelings of victimhood by both Indian and African Guyanese--African Guyanese point to economic and political marginalization and police repression, while Indian Guyanese point to terror at the hands of both the African Guyanese criminals and other sections of the African Guyanese community. But the problem with the debate is that neither side recognizes the legitimacy of the concerns of the other. Indian Guyanese politicians and activists deny there is African Guyanese marginalization and dismiss extra judicial killings by the police as the just reward for criminals. African Guyanese politicians and activists, on the other hand, either dismiss the physical violence against Indian Guyanese as "collateral damage" in the quest for justice or refuse to locate the violence as a particular form of anti-Indian ideological development that is inimical to the creation of a national community. This refusal to acknowledge the fears of the other side reinforces the ascendancy of extremist tendencies on both sides of the ethnic divide. The "African Freedom Fighters" benefitted from the Indian refusal to recognize the legitimacy of African concerns while the emergence of Indian Guyanese support for the "Phantom Groups" is largely a result of the African Guyanese refusal to treat the anti-Indian violence as an unacceptable ethnic extremism.

A second criticism is the misuse of history. A proper appreciation of history is indispensable to understanding the present and crafting the future. Yet, if history is manipulated, it becomes a dangerous destabilizing tool. Indian Guyanese critics present the PNC's reign as something in and of itself, while African Guyanese critics present the current PPP government as the sum total of Guyana's history. Both the PNC and PPP regimes are historical formations. While the PNC regime was controlled and buttressed by African Guyanese, its emergence was not simply a result of an inherent African Guyanese need to dominate Indian Guyanese. It was a direct consequence of choices made by the African and Indian Guyanese leaderships and followers between 1953 and 1964 both in relation to the internal ethnic situation and in relation to the Cold War. The point here is that the actions and counter-actions of the two parties in concert with external forces facilitated the rise of PNC authoritarianism.

Dr. Jagan's choice of ethnicity over class after the 1955 split alienated key African allies who had stayed with his faction at the time of the split, thus speeding up the consolidation of African Guyanese solidarity. Further, the PPP's concern with toeing the international communist line and its less than vigorous concern about the democratization of the authoritarian system beyond free and fair elections helped to create the ground for the rise of Burnhamism. By the same token, the present PPP regime is a direct consequence of choices made by the PNC during its reign and by the PNC and the PPP during the transition from authoritarian rule presided over by Desmond Hoyte. The fact that the PNC, during its reign, did not seek to genuinely empower African Guyanese nor did it negotiate hard enough for African Guyanese political security in the closing stages of its regime is largely responsible for the socio-economic marginalization of Africans. The Hoyte regime opted for a strategy of trying to win over Indian Guyanese voters so that it could continue to rule rather that negotiating the security of its supporters in the event that it lost power. Finally, the PNC helped to create what it now sees as a stubborn government when in the post-1997 period it failed to support or push for more comprehensive constitutional reform that would have fostered a more inclusionary form of governance. Similarly the PPP boxed itself into an isolated ethnic corner when it failed to recognize and utilize Hoyte's political goodwill as genuine patriotism and when it dumped the WPA instead of recognizing and utilizing that party's potential for holding the country to the ethno-political center.

5

Power Sharing Proposals and Discourse

One of the interesting features of ethno-politics in Guyana since 1955 is that the conflict has been accompanied by periodic initiatives towards national reconciliation. Most of these initiatives have centered on proposals for some form of consociational power sharing government. But while both of the major political parties have expressed interest in a joint government and have been the architects of several proposals in this regard, they have not succeeded in setting up a power sharing government. This chapter looks at the various proposals since 1961 and the reactions to them by the political actors. The central thesis is that the proposals usually emanate from the party which represents the group that feels threatened with disenfranchisement or fears the loss of political power. In turn the reactions of other political actors are usually determined by their perception of their own strength and the weakness of the party which makes the proposals.

Some forces, in particular the WPA--both as a party and through some of its members who have functioned in the academic sphere such as CY Thomas, Walter Rodney, and Eusi Kwayana--have argued that development in Guyana would at best be stifled without a political solution. During the first two decades of independence when the country, unfortunately descended into authoritarianism, the main focus of that political solution was the return to electoral democracy and the unlocking of the police state. While attention was given to the underlying problem of ethnicity, in hindsight, perhaps not enough emphasis was placed on the potential impact of this democratization on the historical ethnic competition and vice versa. My contention here is that while due attention was paid to the mobilization of ethnic solidarity and unity as a means of confronting authoritarian rule, enough attention was not given to the ethnic consequences inherent in democratization in an ethnically divided country. The WPA was the exception in this regard; its 1979 proposal for a Government of National Unity stressed the need for a national solution with the widest possible participation.

As the prospects of electoral democracy materialized the opposition parties made several assumptions. First, it was assumed that the Indian and African Guyanese working classes had developed a high degree of solidarity that would carry over into the post-authoritarian period. Second, it was thought that because the PNC presided over the authoritarian state its support would be seriously diminished with the return of electoral democracy. Third, it was assumed that the anti dictatorial parties would transfer their institutional relationship into a broad-based government. Fourth, many thought that the WPA, with its multi-ethnic credentials, would have been a serious electoral contender, thus becoming a balancer in the system. Finally, and perhaps the most damaging, it was assumed that the demise of authoritarianism would translate automatically to democratization. These assumptions have turned out to be costly miscalculations. While the democratic form of competitive elections has been maintained, it has not led to more substantive democratization. As was noted in previous chapters, the underlying factor has been ethnicity or more particularly, ethnic competition arising from ethnic insecurity.

Because the country tethers on the brink of anarchy and disintegration, the temptation to use coercive means under the guise of law and order is real. Resort to such means has increased ethnic hostility and raised the possibility of a return to a full blown police state and authoritarian government. In this atmosphere of polarization, the tenets of Westminster democracy, which are meant as stabilizing influences, have instead served to deepen the polarization and stifle democratic evolution. In particular, the government-opposition and winner-take-all majoritarian principles have facilitated the consolidation of a segmented state based on party paramountcy and ethnic domination. In effect the Westminster model has failed to translate formal democracy into a more substantive democracy that centers ethnic equality of the political economy. Most political parties, political activists, commentators and civil society groups have agreed that the solution to the problem requires a national effort. It is against this background that since 1961 there have been repeated calls for either a modification or abolishment of the Westminster model, in particular the winner-take-all and government-opposition principles and its replacement with a consociational power sharing system.

Kwayana's Joint Premiership

The idea of a consociational power sharing government was first raised in Guyana in 1961 by Eusi Kwayana. He and his colleagues in the African Society for Racial Equality (ASRE), an African-centered organization, in the face of mounting ethnic tensions called for what they termed "joint premiership" between the leaders of the two ethnic-based parties. They reasoned that since the ethnic polarization that resulted from the split of the movement in 1955 had progressively hardened, a joint government was one of the ways to guarantee each group that it would not be disenfranchised. The PPP's victory at the 1957 election in which the numbering seats were disproportionate to its share of the popular vote, along with its embrace of an ethnic agenda, had caused much concern in the African Guyanese community. As Kwayana (2001:1) later observed:

> I proposed a solution, which had not been heard of before, a joint premiership between the rulers of the Indian and African races. It was a solution, so far as I was concerned, posed by the social and political logic of the situation then before us, and not by me.

According to Kwayana, because the two ethnic groups had lost trust in the leadership of the opposite group, governance by one group would most likely be resisted by the other group. He anticipated that should this occur there was the likelihood of violence or what he called "blood baths." Towards this end he viewed his proposal as "special" and called on the leaders to stop pretending that the situation was not serious.

> We have known all along that the Indians would not trust a Black leader and that the Africans would not trust an Indian leader. We could see then that any attempt of the one to rule the other will lead to blood baths... your people, Jagan, do not trust a Black leader; and my people do not trust an Indian leader. Therefore, we must find a special solution and not pretend (1961: 3).

Kwayana's proposal was advanced as both a solution to the ethnic tensions and more importantly as a democratic solution. He also sought to situate it within the context of Guyana's independence from external influences and the struggle for socialism, which both major parties had embraced. As he stressed, the proposal "would give us all what we want—Freedom, Socialism of a Guyanese form, ethnic equality," and would end the escalating ethnic tensions. As he observed at the time:

> That is the plan. Equality of rights and power for African and Indian as custodians of the whole. Justice by law for minorities. Socialism without the blackmail of Russian might or American bayonets on either side. Joint and equal premiership. Partition as a last resort. This plan can end all cause of ethnic antagonism and mistrust. Our co-ops will lay the economic foundation for better race relations (1961:3).

Both parties rejected the proposal and Kwayana was expelled from the PNC for advocating racism. The charge of racism arose from the section of the proposal which suggested that should joint premiership be rejected partition should be considered as a "last resort." It is clear that both parties highlighted "partition," which was not the essence of the proposal, in order to avoid engaging joint premiership. "Partition as a last resort" was less a proposal and more a warning of the possible consequences of one-party/one race rule in the prevailing circumstances. Interestingly Kwayana has revealed that he had anticipated the negative reaction to partition and was not in favor of including it in the statement, but his colleagues insisted on its inclusion (Personal Interview: August 2001).

This proposal was one of the earliest attempts to construct an approach to conflict resolution in ethnically plural societies; it predated Arthur Lewis' 1965 treatise, which is often cited as one of the earliest attempts at advancing a power sharing theory. In this regard, Kwayana feels that the rejection of the proposal was a big mistake. According to him, it was an opportunity to lead the world on how to confront and solve ethnic problems:

> Our proposals for sharing government were extreme and not half-baked. Joint premiership was the most extreme form of joint government at the executive level. It had not been heard of anywhere. We could have given a lead to multi-ethnic ex-colonies. Neither party at that time saw the recommendation for joint premiership as anything but the utmost madness. It was not even worth discussing...The joint-premiership recommendation was far from finished or perfect. It was rejected not as imperfect, but as subversive of harmony. It was treated as wicked and crazy. The leading parties saw no need to improve or refine it. For both of them government was something to be copied from an established model. The established model was the "successful" democracies. Of course it worked in Britain. To their credit, our leaders were not about to re-invent the wheel (Kwayana, 2001:2).

PPP's overtures to the PNC

The rejection of the Kwayana proposal was followed by three years of political instability and ethnic violence; thus confirming Kwayana's prediction of a "blood-bath" in the absence of a political solution. Given its inability to govern the country effectively, the PPP sought to engage the PNC in talks aimed at forming a power-sharing government, without using the term. The PPP requested the assistance of the Ghanian government, the Prime Minister of Trinidad, Dr. Eric Williams, the United Nations and the Commonwealth. It agreed to almost all of the PNC's requests, including parity in the cabinet before the election. The agreement would have been revised to take into consideration the election results:

> The PPP and the PNC to have an equal number of Ministries - 5 to each party - with the Leader of the PPP being Premier and the Leader of the PNC being Deputy Premier. The Deputy Premier shall be the Leader of the Legislative Assembly. The term of office of the coalition government is to be two, three or four years with the minimum period until August 1965, the life of the present Government. It is my considered view that in the charged atmosphere of today, a holding government for a short period until the proposed general elections later this year will not suffice to create unity, peace and harmony which are so necessary today at all levels. It is my view that the coalition should continue after the next general elections on an agreed basis and that the party Leader of the majority party should be the Prime Minister and the other Leader the Deputy Prime Minister. On Independence, the Ministry of Home Affairs should go to one Party and a Junior Minister to the other Party; the Foreign Affairs and Defense Ministry should go to the Party which does not hold the Home Affairs Ministry, and the Junior Minister to the other Party... (Jagan 1972: 318).

In making the proposal Dr. Jagan observed that "that the situation has now deteriorated to such a point that something dramatic must be done to prevent further ethnic strife between the two major ethnic groups, to unite the working class and to create a stable and strong government" (Jagan1972: 317-318). A closer look reveals that Dr. Jagan's observations were similar to those made by Kwayana two years before, which he had ignored. This would later become a pattern of the PPP—it becomes most amenable to power sharing when its hold on power is severely threatened. But the PNC rejected the PPP's offers. Although it participated in the negotiations and the PPP agreed to most of its demands, the PNC found ways to wriggle out of any commitment. This approach was influenced by the party's recognition that the PPP government was losing ground on account of domestic challenges and Cold War imperatives which made the PPP an unattractive option for the USA and Britain.

PPP's National Patriotic Front

The PNC eventually came to power in 1964 as part of a coalition with the right wing United Force (UF). After ditching its coalition partner in 1968, it proceeded to rig successive elections and in the process constructed the most authoritarian regime in the Anglophone Caribbean. It, however, declared itself socialist and instituted policies such as nationalization of the sugar and bauxite industries, government take-over of private schools and the introduction of free education. The PPP supported these initiatives and consequently declared "critical support" for the government. Dr. Jagan and Mr. Burnham appeared on the same platform in 1976 at the annual Trade Union Congress (TUC) May Day rally at which Dr. Jagan committed the PPP to unity with the PNC. This announcement came shortly after a meeting of the Latin American and Caribbean communist parties held in Havana, Cuba in March 1975, which decided to support Third World governments which, though not socialist in character, were willing to take anti-imperialist positions.

Unity talks between the two parties were launched in July 1976, but before the talks commenced, the PNC pulled out. It cited an editorial in the PPP's *Mirror* newspaper that chided the PNC for removing subsidies on basic food items and for increased military spending as the reason for breaking off the talks. Despite the breakdown of the talks the PPP, in August 1977, called for the setting up of a National Patriotic Front (NPF) government including "all parties and groups which are progressive, anti-imperialist, and who wish to see Guyana take a socialist-oriented path of development" (PPP August 1977:1). The NPF proposal, which in some respects were similar to the PPP's 1964 proposal, would have ensured power sharing between the PPP, PNC and other progressive groups after free and fair elections. According to the PPP:

> The Prime Minister will be drawn from the party or parties, which have majority support in the National Assembly. He will preside over a Cabinet or Council of Ministers drawn

from each party (which is revolutionary and agrees to a socialist-oriented program) in proportion to its strength in the National Assembly. Whichever party wins the elections should not oppose the candidature for the Presidency from the other major party. At the local level, district councils should be directly elected and be based on small historically evolved communities. Regional councils, indirectly elected through the district councils, should be given a substantial degree of autonomy (PPP 1977:2).

The newly formed Working People's Alliance (WPA), the PPP's principal ally in the opposition, expressed general support for the NPF, but disagreed with the specifics. The WPA argued that a well thought out program was a prerequisite for such a front. In a statement, it said in part:

Prior to the formation of a National Patriotic Front Government, we believe that there must be an agreed social, political and economic program. A real alliance let alone a revolutionary alliance must be founded in a thoroughly worked out program. It is this program, which gives specific social content to the policies of the alliance. We do not believe that the PPP's proposals pay enough regard to this (WPA: January 1978).

As it did a decade before, the PNC rejected the PPP's proposal. Its leader said at the time that the PNC was the vanguard party and it alone could solve the country's party. He reminded the PPP that "if the Bolsheviks had sought unity or coalition terms the history of the Soviet Union would have been differently written." The PNC also rejected the sharing of cabinet positions as not representing the essence of national unity and lamented the lack of "socialist content" in the PPP's proposals, which was not "based on class but on ethnicity regardless of class" (PNC 1977). Despite the PNC's rhetoric, it was clear that it took advantage of the weak position of the PPP, which had been in opposition for twelve years and had in the process suffered the defection of some of its most able leaders. The PNC also was obviously privy to information that the PPP's position was driven by the dictates of the international communist movement. Despite the party's insistence to the contrary, the PPP's initiative was clearly influenced by the position of the Latin American Communist parties. According to a party insider, the party's Central Committee was divided on the issue, but in the end Dr. Jagan used his enormous influence to push it through. Ferguson (1995:145) supports this thesis. He contended that "Jagan in effect was left with no other option but to adjust strategically his position vis-à-vis the PNC, if he were not to going to be simply bypassed politically" and that "he was under significant pressure from his communist sponsors overseas."

While the PPP in the 1970s argued for the inclusion of the PNC in a power sharing government, it by definition excluded parties which did not subscribe to socialism. The National Patriotic Front proposal was for the most part a proposed coalition between the PPP and the PNC. It did not explicitly name the WPA with which it had cordial relations as a participant. However, the WPA was the only party that engaged the proposal. The two parties held joint meetings to discuss the proposal while the WPA agreed with the NPF in principle it disagreed with the inclusion of the PNC and the ideological litmus test.

By 1978 the WPA concluded that given the dictatorial nature of the government a broad anti-dictatorial alliance was a more feasible form of resistance than a left alliance with the PPP. Towards this end the WPA took the initiative in organizing the Committee for the Defense of Democracy (CDD) to boycott the proposed referendum to change the country's constitution. The CDD included all of the opposition parties, except the United Force, and several social, religious and professional organizations. The success of the boycott fueled hopes that the CDD would continue as an opposition unit. But the PPP withdrew from the body shortly after the referendum. While it did not give a public explanation for the withdrawal it would have been disappointed at the criticism it received from some of the parties over its decision to remain in parliament which was extended beyond its stipulated term. It also would have been uncomfortable working with parties which were ideologically anti-communist.

The WPA made another attempt at an all-opposition alliance

after the Jonestown massacre in November 1978 in the form of the Council of National Safety (CNS). The CNS, which included the opposition parties that belonged to the CDD, held public meetings and a march in Georgetown and called for an enquiry into the massacre. But was it did in the case of the CDD, the PPP withdrew from the CNS because of the involvement of non – socialist forces. The non socialist force, which most irritated the PPP was the Liberator Party (LP), which did not attract much mass support and had far less influence on public opinion than the left wing parties. In this regard the PPP inflated the importance of the ideological differences.

WPA's Government of National Unity and Reconstruction

Of the political parties he WPA has been the most consistent advocate of power sharing. In keeping with its multi-ethnic thrust, it has argued that a power sharing government is central to a political solution. The WPA's conception of power sharing emphasized national unity and reconciliation that cut across ethnic and class lines. Except for its initial exclusion of the PNC, it advocated the widest possible participation. Its 1979 proposal for a Government of National Unity and Reconstruction to replace the then PNC regime was premised on the belief that "no one political party can resolve the prevailing crisis" (WPA 1979: 2). For the WPA the GNUR had six major objectives: the restoration of the national economy; the restoration of civil liberties and the rule of law; the removal of arbitrary rule and corruption in public life; the restoration to trade union members of the rights to strike, free association, free and fair elections of their officers and effective representation of their interests; the abolition of private armed bodies and the end to partisan control of the security services of the state; the rapid establishment of the foundations for a return to free and fair elections under a new and secure political system. (WPA 1979)

The WPA's proposal for the GNUR was made in the context of its conclusion that the country was under authoritarian rule. In this regard it did not see a place for the PNC in such a government; it contended that since that party was the problem it could not be part of the solution. The WPA also was not in favor of an ideological litmus test for participation in such a government. On both counts the WPA approach differed from that of the PPP, which insisted that the PNC must be included in any power-sharing government and that participation must be premised on the acceptance of socialist orientation as the guiding principle. The PPP's rationale for the PNC's inclusion was its belief that the government was not a dictatorship and that there was a genuine socialist bloc in the PNC. The latter view was also counter to that of the WPA's which viewed the PNC's embrace of socialism as a mask for one-party domination. Making the WPA's case for the GNUR, Rodney (1979:26) contended:

> This is a time for calling on our resolve of patriotism. The road to recovery of national purpose lies through the restoration of democracy. All parties and all interest groups must somehow be represented in a Government of National Reconstruction and National Unity. Burnham Must Go! Yes, but that is only one side of the coin. There must be an alternative to replace the dictator. Let that alternative be a Government of National Unity. A clear alternative is a powerful political force. It gives our people something to mobilize around. It gives the outside world something to think about as the force of the future in dealing with Guyana (p.26).

The WPA proposed that the three opposition parties -- PPP, WPA, and the small Vanguard for Liberation and Democracy (VLD) -- be equally represented (nine members each) in a 50 member Council of National Reconstruction. The other 23 seats would be divided among labor, peasant and citizen organizations. Executive authority would lie in the hands of a fifteen member committee reflective of the Council's membership (WPA, August 1979). The proposal was greeted with enthusiasm by the VLD, a newly formed citizens group, COMPASS and four dissident trade unions called "The Four Unions," but the PPP was hesitant.

Civil Society Initiatives 1979-82

In 1979 members of the Citizens Committee, a coalition of prominent citizens and civic organizations which had organized alongside the CDD for the boycott of the referendum, invited the PPP, WPA, VLD and organizations affiliated with the Citizens Committee to a conference on the future of the country. After several meetings the group agreed on a general program and released a joint statement to that effect. But the talks soon stalled as the PPP insisted on the nationalization of banks and insurance companies, a proposal with which none of the other participants agreed.[33]

Two years later, in April 1982, the Guyana Council of Churches invited all political parties and social organizations to a meeting which agreed to the need for a broad based government as a way forward. But as was the ease with previous initiatives, the PPP was not willing to commit itself to a program that was not socialist while the WPA insisted that ideology should not stand in the way of national consensus. As a compromise the WPA proposed a caretaker government for no more than one year with a limited mandate to prepare for free and fair elections. It also proposed that the election be held under the electoral rules of the 1966 constitution after review by a constitutional jury or commission. While the PPP agreed in principle with the idea of a caretaker government, it felt that it should not be limited to one year and that the 1980 constitution should also be considered. Further, it objected to the WPA's proposal that non-alignment and ideological pluralism be the guiding principle of the government; it instead expressed its preference for an anti-imperialist orientation. In the end the PPP presented its own program for consideration.

The PPP charged the VLD with supporting imperialism and capitalism and criticized the WPA for preferring the VLD's position to the PPP's. It contended that the WPA insistence that the program of the caretaker government should not be "anti-anything" was more "neutralist" than anti-imperialist and pointed to the inconsistency between the WPA's programmatic commitment t socialism and its lack of support for it at the talks. According to the PPP:

> It is wrong to be silent on the question of imperialism, and to call for some of the same things which imperialism is now, through the IMF and the World Bank pressing for... We believe also that it is wrong to couch the language in such a way as to skirt around the question and blame both 'power blocs' or what some prefer to call 'super powers' for the situation in this world and the Caribbean... We perceive

that there are, apart from ideological, tactical considerations for the refusal to take a position against imperialism... The WPA has stated during the discussions that the program of the caretaker government should not be anti-US imperialist, anti-Soviet or anti-anything. It should be noted that this is a neutralist, not a non-aligned position. (PPP: 1982)

The PPP also took issue with the WPA's position on the inclusion of the PNC in the caretaker government. It contended that although the PNC came to power with the aid of imperialist forces, it had since taken progressive positions and instituted socialist policies such as nationalization:

Although the PNC was brought to power by imperialism, it took at a certain stage due t objective and subjective considerations certain anti-imperialist steps through the nationalization of the imperialist strongholds – the sugar and bauxite industries, which dominated the economy and the lives of the people. Moreover, the pre-requisites for the transition to socialism have not been established (PPP: 1982)

The WPA responded to the PPP's criticisms by arguing that a common program arising out of a broad alliance should not be the program of any of the participating parties. It accused the PPP of appearing to be reasonable in public while being inflexible in private. The WPA also was unconvinced by the PPP's contention that the PNC was building socialism, preferring to focus on the party's authoritarian rule. Using the frame of criminals versus vigilantes the WPA opined that the PPP wanted the criminal to "join the vigilantes, not as a convert, not as one who is 'pushed to the left', but as one clever enough to find himself an acceptable cover for his banditry." On the issue of foreign policy the WPA described itself "a partisan of the Caribbean revolution of the working people." Towards this end it eschewed an "over-active" foreign policy in which it is seen as "an agency of a rival bloc." (WPA 1982).

The WPA shifted its position in 1985 when it declared that should the PNC agree to free and fair elections it was prepared to work with that party in a power sharing government. This shift occurred in the wake of the demise of the Grenadian revolution which forced the Caribbean left to reassess its approach to political mobilization. The WPA concluded that building socialism in Guyana was not possible at that juncture. Speaking at a conference organized by the Critchlow Labor College, Eusi Kwayana reiterated the WPA's position that the PNC's clam to be building a socialist society was not borne out by the actual experience. He argued that the PNC had instead created a form of state capitalism accompanied by an authoritarian state and recommended as a solution a democratic republic that guarantees civil liberties, free and fair elections, eschews ethnic domination, respects he sovereignty of the people and trade union rights and defend the national independence of the Caribbean (Kwayana 1985: 9)

On the specific issue of power sharing, Kwayana called for a "plural government" representing the will of the people. According to him:

> The party which comes out as a majority should undertake to set up a plural government on the bases of the expressed will of the whole people, including trade union representation if the TUC wishes it. The WPA will accept the decisions of such an election and such a government on broad policy (1985: 10)

The PPP-PNC 1985 Unity Talks

In an apparent admission that matters were beyond its control, the PNC opened unity talks with the PPP in January 1985. The PNC explained that the decision was taken in the interest of nation- building and national defense against imperialism. Halim Majeed, one of the PNC participants, reports that the talks towards agreement on a "Fatherland Front" between the PNC and the PPP was making positive progress when the project was scuttled by new president, Desmond Hoyte, who assumed the leadership of the PNC when founder-leader, Forbes Burnham, died suddenly in August 1985. Both Burnham and PPP's leader Dr. Jagan had reportedly agreed in principle to the planned unity government.

Majeed (2007) has speculated that Hoyte's rejection of the plan may have stemmed from his conception of a PPP-PNC arrangement as too narrow and of his preference for relating to the WPA whose leadership he found more intellectually stimulating than the PPP's. There is also a strong case to be made that Hoyte felt that the PNC's retreat from its socialist policies both politically and economically had dramatically changed the situation (Ferguson 1995; Majeed 2007). While there is a lot of merit to those interpretations, Hoyte's mixed responses to power sharing later on shows that he was also not intellectually convinced that power sharing was an effective solution to the country's problems. Further, he may have reasoned that a party does not share power when it has a firm hold on it.

The PCD and WPA Proposals

Despite ongoing disagreements with the PPP and its disappointment at the lack of consultation on the PPP's talks with the PNC, the WPA in the wake of the rigged election in 1985, took the initiative to bring the parties together in the Patriotic Coalition for Democracy (PCD). Unlike previous alliance efforts, the PCD lasted for a relatively long period--1986 to 1990. This was due in part to the fact that the alliance was more concerned with agitation for free and fair elections rather than creating a government. Predictably, when the issue of a post-PNC joint government arose, the alliance collapsed.

In the meantime the WPA, in 1990 suggested the formation of a caretaker government to oversee the preparation of the pending elections. It proposed that the government include the PNC and the PCD parties with the PNC leader retaining the presidency. While the suggestion did not find favor with PPP, the PNC expressed a strong interest. This change in the positions of the PPP and the WPA over the inclusions of the PNC as part of a national solution marked the beginning of the end of the PCD.

PPP's Inclusive Governance

Given the PPP's firm embrace of power sharing from the 1960s it was, therefore, surprising that with the imminence of free and fair election, the PPP began to retreat from this commitment. Despite differences with the WPA on the presidential candidate for a joint opposition slate to contest the 1992 election, the door to a broad-based government was firmly closed when the PPP, upon winning the election, decided to form the government on its own. This move was a fatal blow to the cause of national reconciliation as it effectively destroyed the ethnic unity that had begun to take shape during the anti-dictatorial struggle. Further, the PPP created for itself two sources of hostility—the PNC and its former allies in the anti-dictatorial struggle.

The PPP has become the only major political force in the country that is opposed to a broad-based multi-party Government of National Unity. One may conclude that the party, since its assumption of office, has stood in the way of a national solution and in the process has dragged the country to the brink of disintegration. Given its own negative role over the years, the PNC shares responsibility for this outcome, but by coming out in favor of "power sharing" in 2002, it signaled its willingness to accept a national solution that includes sharing office with the PPP. This PNC olive branch has not, however, shifted the PPP, which continues to close the door on any meaningful unity.

The PPP has advanced a holding agenda of "first build trust," "dialogue," and "power sharing in parliament." At first glance this position seems reasonable, but that quickly fades because it is advanced in the interest of party survival rather than the country's survival. It represents an about turn for the PPP which up till the eve of the 1992 election advocated a winner-does-not-take-all form of governance. It has labeled calls for power-sharing undemocratic and argued it is a means of denying the party its legitimate right to control the government. This position is a direct contradiction of the party's stance when it was in the opposition; it tirelessly argued that shared governance was a prerequisite to political peace and economic development. Four years before its return to power, its leader, Dr. Jagan reiterated the PPP's position:

> We in the PPP in Guyana are calling for a revolutionary democratic National Patriotic Government. For many years, for economic, ethnic/cultural/ and security considerations, we have advocated "winner-does-not-take-all" politics; namely, that even though we consider that we alone could win a free and fair election, we would form not just a PPP, but a broad-based government including other parties, groups

and social organizations. Only through such a government, with the people's fullest involvement, can a nation of one people and one destiny be built (Jagan, 1993: 31).

Speaking in 1997, just before he died, Dr. Jagan still harbored dreams of a power-sharing arrangement:

> This issue has a long history in Guyana. Before we entered politics in the 1940s - long before Mr. Mandela came up with the formula of bringing the opposition in - we had made several attempts to bring about unity in our country. In 1957, we failed to create a political coalition between East Indians and Afro-Guyanese. In 1961, we won and I tried again. I went to the UN in support of Afro-Asian states to work out the formula, but then the foreign governments were working with [coup leader] Mr. Burnham to put him in power. As the opposition for 28 years, we again tried to bring about some unity but failed. In 1977, we came out with a slogan and a policy proposal called "winner will not take all" even if we win the election. We alone will not form the government. So, the policy is still to bring about unity along ethnic and religious lines in Guyana (Jagan 1997).

But according to the party the pre-1992 position was motivated by the authoritarian regime, but with the return of electoral democracy, power-sharing is no longer relevant. As then leader Janet Jagan argues:

> Democracy then is based on the concept of the wishes of the citizens at regular free and fair elections. Whatever the result of the will of the majority of voters then that is how governments are formed...there is no such thing as the winner-takes-part or winner-shares-seats-to-losers (Jagan: 2000)

The PNC's Shared Governance

As announced at its 2002 Congress, the PNC duly released a comprehensive document laying out its arguments for power-sharing and a plan on how it should be implemented. For the

PNC, power-sharing was "necessary" for the country's future". It advanced the following reasons: protection of the rights of "the marginalized and the vulnerable"; the need to turn back the country's social and economic downturn; and the protection of the country's sovereignty (PNC 2003). The PNC proposed a return to the independence formula of a split-executive with a non-executive president and a Prime Minister. The President would serve as commander-in-chief of the armed forces and mediator in political disputes, while the Prime Minister would be the head of government and chair the cabinet or Council of Ministers. Cabinet decisions would be by consensus and unresolved issues would be referred to the President. The proposal also included "Ministerial Working Groups," which would examine policy issues before they are submitted to the cabinet for consideration.

The PNC argued that its proposal would "redefine opposition politics" by making opposition parties "partners in the governing executive." It would also improve government accountability. Towards this end it proposed that meetings of parliamentary committees by in the form of public hearings and that parliament be more vigorous in its oversight of the executive. Finally the PNC proposed that there should be a referendum after ten years to determine whether the power-sharing arrangement should continue.

From Herdmonston to Big Tent

The WPA made yet another attempt to get the parties to form a national government following the PPP's decision to curtail its term by two years as part of the Herdmonston Accord. It proposed an interim power sharing government with the expressed task of overseeing the implementation of constitutional reforms and preparing for new elections. On this occasion neither the PNC nor the PPP entertained the idea. A further suggestion in 2001 by WPA' co-leader, Rupert Roopnarine for power sharing at the local government level was similarly ignored by the two major parties.

The PNC, which since its dramatic embrace of power sharing in 2002, had sent mixed signals about its commitment to the idea. While it continued to agree that power sharing was the best solution to the country's problem, it never made the issue a central part of its agenda. The party seemed to be split between those who preferred the inclusive domination model and those who fully embrace power sharing. The latter group itself was divided between those who wanted a negotiated settlement based on political equality and those who preferred the PNC to first win at the polls and then invite the PPP to join it in a power sharing government.

It was this latter tendency which seemed to be behind the PNC's announcement that it intended to pursue a "big tent" coalition of opposition parties to contest the 2006 election. According to the PNC it was prepared to work in a coalition but not dominate it. Some observers interpreted that to mean that the PNC would not insist on its leader as the presidential candidate. But this was not enough to attract other opposition parties which were either wary of the PNC's sincerity or did not want to associate with a party which had a terrible reputation among Indian Guyanese.

It was in the context of this negative attitude towards the PNC that the opposition parties responded more enthusiastically to the call by ROAR's leader, Ravi Dev, for a "Center Force" to serve as a counter to the hegemony of the PPP and the PNC. There was much excitement when a group of parties--the newly formed AFC, the WPA, ROAR, the Guyana Action Party (GAP) and individuals including Joey Jagan, son of Dr. Jagan, and Peter Ramsaroop, a former member of the REFORM wing of the PNC--announced the formation of the Third Force. However, the coalition began to unravel shortly after the announcement. Some of the parties charged others with a secret plot to take the Third Force into an alliance with the PNC. Despite strong denials by those accused, the coalition disintegrated.

The decline of the Third Force led to a new initiative by some individuals associated with the REFORM wing of the PNC. The One Guyana Platform comprising the PNC, WPA, the National Front Alliance (NFA) and a group of pro-PNC trade unions was ambivalent about its objective. Although speakers at its public meetings described the group as one committed to ensuring the transparency of the electoral preparation, some PNC speakers appeared to be in campaign mode. The WPA under pressure from some of its supporters declared that its participation in the coalition was limited to agitation for electoral transparency. But the strategy of a section of the One Guyana Platform seemed to be to use the agitation to garner support for the revival of the PNC's Big Tent. The group, therefore, hoped to delay the election as long as possible. This hope was dashed when the Elections Commission announced that despite opposition concerns about the voters list, it was ready to proceed with the elections. This led to a flurry of behind the scenes negotiations between the PNC and the WPA over a joint state. As was the case with similar initiatives in the past, the negotiations stalled over who should be the presidential candidate. The PNC's insistence on its leader as the candidate was not accepted by the WPA, which had problems selling the idea of the alliance to its membership. At a meeting held in New York emotions ran high as most members rejected any alliance with the PNC. Sensing that the WPA would not join it in a pre-election alliance, the PNC began to make arrangements to contest the elections on its own. In the end the PNC contested as the PNC-One Guyana which was in effect a PNC slate, as the only non-PNC candidate was the leader of the small NFA. The WPA did not contest the election while the AFC, which was adamantly against any alliance with the PNC, contested on its own and GAP and ROAR contested as the GAP-ROAR alliance.

The Discourse

The PPP's return to power in 1992 has been accompanied by a renewed debate on power-sharing as a solution to the ethnic problem. The vigorous discourse since 1992 is largely due to four factors. First, as was the case during the PPP's previous term in office, electoral democracy has been accompanied by intensified ethnic conflict. This has led to a re-opening of the debate of the suitability of the Westminster system to the Guyanese political realities. Second, individual members of both major parties publicly expressed positions on the issue that were counter to the official party positions. Third, civil society organizations and individuals have been more outspoken than on previous occasions. Finally, the presence of a free media has provided a medium for a public discourse. The independent *Stabroek News*, in particular, has through its editorial pages been part of the debate. The debate, which has largely been carried out in the letter section of the daily newspapers and on the various television talk shows, has been between three groups—the advocates of power-sharing, those who do not oppose it but are skeptical and those who completely reject it.

Advocates

The strongest and most consistent advocates have been members of the WPA whose advocacy dates back to the 1970s. With the decline of the party as an influential voice since 1992, some members have expressed the party's positions on the issue in their individual capacities. They have been joined by members of the PNC and the PPP and independent individuals. Finally organizations such as the Trade Union Congress and the ethnic groups ROAR and the African Cultural and Development Association (ACDA) have also weighed in on the debate. These advocates have premised their case on the following arguments. First, ethnic polarization is a given in the Guyanese situation and as such any solution has to begin with an acknowledgement of that reality. Second, the Westminster winner take all model has exacerbated the ethnic problem. Election results are predictable, leading to a permanent majority and a permanent minority. Third, neither ethnic group is willing to be led by the party of the other. Fourth, the country's economic underdevelopment arises in large part from the ongoing ethnic polarization and conflict. Fifth, the right of the minority African group to participate in the governance of the country is both a democratic and human right.

In 1961 Eusi Kwayana observed that neither group was willing to accept the leadership of the opposite group. Revisiting the issue forty years later he observed that since the 1955 split each group had begun to develop its own "pre-nation" institutions, a development he did not see in negative terms. Kwayana, therefore, views separate organizing as a necessary prerequisite for achieving "national wholeness". He argues that the issues of equality and domination were still central and opines that his 1961 joint premiership proposal was rejected largely because it denied any opportunity for domination by stressing human equality. Kwayana also argues that the rejection was a fatal mistake; he felt it could have prevented the ethnic violence of the 1960s. He acknowledges that his conception of power in 1961, which focused on the two leaders, was narrow and welcomed the broader conception in the current debate. For Kwayana, then, power-sharing is a means towards an end- national wholeness. (Kwayana 2001).

But he challenges the contemporary advocates to go beyond a narrow power-sharing based only on ethnicity, masculinity or class. Kwayana develops this theme in another article, *"Power Sharing: Who's Power."* He concedes that current conditions for power-sharing were less encouraging than when he first proposed it in 1961. He notes that ethnic violence and the length and nature of PNC rule had combined to make national reconciliation difficult but he chastised the Guyanese leaders for lack of creativity. According to Kwayana the British did not design the Guyanese society to be governed by the Westminster winner – take-all system. He was also critical of the leadership for their use of power as a "trophy" and the manner in which it was coveted and guarded. He called for a "civilizing of power" (Kwayana 2001a). Kwayana's intervention is critical. Although he had since 1961 been very much involved in shaping the discourse on ethnicity and race he had hitherto avoided the current debate largely because of his belief that previous generations should not impose their views on their successors. But given his long experience and the respect he enjoys, his intervention was welcomed by the power-sharing advocates.

Moses Nagamootoo, an executive member of the PPP, broke ranks with his party and argued for a redefinition of democracy. Noting that the late PPP leader, Dr. Jagan, was instrumental in frustrating open ethnic challenges to the PPP government between 1992 and 1997, he chided PPP supporters for turning against power-sharing. He described the Herdmonston and St. Lucia accords as "palliatives" which "gave us time but did not take us over the road of distrust/hostility to tolerance/engagement much less on the road to reconciliation." He also criticized the dialogue between the two leaders as being less about reconciliation and more about "pressure politics". The failure of the dialogue, according to Nagamootoo, left power-sharing as the only viable alternative. Towards this end he advocates the institutionalization of power-sharing. Unlike the PPP, Nagamootoo admits that ethnic voting patterns and ethnic party loyalties are a given and urges the parties to take cognizance of that fact (Nagamootoo 2002).

This view is shared by three executive members of the PNC who contend that despite the fact that both parties claim to be inclusive when in power, supporters of the opposite party feel excluded and discriminated against. (Lowe, Mc Allister and Norton 1999). Like Nagamootoo, Lowe et al deviated from their party's official stance. Party leader, Desmond Hoyte, who had described power-sharing as "nebulous," "protean" and "horse trading," later changed his mind and embraced the idea just before he died in 2002. Observing that it "was an idea whose time has come" he premised his case on the "imperfections" of the winner-take-all system which he called an "obstacle" to national cohesion and development. (Hoyte 2002).

Eric Phillips, a former member of the REFORM wing of the PNC and current member of ACDA, has emerged as another strong advocate of power-sharing. Calling it a human right, Phillips grounds his advocacy in the need to recognize African security as integral to the security of the country. He sees African marginalization as unhealthy for the future of the country. For him power-sharing must be premised on the respect for the rights of all ethnic groups. Phillips also sees the health of the economy as being linked to political stability which he argues will be guaranteed by a power-sharing government (Phillips 2008).

Kwayana's party, the WPA has been the most consistent advocate of power-sharing. From its proposal for a Government of National Unity and Reconstruction to replace the then PNC authoritarian regime to the present, it has linked its multi-ethnic philosophy to power-sharing. In its submission to the constitutional reform commission the party reiterated its commitment to the idea. It has since 1992 repeatedly called for the setting up of a power-sharing government as an interim arrangement. According to its co-leader, Rupert Roopnarine, such an arrangement would "suspend" winner-take-all and single party government and give the country space, if well used, to reconcile (Roopnarine 2000).

Another WPA executive, Clive Thomas, has drawn attention to the relationship between the country's ethnic problems and the persistent decline of the economy. He locates the poor state of the economy in the ongoing ethnic strife and posits that any economic improvement must be tied to a political solution. While conscious of the threat of gridlock in a power-sharing arrangement, Thomas argues that extremism arising from ethnic exclusion is a far greater threat. He also contends that despite the reforms arising from the 1999 constitutional reform process, given the lack of real separation of powers, there is not likely to be any fundamental charge of the political process. Finally he expressed the view that free and fair elections did not alter the "executive totalitarianism" that developed under the PNC and warned of the threat of social breakdown (Thomas 2003). Another WPA activist, Tacuma Ogunseye, agrees that power-sharing is aimed at empowering all ethnic groups including the Amerindians who are usually left out of the national discourse. Towards this end he disagrees with those who think that political education by itself could solve the problems of ethnic voting. Like most supporters of power-sharing he contends that such an arrangement could be "a vital tool in the political education of Guyanese for meaningful change" (Ogunseye 2009).

My own views on the need for power-sharing are premised on the Kwayana perspective which combines the need to avoid domination and an acceptance that neither ethnic group has shown an inclination to accept the leadership of the other. Towards this end I reject the integrative approach which encourages ethnic parties to try to encourage other groups to join its ranks. This invariably leads to inclusive domination whereby leaders of the opposite group are included not as equals but with the understanding that they accept the lead of the dominant group. This has been the case with the Civic component of the PPP, which is not an equal part as none of its members could be the party's presidential candidate (Hinds 2004).

I also opposed the dialogue between the two leaders as counter productive in the final analysis. While it helped to halt the violence it became a matter of convenience for both parties, which did not want to embrace power-sharing. The PPP used the dialogue to contain the PNC and as substitute for meaningful power- sharing. Similarly the PNC engaged in the dialogue as a compromise between its power-sharing and hardline factions and as a form of power politics from outside of the process. Since the PPP did not see the two parties as political equals and since as the government it could determine which of the joint agreements gets implemented, in the last analysis the PNC was powerless to sustain the process. I argued that because the dialogue raised expectations among African

Guyanese of a political solution its failure would invariably lead to a return of violence. The move to power-sharing then, arises from the failure of majoritarian democracy, inclusionary domination and the dialogue to significantly reverse the ethnic conflict. While power-sharing would not by itself reverse conflict by eliminating the competition over who governs it, would create space for ethnic cooperation among the people (Hinds 2004).

Ravi Dev, the country's foremost Indian Rights activist, has also argued for a power-sharing arrangement based on the acceptance that ethnic polarization is a fact of life. For Dev, the case for power-sharing would be strengthened when the major political parties accept that they represent the two major ethnic groups. Further, Dev posits that the security dilemma, whereby both major groups despite their dominance of strategic sectors of the political economy remain insecure especially when they are out of political power, as the major factor in favor of power sharing.

Dhanpaul Narine and Tara Singh, two PPP supporters who initially opposed power-sharing, advocate a new vision for Guyana in which power-sharing should be a central factor. They view such an arrangement as helping "to move Guyanese away from the politics of 'them' and 'us' and laying the basis for restoring citizens faith in the political system." While acknowledging inherent problems such as gridlock, Narine and Singh felt that these can be overcome by mechanisms with special constitutional powers to break deadlocks. They also do not confine power-sharing to executive branch, but extend it to the legislative branch, state boards and commissions (Narine and Singh 2002).

With the return of electoral democracy and the PNC's loss of power, it pinned its hopes of victory on the combination of a possible crossover Indian vote and other Indian-based parties' splitting the Indian vote. While a majority of the PNC leadership had opposed or has been, at best, lukewarm towards power-sharing, the party had nevertheless challenged one-party governance of the country on the grounds of discrimination and ethnic dominance. One may conclude, then, that the PNC found itself in the dilemma of embracing the winner-take-all principle but rejecting its consequences when the party loses an election. But as the prospects of winning a fair poll progressively diminished, and faced with pressures from within its ranks, the party opted for power-sharing.

Some observers have viewed this changed position with skepticism, especially since the PNC has not made it the centerpiece of its campaigns. One critic, Clarence Ellis, a PNC supporter observed at the time of the announcement:

> Mr. Hoyte says that an adjusted system of governance "appears" to be an idea whose time has come. The operative word is "appears". . . . We are, therefore, forced to believe that Mr. Hoyte has some concept of shared governance in mind when it is obvious that he is prepared to walk the walk by laying down some markers on shared governance (2002: 5).

Ellis would later return to the theme during the 2006 election campaign when he chastised the PNC for not making power-sharing a part of its election manifesto:

> In the first place, the manifesto does not represent a point of departure from the Westminster model even though the Party has endorsed a power sharing government. Stabroek News reports that "[a] top priority for the PNCR-1 Government will be the early construction of a paved highway connecting Guyana to the north central states of Brazil." For a party that believes in power sharing, a top priority ought to be the pooling of ideas for an agreement of a strategy of development for the way forward. Power sharing has to be steeped in the party's thought processes and Westminster has to be jettisoned. The first criticism of the manifesto therefore is that it is not consistent with the Party's declared preference for a new way of governing (Ellis 2006).

Later two leading members of the PNC resigned from the leadership over the party's apparent ambivalence on the issue. According to one of them, Sherwood Lowe: "I feel that the party has to push the shared governance issue more, which was not being done; and I feel that I could make a greater impact outside the executive because this issue cannot wait until 2011. It has to be done now" (Lowe 2006).

Anti-Power-Sharing

The PPP has been the leading opponent of power sharing. One of the fiercest opponents of Power Sharing is Prem Misir, a government spokesperson. He argues that there is no need for power-sharing since the justification for it, African marginalization in the political economy, is a myth. He contends that the similarity of the African and Indian Guyanese socio-economic status is evidence that African Guyanese are not the victims of "large-scale institutional discrimination." Instead the power-sharing advocates "transformed" African Guyanese insecurity into racism against them. He dismissed federalism as an impractical alternative largely because it has not reduced ethnic conflict where it exists. He similarly rejected executive power-sharing as "bureaucratic" and "ethnic separatism" and called for a referendum on the issue (Misir 2006).

PPP executive member and speaker of the National Assembly, Ralph Ramkarran also opposes power-sharing. According to him the opposition calls for it are "motivated by and are a confession of political failure" to win over votes from the opposite group as the PPP has done. Consistent with the PPP's line he advocates "courtship before marriage" and sees the issues as political rather than constitutional (Ramkarran 2010). Randy Persaud, another PPP spokesperson, refers to power-sharing as an "extra electoral concept" that is aimed at undermining electoral democracy. He views it as a function of Black Nationalism: "it has become the fulcrum" (Persaud: July 1 2006).

President Jagdeo contends that the constitution makes provision for power- sharing in the form of independent commissions on human rights and ethnic relations. As he declared "that's an inclusion form of governance, because nowhere in the region does an opposition have so much say" (Guyana Chronicle: August 22, 2002). The President also claimed that power-sharing would lead to dictatorship and institutionalized racism (Guyana Chronicle July 21, 2003). Jagdeo further argued that trust is a prerequisite for sharing power. Towards this end he favored the implementation of constitutional reforms as a first step (Stabroek News: February 9, 2003).

Skeptics

While there is widespread support for power-sharing among the country's political elite, some are skeptical about how it would be implemented. This group shares the PPP's position that the lack of trust between the two parties is an obstacle to power-sharing. It also tends to ground its skepticism in the belief that the country's ethnic problems can be overcome by reforming to the Westminster winner-take-all model. Khemraj Ramjattan, a former PPP executive member, argues that in Guyana's ethnic environment one-person-one-vote leads to "an elective or majoritarian democracy." He observes that in such a scenario African Guyanese are permanently shut out of power but he rejects power-sharing on the grounds that there is lack of trust between the two parties and that the implementation of power sharing would lead to a lack of opposition. He, therefore, argues that African Guyanese insecurity would be minimized when the two major parties democratize themselves. According to Ramjattan in a democratic environment, moderates would dominate and ethnic hardliners and extremists would be pruned (Ramjattan, 2004). Fredrick Kissoon, an anti-PPP Indian columnist and University lecturer, is also skeptical of power-sharing. He dismisses the security dilemma argument as outdated. Like Ramjattan, he acknowledges that the current system leaves African Guyanese outside the councils of power and he is even more strident on the elective dictatorship thesis. Although he has become less critical of power sharing, he sees the evolution of an effective multi-ethnic party as the better solution to the problem.

Perhaps the most consistent skeptic has been one of the country's independent newspapers, the *Stabroek News*. A product of the political liberalization introduced by the PNC after the death of its founder-leader in 1985, *Stabroek News* has consistently taken an independent moderate position which is grounded in a British style liberal democracy and free market capitalism. Its outlook is, therefore, much more reformist, and it prefers gradual change. Its founder and editor in chief until 2008 had been involved in the country's political discourse dating back to the 1960s. Although his moderate-to-conservative views were well known, he was nevertheless not hostile to radical activists, some of whom have been *Stabroek News* columnists. The newspaper's editorials, for the most part, raised questions about the viability of power-sharing without dismissing it as un-workable.

They have been less optimistic about the possibility of success and tend to share some of the PPP's approaches to the issue if not the motives. For example, *Stabroek News* endorses the PPP's view that the lack of trust between the two parties is a significant roadblock which has to be overcome if power-sharing will get off the ground (Stabroek News: December 17, 2002). Consequently the newspaper prefers a gradual incremental approach along the lines of those proposed by the PPP, although it was quick to point out that its notion of incrementalism does not mean stalling (Stabroek News: August 11, 2002). Other areas of concern for *Stabroek News* include the threat of gridlock, the diminishing of the role of the parliament the abolishing of the opposition, and the hardening of ethnic blocs. It has been particularly concerned about gridlock which it views as "as area that would require careful negotiation if a power sharing agreement was to be reached" (Stabroek News: July 22, 2004). This incrementalist approach meant that *Stabroek News* was a firm supporter of dialogue between the two parties. It felt that it is better to have the two parties talking rather than having one on the streets (Stabroek News: August 13, 2002).

Stabroek News' concerns are shared by Selwyn Ryan, a Trinidadian political scientist who has been a keen observer of the Guyana situation. But unlike the *Stabroek News* Ryan thinks that given the advanced nature of the conflict, power-sharing could usher in some form of stability. As he observes "It is however clear that unless some such consociation formula is put in place in Guyana, that country that will lurch from crisis to crisis, the cumulative effect of which would destroy Guyana's economy, civil society an in time may make Lebanon look like a picnic" (Ryan 1998). Ryan expanded on this thesis four years later as the Guyanese problem escalated. In comparing Guyana to his native Trinidad and Tobago he observes that in Guyana where civil society and the middle class are consumed by the ethnic conflict and where ethnic narratives of victimhood are entrenched there is much more justification for power-sharing. But he cautions that power-sharing should be preceded or accompanied by "social reconstruction" (Ryan 2002).

Conclusion

The discourse on power-sharing in Guyana shows two dominant tendencies. First, those who advocate a power-sharing government tend to accept ethnic polarization as a given. It is not surprising that in this regard African Guyanese spokespersons tend to be more forceful in their advocacy. Many view power-sharing as both a way of addressing the African Guyanese fear of disenfranchisement and as a form of democratization. Others argue that it is also a way to check violence. Those who oppose power-sharing take a purely partisan position; while they point to problems such as lack of trust and the loss of opposition, they have not philosophically engaged the issue. The skeptics, on the other hand, are unwilling to conceptualize governance outside of the liberal democratic majoritarian government-opposition framework. The argument that trust is essential for a workable power-sharing government seems plausible at first glance. But trust between adversaries is best achieved when the causes of the distrust are removed. Since the major cause of ethnic distrust in Guyana lies in the mutual fear of disenfranchisement, domination and disrespect, them it makes sense to begin the process by addressing the conditions that facilitate those fears. If the political process guarantees freedom from these fears, the possibility of trust will be vastly increased. Power-sharing, therefore, can be a catalyst for ethnic trust as the ethnic representatives would gain experience working together on critical national issues.

6

The PPP's Betrayal of Power Sharing and National Reconciliation in Guyana 1990-92

The October 5, 1992, election, which resulted in the defeat of the incumbent People's National Congress (PNC) after 28 years in office, brought an end to a significant chapter in the country's history. The outgoing government, despite significant political and economic reforms in the last seven years of its tenure, had presided over the most authoritarian postcolonial Caribbean state. In the process of consolidating this authoritarian state, the PNC had transformed it into a de facto one-party state over which the party was paramount, and which systematically trampled on civil rights and liberties while closing all legal and constitutional means of removing it from power.

Despite the realization of free and fair elections, two critical areas of concern remained. First, although the PNC lost the election, the authoritarian state over which it presided remained intact. Second, by the time of the election, marked advances in multiethnic solidarity, engendered by a convergence of the PNC's authoritarian and anti-people policies and the deliberate work of the WPA, the PPP and others, had been seriously eroded. Attending to these two areas was pivotal to transforming the democratic opening to actual democratization. It was, therefore, a mistake to believe, as many inside and outside the incoming PPP government did, that the defeat of the PNC meant the end of the transition from authoritarianism and the return of democracy. In other words, governmental change is not necessarily regime change, and democratic opening in the form of free and fair elections is not the sum total of democracy. This miscalculation led the PPP government to assume a mandate that exceeded its capacity, and crucially, it led to the failure of other political and civil society forces to press for necessary safeguards and guarantees for completion of the transition.

Since 1992, the country has faced the daunting challenge of balancing the two major consequences of the election results - the democratic expectations arising from the first phase of its transition from authoritarian rule, and the renewed racial rivalry and insecurity that accompanied the return to electoral democracy. The dominant feature of this period has been the convergence of intensified ethnic antagonism and persistent political instability. This development has had a devastating effect on the country's political economy. In short, the anticipated democratization and economic revitalization following the initial transition from authoritarian rule have not materialized.

This development is not uncommon in countries emerging from authoritarian rule. O'Donnell and Schmitter (1986:3) point out that one of the outcomes of the transition from authoritarian regimes can "be simply confusion, that is, the rotation in power of successive governments which fail to provide any enduring or predictable solution to the problem of institutionalizing political power". They also contend that transitions can also be followed by "widespread, violent confrontations." Huntington (1997: 6), in his discussion of the problems of democratization, goes to the heart of the matter as it relates to Guyana when he argues that "democratization is the solution to the problem of tyranny, but the process of democratization itself can also create or exacerbate other problems with which new democracies must grapple". He further observes:

> The initiation of elections forces political leaders to compete for votes. In many situations, the easiest way to win votes is to appeal to tribal, ethnic, and religious constituencies. Democratization thus promotes communalism and ethnic conflict and relatively few democracies have structured their institutions to minimize the incentives to make such appeals.

The last point in the above quotation points to the question of conflict management within the context of democratization. In other words, how does a country emerging from authoritarian rule manage problems such as ethnic conflict while simultaneously enhancing the democratic process? Realization of this synthesis is determined largely by the deliberate choices and actions of the major political actors. They must carry out a delicate balancing act, as the transition from authoritarian rule imposes pressures for democratization while the very democratization process encourages political competition, which in racially segmented societies takes the form of racial rivalry. Democratization in ethnically segmented societies emerging from authoritarian rule, therefore, faces stern challenges that, if not properly managed, can lead to a return to authoritarianism (O'Donnell and Schmitter 1986 and Huntington 1997).

What accounts for this state of affairs? Why has the end of authoritarian rule led to instability and confusion instead of democratization? While the ethnic factor is a constant in Guyana, it is argued that the adversarial actions and choices of the two major parties have been the driving force in shaping this outcome. The contention is that the parties, separately and together, have failed to meet three major challenges: (a) the need to manage and contain the intensified racial polarization; (b) the need to develop an alternative form of governance and political culture that is more conducive to racial peace and cooperation; and (c) the need to transform the state and the political economy away from its authoritarian past. The key to this failure lies in the choices and actions of these parties at critical junctures.

This chapter examines the choices made by the PPP at one such juncture - the very election that brought that party to power. It argues that the choices made by the PPP just prior to the elections and immediately afterwards laid the foundations for the adversarial and zero-sum politics that have characterized the period under study. While adversarial politics in Guyana can be traced as far back as 1955, when the national movement split into two ethnic camps, it is argued that the 1992 election presented an opportunity to alter that process by introducing a new form of political behavior among the political elites, which, had it been taken, could have gone a long way towards frustrating impediments to racial peace and democratization.

The First Failure

The attainment of free and fair elections, after almost three decades of electoral fraud, was a deserving victory for pro-democracy forces spearheaded by the Patriotic Coalition for Democracy (PCD), a coalition of opposition parties that had since 1986 made free and fair elections the focus of their campaign. But would free and fair elections, even if they lead to the removal of the authoritarian regime, lead to democratization? Previous instances of free and fair elections, in particular those of 1957 and 1961, both of which were won by the PPP, had led to political instability and racial disturbances, which in turn facilitated, to a considerable degree, the rise to power of the PNC. It meant, therefore, that the political actors, if serious about democratization, would have sought to encourage an atmosphere of racial cooperation and discourage a situation that encouraged racial mobilization. Such a development would have been most effective had it preceded the election.

These considerations seem to have been uppermost in the minds of the WPA. In a statement made seven years before the 1992 elections the party said:

> There should be an honorable understanding that any political party that wins an overall majority will, in spite of this and because of the total crisis, seek to create a national government based on the votes of the people, and not seek to run the country by itself. The party chosen to run the government should at once consult with the nation about the drafting of a patriotic pact or understanding for the reconciliation of the Guyanese nation within a Caribbean framework (WPA 1985: 9).

Four years later, in 1989, the WPA moved a successful motion in the National Assembly for a "national dialogue of all social forces... aimed at an internal solution of the elections issue and a full dialogue of the many sided crisis" (Kwayana 1999: 10). The dialogue never got off the ground as the PNC insisted on taking elections off the agenda. With elections due in December 1990, the parties were working against time. Not all of the reforms had been put in place, and the opposition parties were skeptical about holding the election without clear guarantees that it would be free and fair. The WPA, in particular, favored postponing the poll until all the reforms were in place. It proposed, both in parliament and in the

PCD, an interim government for the period between the end of the PNC's tenure and the holding of the election whereby the ruling party and the opposition would evenly share cabinet posts with the presidency going to the incumbent PNC. According to the WPA this "caretaker" government would be in office "for a limited duration with a commitment to the completion of the electoral reforms for genuine elections at the end of the agreed period, and a minimum economic programme" (Roopnarine 2002:2).

The PPP surprisingly did not support the proposal. According to Rupert Roopnarine, who presented the proposal to the PCD on behalf of the WPA:

> We were asking the PCD to consider a power-sharing cabinet shared equally between the PNC and the PCD and chaired by President Hoyte. The discussion did not get as far as the details of an arrangement. The overwhelming opinion of our colleagues in the PCD was that Hoyte and the PNC would never agree to any such thing and that the WPA was dreaming if they thought they would (p. 2).

Although Roopnarine does not name the PPP, other attendees of the meeting confirmed that the PPP led the charge against the proposal. The other functioning member of the PCD, the Democratic Labor Movement, did not object to it. So certain was the PPP that the proposal would fail, it did not object to the WPA approaching the PNC on its own. The PNC unexpectedly treated the proposal with much seriousness. This long quotation from Roopnarine confirms the high degree of seriousness:

> Within days we received a reply inviting us to a meeting at the Office of the President to discuss the idea. It was the first time that the WPA and the PNC were to be face to face since the days of the civil rebellion of the late seventies. I led the delegation to the meeting and was surprised to find that several senior ministers were present, including Mr. Keith Massiah, the Attorney General, armed with his constitution, and Foreign Minister Rashleigh Jackson, among others. The presentation of the proposal led to a number of discussions

on points of detail, such as, how would portfolios be allocated, what were the constitutional provisions, and so on. We had some suggestions of our own, but felt that those details could be worked out once the proposal was agreed on by all sides. The meeting ended with President Hoyte responding that if the WPA could persuade our colleagues on the PCD, he would be prepared to discuss the matter further (p.2).

Faced with this positive response from the PNC and perhaps caught off balance, the PCD confronted a serious challenge, to which it did not respond positively. According to Roopnarine:

At a specially convened meeting of the PCD at Freedom House, I reported on the meeting with the President and his colleagues and relayed Mr. Hoyte's response, urging that the invitation to further discussions be taken up. After some debate, the response was rejected by our colleagues of the PCD and the WPA was accused of entering into a conspiracy when we were on the verge of victory in the fight for genuine elections (p.2).

It is clear from the above quotation that the PPP paid little attention to the potential problems of the post-election period. The party seemed to be content with "victory" rather than the larger democratic project. Since the PPP had eschewed winner-take-all governance and had expressed a desire to join with its PCD partners in an electoral alliance and coalition government, should they win the election, it could not be charged with being anti-alliance. Its objection, therefore, was alliance with the PNC. The party may have been concerned that the presence of the PNC would prevent it from being the dominant partner, a position it would occupy in a PCD government. Or it may have underestimated the PNC's strength. In that sense the PPP placed party interest above national interest. Kwayana (2003: 1) sums up this aspect of the PPP's political attitude this way: "The present ruling party has a dominant craving for unimpeded one party rule...The PPP privately defines democracy to allow for their subconscious dream of one party rule, which is what they mean by democratic centralism in the state." It should be noted here that unlike the PNC, which was split between "hardliners" and "softliners," the PPP's leadership seemed united on the positions taken, even though Janet Jagan was cited by PPP insiders as being the most rigid (Private interview with PPP member: December 1988).

The irony is that it was the PPP that had consistently argued for governmental alliances with the PNC while the WPA had for a long time rejected any such idea. However, the WPA's call for the interim government was consistent with the position the party had taken since 1985 that it would cooperate with the PNC if it agreed to free and fair elections (Kwayana 1985). According to the WPA, its proposal was guided by the need to "provide a neutral line for the elections" (Kwayana 1999: 10) and its anticipation of the consequences of a post-transition government that excluded the PNC. Roopnarine puts it this way: "We proposed the Caretaker Government, sensing the likely social tension between a long entrenched regime and a new one, however legitimate in all the circumstances of Guyana" (p. 3).

The PPP, for its part, did not seem to have taken into account that since 1985 the PNC had split between the "hardliners," who wanted to continue authoritarian rule in all its forms, and the "softliners," who preferred a reformed authoritarian regime in which selected and incremental political and economic reforms were granted. Further, the softliners, led by President Hoyte were in control of the party and government and were prepared to distance themselves from the hardliners.

Had the PCD parties entered into a pact with the PNC in 1990, there would have been several benefits for post-election politics. First, it was possible that a pre-election power-sharing government with two years of working together could have been carried over into the post-election period. This would have ensured less political instability and quickened the completion of the transition period. Second, even if the above did not occur, the election would not have been as high intensity as it turned out to be since the experience of the parties working together would have reduced the political space for ethnic mobilization. Third, the PNC's participation in a joint government would have strengthened the hand of the softliners and substantially weakened the hardliners. This failure to fashion a government of national unity in 1990, therefore, had direct consequences for the 1992 election and the post-election period.

The Second Failure

Despite the differences over the proposed caretaker government, the opposition parties agreed, in principle, to contest the election as a unified force under the banner of the PCD. This was a shrewd decision, as it had the potential not only of defeating the PNC by avoiding a fragmented opposition, but more importantly, it had the potential of blunting any attempt to mobilize along ethnic lines as the PCD would be a multi-ethnic alliance. Further, a broad-based government, representing a wide cross-section of the electorate both in ideological and ethnic terms, stood a better chance than a single-party government of effecting democratic consolidation after the election.

Given the PPP's stated commitment to a winner-does-not-take-all government and the WPA's historic embrace of executive power-sharing as a solution to the ethnic problems, negotiating a PCD pre-election and post-election arrangement seemed a foregone conclusion. However, there was one important stumbling block—leadership. When the issue of a consensus PCD presidential candidate arose, the PPP proposed its leader, Cheddi Jagan, but the WPA preferred a neutral candidate outside of the political parties. The WPA felt that given Jagan's central role in the ethnic acrimony of the past, his candidacy would alienate African Guyanese voters. But the PPP, confident that it could attract the majority Indian vote, refused to budge; thus once again sacrificing unity for party superiority. After intense and sometimes acrimonious negotiations, the PCD parties failed to arrive at an agreement and went their separate ways.

The PPP blames the WPA for the demise of the PCD, but the WPA's position, unlike the PPP's, seemed to take into consideration not only triumph at the poll, but more importantly how the inevitable racial polarization would be managed after the election. The PPP's decision to contest the election with a group of non-party supporters called CIVIC, had three major negative consequences for democratic consolidation. First, it had the effect of reducing the contest to one between the PPP and the PNC, which in the context of Guyana meant a contest between the two major ethnic groups. According to Ralph Premdas who observed the election, "The PNC and the PPP acted in ways that suggested that the major contestants were the PNC and PPP and others were of little consequence" (1993:13).

Second, as a result of the above, the PNC, which had lost a lot of its African Guyanese support to the WPA over the years, could now easily appeal to ethnic sentiments to regain lost ground. Again Premdas reports: "At several PNC meetings which I attended the issue of racial domination was woven into a history of African liberation from slavery suggesting that the PPP was about to re-enslave the Black Guyanese population" (1993: 118-119). Premdas failed to report similar ethnic appeals at PPP meetings, which equated the return of the PNC to power with African domination. The WPA suggests that both parties pursued "the politics of racial solidarity by other means. That is, each of them took steps to secure a loyal ethnic vote and at the same time had a marginal campaign to capture others outside its own ethnic camp. Both failed to do this (1992:1)." Premdas, however, did report that the PPP failed to address the PNC's claims of ethnic domination. He says that the PPP "cleverly omitted any suggestion that the destruction of Guyana's social and economic well-being was due to the ravages of intercommunal strife in which it played along with the PNC an equal role" (p. 121). He also charges the PPP with erasing the role of African leaders, in particular Forbes Burnham, in building the early independence movement.

The third negative consequence of the failure to field a PCD slate was the weakening of the WPA, which represented the racial center around which the multiethnic anti-authoritarian movement was mobilized. According to the WPA (1992:1), its African and Indian support responded to the ethnic appeals of the PPP and PNC:

> The PPP felt forced for its own survival to tell Indo-Guyanese that the WPA was not what it claimed to be, but was an African party with a secret plan to join the PNC in a coalition. The PNC was equally vicious. It told the Afro Guyanese that the WPA was an Indian party with a secret plan to

join the PPP in a coalition.

Had the WPA and the PPP contested the elections as a single entity, the WPA could not have been charged with having "secret plans." Further, the PNC would have had a difficult time making the case that a PCD slate with known and respected African leaders such as Eusi Kwayana, Clive Thomas, Andaiye, Bonita Harris, and Tacuma Ogunseye, would have participated in Indian Guyanese domination of African Guyanese. The weakening of the WPA meant the removal of any potent third force and the transformation of the political landscape from a "tri-polar" system of two race-based parties and a strong multiracial party, to a bi-polar system of just the two race-based parties. Whereas under the tri-polar system the two race-based parties are balanced by the multiracial party, which often serves as a check on open racial appeals and mobilization, the bi-polar system, with the removal of the balancer, is more conducive to racial appeals that often lead to conflict.

The results of the election, not unexpectedly, confirmed this development. The PPP won with a slim majority (55 percent) based on the majority Indian vote. The PNC secured a large minority (40 percent) while the WPA and the resuscitated United Force (TUF) got approximately 2 percent each. The returns of the PPP and PNC mirrored the ethnic breakdown of the electorate. Two crucial developments on Election Day and during the immediate post-election period signaled a political realignment that would prove pivotal in the period ahead. First, the PNC, led by its deputy leader, Hamilton Greene, on Election Day attempted to abort the election by claiming that many of its supporters were disenfranchised. Hundreds of PNC supporters took to the streets to make their case and calm was restored only when party leader Desmond Hoyte called off the protest. He later accepted the result of a quick count, conducted by the Carter Center under the supervision of former US President, Jimmy Carter, which gave victory to the PPP.

Hoyte's statesmanlike action was unexpected, as there were some grounds for the PNC's claim, given problems with the voters' list. Three factors seemed to have influenced his actions. First, he was obviously aware that the USA was observing the situation with keen interest and would not look favorably on a reversal of the process. In this regard President Carter's presence in the country was crucial. Second, because of an internal feud with Hamilton

Greene that became public after the election, he seized the opportunity to distance himself from Greene. Finally, Hoyte, despite his autocratic leadership style and his unconditional support for Burnham's authoritarian rule, had become committed to what Ferguson (1995:220) calls the "democratic ethos." Ferguson suggests that this commitment to political democracy was born out of his need to avoid erecting barriers to the success of his economic liberalization program. As Ferguson says, Hoyte was "consumed" by the economic liberalization programme and "was not prepared to allow partisan, political calculations to threaten this overriding national imperative" (p.216).

Hoyte's actions, therefore, were pivotal to the short term and long term future of the country. First, his concession of the elections consolidated the hardline faction both inside and outside the party that saw his action as a "sell out." This faction included both those driven by an intense fear of Indian domination and others who believed it was the PNC's right to rule indefinitely, even if it did so as a result of fraudulent elections. Many of these left the party when Hamilton Greene was expelled and provided the base for his new party, Good and Green Guyana (GGG), which gained the most votes and the mayorship of the capital city, Georgetown, in local government elections held in 1994. The sentiments of this group were best captured in the Mighty Rebel's winning calypso of the 1993 Mashramani carnival season titled "Desi you wrong." In typical calypsonian style, Rebel invoked the spirit of Forbes Burnham who admonishes Hoyte for allowing the PPP to return to power. This hardline faction was to prove crucial to the PNC's strategy in 1997. On the other hand, Hoyte's concession raised his standing in the African Guyanese middle class community and among some moderate Indians of the commercial class. This had the effect of maintaining the PNC as a legitimate force despite its dismal past and in spite of the split in the party.

The other major development in the political realignment of the country resulted from the PPP's decision to renege on its pre-election promise to eschew winner-take-all politics. After some exploration of a possible PPP-WPA coalition, the PPP decided to form a PPP government euphemistically called PPP/CIVIC. While relations between the WPA and PPP were strained as a result of the pre-election disagreement over the PCD slate, and although the WPA, contrary to popular expectation, garnered only 2 percent of the vote, the party was thought by some observers to be a potential mediating force in the context of heightening racial tensions. As Premdas (1993:113) says of the WPA's electoral return:

> This score certainly underestimated the substantial role that the WPA played over two decades of persistent opposition that it waged against the PNC regime. Further it belittled the massive part the WPA played at all stages in sanitizing the election machinery.

The WPA itself was split over participation in a PPP-dominated government. No doubt the risk of being perceived as siding with one ethnic group and being seen as an appendage of the PPP may have been uppermost in their minds. Another stumbling block was the PPP's insistence on having the WPA's co-leader, Clive Thomas, in the government in an individual capacity rather than as a WPA member. On the other hand, a PPP-WPA government would have made the government's legitimacy less questionable with the WPA serving as a bridge to the African Guyanese community.

Conclusion

Democracy and democratization in Guyana cannot be separated from ethnicity, for it has the capacity to frustrate and derail the process. This must be a paramount consideration for those who preside over the transition from authoritarianism in similar societies. The makeup of the government along with its policies must be geared towards ensuring security for all groups. In this regard, two considerations are pertinent. First, unlike most "Third Wave" transitions, the transition stage in countries such as Guyana has two phases. The period 1985-92 is the first phase or the "political liberalization phase" whereby the extreme form of authoritarian governance and the authoritarian government are dismantled, but the old regime structures remain in place. The second phase or the "political engineering phase," which follows the election, must aim at ensuring ethnic peace and security, while simultaneously transforming the nature of the state away from its authoritarian foundations.

A related conclusion concerns the role of the old regime. Since the transition is not completed with the election, the defeat of the old governing party should not be seen as a signal to marginalize it. This is even more urgent when that party still commands considerable support, especially if that support is within the military, the bureaucracy or in the form of a sizeable ethnic bloc. To marginalize that party is to create immediate obstacles to stability and democratization.

A third conclusion relates to the dismantling of the tri-polar system. Ethnic-neutral parties play important roles in the first phase of the transition in that they give the anti-authoritarian alliance a multi-ethnic outlook that is crucial to the defeat of an authoritarian ethnic-based government. The irony for parties like the WPA is that the very democracy that they fight for often turn out to be the harbinger of their demise, particularly on the electoral front. Yet they can play an even greater role in the second phase where the need for a mediating force is crucial to the success of political engineering. But their political survival is dependent on an electoral atmosphere that is devoid of extreme ethnic rivalry. Democratic consolidation in ethnically segmented societies is enhanced by the presence of parties that sit at the center, as they serve as the bridge between the two contending forces. This role is even more crucial given the fact that Civil Society in these segmented societies is for the most part underdeveloped.

Finally, in situations of ethnic rivalry, political missteps are not easily corrected. For this reason the first step in the process is critical; it signals the intentions of the actors. Rulers in segmented societies do not have much room for maneuver; they must hit the ground running in the right direction. And it is always risky to run alone if the party's base is drawn from one segment, for that instantly creates the conditions for rivalry, which quickly turns to instability.

7

Benefits, Concerns and Prospects

Benefits

Perhaps the foremost benefit of consociation power-sharing is its potential for ensuring that no ethnic group dominates the other politically and by extension culturally and economically. In Guyana the executive branch has evolved as the engine of government with the other two branches serving for the most part in a supplementary manner. One can argue with much justification that there has been an executive supremacy that borders on executive tyranny. The party which wins the election gets a majority in the parliament, which then gives it automatic control of the executive branch. This guarantees the governing party enormous power, which in a situation of ethnic conflict is an unfair advantage that eventually leads to authoritarianism or democratic exclusion as exclusionary domination. With the built-in parliamentary majority, government bills are guaranteed passage unless there is a revolt among government parliamentarians, which has never occurred in Guyana.

However, with both parties in the cabinet the fear of the power of the executive by the minority would be greatly diminished. Since ethnic insecurity is premised on the fear of domination, institutional assurances of security will most likely lead to a decrease in the intensity of this fear. Because the executive branch of the government has a monopoly on decision-making within the Guyanese state, it has become the symbol of domination along class, gender and ethnic lines. Given the fact that ethnicity has greatly influenced political behavior in Guyana since 1955, control of the government is seen largely, though not exclusively, in ethnic terms. The power of the state in determining economic policy and distributing resources places it in an extremely powerful position. In an economy in which the state is the largest employer and the private sector is relatively small, the power of the executive is enhanced.

This leads to a second benefit of power sharing--the enlarging of multiethnic space. The creation of multiethnic space in ethnically polarized societies is directly linked to ethnic security. When ethnic insecurity is high multiethnic space contracts and when it decreases multi-ethnic space grows. The significant achievement of Walter Rodney and the WPA was their success in increasing multiethnic space by encouraging a power-sharing arrangement in the opposition at three levels--between the WPA and the PPP, among all political parties regardless of ideological leanings and between the political parties and labor, religious and other professional organizations. These power- sharing arrangements created spaces for ethnic solidarity among workers, between ethnic communities and between the working classes and professionals.

The PPP's retreat from the power-sharing pact with the opposition parties and its refusal to enter into a similar pact with the PNC after the 1992 election greatly decreased multiethnic space. The threat of Indian domination forced many Africans, including those who opposed the PNC government, back into the PNC's orbit. On the other hand the potential for Indian ethnic security under the PPP forced Indians who had deserted the PPP back into the fold. With the decrease of multi-ethnic space, the multiethnic coalition and the WPA declined. The consequence was the heightening of ethnic insecurity and conflict that exploded in the wake of the 1997 election and has since all but consumed the society.

The removal of the threat of political domination would most likely decrease the ethnic temperature. The "soft" ethnic constituencies, which were part of the multiethnic community of the Rodney-WPA tendency would be freer to pursue cross-ethnic politics. Some proponents of multiethnic politics have attempted to build a movement without due consideration to the ethnic dynamics. But it is almost impossible to build a multiethnic movement without engaging ethnicity. This was proven by the WPA, which arose out of such an engagement beginning with the work of ASCRIA and

IPRA individually and together. This laid the groundwork for the Rodney period. On the other hand, the attempts by the PNC to create a "race neutral" state outside or above the ethnic dynamics proved to be futile. Under pressure from its constituency that endured African dominance, the PPP has not attempted a similar approach. Rather it has opted for an inclusionary domination model, whereby it allows limited participation by African Guyanese individuals who subscribe to the PPP's agenda and do not have significant following in the African Guyanese community. The AFC, which hoped to be multi-ethnic, drew more than 90 percent of its electoral support from African Guyanese. Consequently it has been unable to mobilize multiethnic pressure on the government.

The group whose party is in power is less likely to experiment with multi ethnicity in the absence of overarching reasons such as authoritarianism. Further, while the "soft" support of the party out of power is more likely to be open to multiethnicity, the majority "hard" support is less likely to do so. Power sharing at the top frees the soft support of both groups from reluctance and tentativeness on class, gender and national issues. Power sharing, then, could be an important facilitator of more overt gender and class politics.

The third benefit of power-sharing is its potential for the enhancement of democratization within the government. One of the problems of governance in the Caribbean, despite its general adherence to the tenets of formal democracy is the concomitant monopoly of power by the ruling party and the exclusion of the opposition. This democratic exclusion has led to virtual a one party-democracy, which has had negative consequences for the rule of law, respect for civil liberties, government accountability, economic management and development, political instability and national sovereignty. In ethnically polarized societies democratic exclusion and one- party democracy often mean ethnic exclusion and domination. The ruling party's obsession with remaining in power to protect the "race" leads to it being unaccountable to either its constituency or that of the opposing parties. Further, the guaranteed ethnic support regardless of the quality of governance makes the government more likely to overreach. On the other hand opposition perception and reality of marginalization drives it to extra-parliamentary tactics, which are then crushed by the government in the name of law and order.

A fourth benefit of power sharing is that it brings the opposition off the streets into the formal councils of government thus denying the government the excuse that it is under siege and the opposition of charges that its supporters are ethnically marginalized. With both groups in the executive branch, majoritarianism gives way to a more consensus form of democracy. But increased democracy within the executive branch will not enhance democracy if it is not supplemented by democratization of other branches and between the central government and local government. While power sharing in the executive does not automatically lead to democratization of the other two branches, it stands a better chance of facilitating this. Increased separation of powers between the executive and legislative branches would lead to more checks and balances than currently exists. If the PNC were to serve in a power-sharing cabinet, African Guyanese would see their own representative in the halls of power and this will likely boost their confidence in their ability to survive in Guyana. This could in turn lead to a decrease in African Guyanese protests and destabilizing tactics. As I have argued elsewhere,

> A power sharing model, whereby parliamentary parties sit together in the cabinet and make and implement decisions is this is like taking the dialogue between Mr. Hoyte and Mr. Jagdeo into the Cabinet. The difference is that with executive power sharing, they will both be responsible for not just taking decisions but implementing them. The PNC in such a scenario will get a chance to share in deciding things like house lot distribution, awarding contracts, staffing state boards, the future of bauxite, village development, what to do with the Black Clothes and all the other things it now complains about (Hinds 2001:1)

Concerns

The possibility of gridlock is a major concern of power sharing skeptics. Gridlock is inherent in any system of governance. While it is theoretically counter productive, it has not proved to be a massive hindrance to actual governance even in systems with inherent gridlock devices such as the USA. Although situations of crisis and emergency demand prompt decision-making, hastily executed decision-making is contrary to democratic governance as it downplays democratic tenets such as consultation, extensive deliberations, compromise and consensus. Even the British Westminster model, which is one of the least gridlocked political systems, has a built-in delay mechanism in the form of a suspensory veto by the British House of Lords whereby that body can hold up passage of a bill for up to six months. Although an all-party cabinet moves gridlock into the executive branch, the same gridlock exists in single party executives where various factions of the party invariably battle over policy.

In ethnically divided societies with a winner-take-all system, gridlock is more the rule than the exception. Since 1992 the government has been unable to get much done as the opposition has used its street power and support within the state apparatus to frustrate decision-making. Although the government has used its majority in the parliament to pass measures, gridlock occurs in the implementation process. First, the decisions must pass muster among various contending factions within the ruling party. While the party may be united on the need to remain in office, its leaders often differ in terms of which section of the support base should benefit from government largesse and to what extent the needs and demands of the rival support base should be accommodated. Second, governments tend to be much more cautious about initiating measures for fear of exciting the opposition which often uses extra parliamentary tactics to frustrate or prevent the government from enacting its policies and programs.

The threat of gridlock has the potential of forcing compromise, if not consensus. It expands the scope for broad discussion and deliberation that make for more broad-based decisions. This is most crucial for deeply divided societies as it institutionalizes a culture of cooperation and produces decisions that have the support of the various factions. Gridlock in a power-sharing arrangement, therefore, is not necessarily a negative thing. In small countries such as Guyana, without the constant threat of external intervention and war, there is seldom need for speedy passage of policy measures. In this regard gridlock can be a tool of democratization if it encourages broader and closer scrutiny of government business.

The argument that power-sharing would harden ethnic feelings fails to take into consideration that ethnic political action is not necessarily an unhealthy phenomenon. Ethnic identification by itself does not cause conflict; it is when it is married to the struggle for dominant power that it becomes lethal. What power sharing sets out to minimize and or eliminate is not ethnic feelings but ethnic domination and conflict. By transforming the current high stake competition into a low stake one, power-sharing could soften rather than harden ethnic antagonism. In Guyana's case any corrective measure must begin with an acknowledgement of the institutionalized ethnic voting patterns. While power-sharing may not solve ethnic problems and or change ethnic voting patterns, it has the potential of neutralizing the consequences of ethnic voting by forcing the contending forces to work together for the common good. It also has the potential of encouraging the less hardcore ethnic voters to vote for a third force which in turn could create a balancer in the power sharing government.

The concept of an opposition operating outside of the ultimate decision-making process has worked well in western democracies where the opposition is actually the government in waiting. However, in ethnically divided societies and most homogenous postcolonial societies in Africa, Latin America and the Caribbean the opposition has evolved more as a source of extra-parliamentary protest; opposition in these societies generally means, at worst, making the country ungovernable and, at best, undermining the government. This negative role of the opposition is linked to the winner-take-all form of governance, which confers absolute power on governments. The formal role of opposition parties has been confined to legislative debate with little power to influence policies. In ethnically divided societies, therefore, the opposition has had a negative impact; in fact it has served to heighten rather than diminish conflict. Power- sharing brings the opposition into the decision making process. Rather than being eliminated, the opposition is relocated directly into the political process.

This is perhaps the most glaring benefit of power-sharing for Guyana where the opposition has functioned more as a parallel government than a government in waiting. Under power-sharing, opposition will be shifted to the legislative branch, which has to be translated into a real oversight of the executive branch. In this regard there has to be more separation of powers then currently obtains whereby the number of ministers who sit in parliament is minimized. This would allow for a fresh set of eyes and minds to look at bills when they reach the parliament.

One key concern is whether warring parties can work together in the same cabinet. There are no simple answers to this question, as political behavior cannot be accurately predicted. But unlike a coalition government, which is a marriage of convenience, a power-sharing government in circumstances of acute division and distrust has to be constitutionally covered. While parties cannot be forced to enter a government, once they enter they have to be subjected to rules that govern the working of the government and must agree to a common program. A party may choose to opt out of a power-sharing government, thus throwing the system in crisis. There is no automatic remedy for such a development, but the potential for withdrawal has to be countered by the institution of mechanisms that encourages the broadest consensus. In other words, as Horowitz (1989) contends, there must be more incentives for a party to stay in the government than to be on the outside. One such incentive is an agreed national developmental program in which the concerns and priorities of all groups are included. This should not be a difficult undertaking, given the fact that in most ethnic societies there is not very much ideological difference between the ethnic parties. The final aspect of the power-sharing model is the civic aspect — sharing of power between the government and Civil Society. This has to be both formal and informal. The Social Partners formulae must be given constitutional cover. In this regard the broadening of second house of the legislature to include representation from Civil Society organizations and Local Government Councils is a viable option.

Separation of Powers

Some critics have argued that a power-sharing government that includes only the two major parties could lead to a dictatorship. The problem is that the Guyanese electorate has become even more reluctant to vote for non-ethnic parties. This trend may change when the fear of domination is minimized or removed, but this is more a medium to long term expectation. And since power-sharing must not veer away from democratic elections and representation based on the results of those elections, the non-ethnic parties must earn their way into the executive branch; they must win enough votes to sit in the cabinet. The next best step is to ensure that power is not concentrated in the executive branch. While power-sharing in the executive branch is central to the short-term objective of reducing the clear and present danger of ethnic insecurity and fear, it is not sufficient to induce substantive democratization and maintain long-term stability. Whereas sharing power within the executive speaks primarily to the ethnic question, sharing power among the three branches of government speaks to the larger issue of democratization.

Separation of powers along the lines of the American system is the most plausible alternative. It would eliminate executive supremacy whereby members of the executive also exercise legislative powers. Those members in effect have two votes on a given policy. However, the composition and rules of the legislature are vital to any effective system. If the parties which dominate the executive also dominate the parliament there is little room for the latter to serve as a check on the former. Hence, the parliament should include, in addition to elected representatives of the parties, representatives from local and regional governments. This would ensure broader representation and more diversity of opinion. This broader representation necessitates a second house comprising nominated members with the majority coming from civil society organizations such as trade unions, the religious community, women and youth groups and professional associations. Because this will not be an elected body its powers should not exceed that of the elected house. But it should have a suspensory veto along the lines of the British House of Lords. In addition to the composition the rules of the legislature should allow for measures to be passed by a super majority rather than the current simple majority. This will force cooperation among the parties.

Unlike other Anglophone Caribbean countries Guyana's chief executive is an Executive President more along the lines of the president of the USA. The holder of this office, who is elected separately from the legislative, has an absolute veto over legislative acts and is vested with sole executive power. Although there is a Prime Minister who is also the head of the government in the legislature and the president's deputy, the power of this office is largely ceremonial. Such a powerful Chief Executive at the head of an executive led by the party with the majority in the legislative is often a recipe for elected dictatorship which in the context of ethnic polarization has negative consequences for shared nationhood. It is against this background that there is need for a split executive whereby executive leadership is expressly shared between a President and a Prime Minister. I favor the PNC's proposal whereby the party with the most votes wins the Prime Minister-ship and the one with the second most votes wins the Presidency. The President holds the position of commander in Chief and Head of State while the Prime Minister is head of government. However, I propose that the two officers have veto powers over the other. The main advantage of such an arrangement is checks-and balances within the executive branch. Further, unlike the traditional Westminster system, where the office of the head of state is largely ceremonial, under this arrangement it is actually substantively involved in the everyday governance.

A second proposal is more separation of powers between the executive and the legislature. Although under the current system the president can appoint some non-legislators in the cabinet, the latter is still dominated by the members of the legislature. This blurring of the lines between the two branches impedes checks and balances and renders the legislature a rubber stamp for executive actions. To correct this problem the number of legislators belonging to the executive branch should be either limited to the barest minimum or the model should be eliminated. The independence of the legislature is more likely to make it a more effective oversight of the executive than currently exists. One argument that could be made against this arrangement is that the parties could still use their legislative seats to keep the legislature as a junior partner. However, this will be mitigated by raising the bar for passage of bills from a simple to a super majority.

Another reform in this regard concerns the judiciary whose makeup is currently determined by the president in "consultation" with the opposition leader. Under a power-sharing government, members of the judiciary should be nominated by the President and the Prime Minister and confirmed by the legislature. This procedure would also hold for other key appointments such as the heads of the police, army, public service, ambassadors and members of key commissions.

Horizontal and Vertical Power Sharing

Horizontal power sharing has two dimensions: the sharing of power within the executive branch based on proportionality and mutual veto and the sharing of power between the executive and the other two branches of government-- the legislative and judicial branches. The sharing of power between the legislative and the executive branches is especially important. The principle of separation of powers and mutual oversight are important here. The second aspect is the sharing of power between the cabinet and the parliament. For this model to be meaningful, the balance of power between the two branches will have to be fundamentally altered. First, all executive control of parliament will have to be removed. As discussed above, there must be some degree of separation of powers. Since I do not think strict separation is attainable in the short term I would as much as possible limit the number of cabinet members sitting in parliament. This separation of powers will ensure less conflict of interest on the part of parliamentarians and it will also solve the problem of whether ministers should sit in parliamentary committees. Because they would not be parliamentarians the question of them sitting in committees should not arise.

A second reform aimed at empowering parliament should be raising the bar for the majority needed to pass a bill. I would suggest 60 percent for ordinary bills and 70 percent for the budget and other money bills. The same rule should apply for the committees and sub- committees. This would ensure that the government does not use its majority to dominate parliamentary decisions. Third, parliament should have the power to summon any member of the executive, including the president, to answer questions concerning governmental operations and other issues of national concern. Fourth, the chairmanship of parliamentary committees should be proportionately divided among the parties. Fifth, the Speaker and

Deputy Speaker should be elected by a 60 percent majority of the members. Should these reforms be implemented, parliament will become an equal partner with and counterweight to the executive, thus allowing for meaningful balance of power. With the institution of a super majority rather than a bare majority, legislative decisions would require opposition consent.

Vertical power-sharing has four dimensions. First, there is the sharing of power between the Central government and Local government. This will necessitate the restoration of Village Councils and other local bodies and the devolution of power to them. It will also necessitate a reduced role for political parties at the local level. Since the total exclusion of parties from local elections will not sit well in a party- centered society, I propose that parties be allowed to contest a maximum of 40 percent of the seats at local government elections. I do not favor the federal system as this would transfer the problem from the center to the periphery, but I think the village system is crucial. Local governments should share decision making in crucial areas such as infrastructure and perhaps education. But the key is that local governments should be answerable to parliament and not to the Minister of Local Government and should be given some scope to independently woo economic projects subject to parliamentary approval.

The second dimension of Vertical Power-Sharing is the sharing of power between Civil Society and the government. This should be actualized through the creation of a second house of parliament--a nominated house-where representation should be shared by the parties and Civil Society organizations. A second aspect of this dimension is the sharing of power between the political managers and the Civil Service. Politicization of the Civil Service has led to its domination by the ruling party. Power-sharing could restore the autonomy of the service and empower it to serve as a check on executive excesses, something that would be most helpful in minimizing corruption.

The final dimension of Vertical Power Sharing is gender power-sharing. This is most important to any successful power- sharing model. It is well known that men dominate the upper echelons of the power structure. I, therefore, endorse the WPA's proposal of a woman's vice- president and recommend that the 30 percent rule, whereby parties are required to have women make up a minimum of 30 percent of their slates, be applied all councils of governance-cabinet, both houses of parliament and local governments. Gender power-sharing holds the prospect of bringing fresh ideas to the table that could well turn out to be a deviation from the acrimony that now characterizes governance.

8
Conclusion

Ethnic groups living side by side have always been suspicious of one another. That suspicion turns to fear and insecurity when the issue of who controls power—decision-making (political) and resource allocation (economic) -- invariably arises. In other words, groups fear domination by the other and act out that fear through the choices they make both at the community and national levels. Group culture is influenced by this need to defend the group from domination. This accounts for the anti African Guyanese element in Indian Guyanese cultural reflexes and the anti Indian Guyanese element in African Guyanese cultural reflexes. What compounds this fear is that both groups have had a taste of domination by the other.

After six decades of ethnic competition, ethnicity has become the overriding motivation in Guyana's political culture both at the level of the elites and the masses. In this regard ethnic voting patterns and other forms of political expression become the norm rather than the exception. One of the problems of political mobilization is that some politicians who are concerned about the disadvantages of ethnic polarization have tended to downplay ethnic expression. This is counter-productive. The tendency to deny that ethnic preferences are a major component of political action by the political directorates and their supporters actually exacerbates the problem. In the final analysis there has generally been a less than honest attempt at tackling the negative consequences of ethnic politics as politicians have been more concerned with denying the existence of an ethnic problem when in office rather than creating conditions and institutions and formulating policies to mitigate the negative outcomes of ethnic politics.

Both major political parties have, therefore, embraced an inclusionary form of domination whereby the opposite party and its supporters, though not totally excluded from the political process, are nevertheless limited to the periphery. This inclusive domination leads to a dual outcome. On the one hand, it provides short term stability as the out-group engages the formal political process as a first resort. This was evident in the actions of the PNC in the period 1957-61 and 1992-97 when the PPP governments were not harassed as much as they were later on. Similarly, the PPP, despite minor protests, functioned solely within the formal framework from 1964 to 1973. But as the group in office consolidates its hold on power, the powerlessness of the out-group becomes self evident, which in turn leads to the embrace of extra-parliamentary tactics. This was the case with the PNC 1961-64 and post-1997 when the party, in the face of entrenched PPP rule, spearheaded street demonstrations, which on both occasions turned violent. The PPP also resorted to extra-parliamentary action after the rigged 1973 elections, which included boycott of parliament, civil disobedience, strikes and economic sabotage.

There are five major conclusions one can draw from the examination of ethnic politics in the post colonial period. First, both ethnic political parties adopted a model of inclusionary domination whereby the primary objective has been to capture power, defend it at all costs and use it to woo members of the opposite ethnic group. Although there was no ethnic cleansing, the out-group was systematically denied any meaningful participation in the governance of the country. Both major parties were supported by their wider ethnic communities, but the Indian support of the PPP has been more complete than African support for the PNC. Second, the emergence of the multi-ethnic WPA in the 1970s served as an obstacle to intense conflict and influenced the creation of a multi ethnic movement. One may conclude that the opportunity for multi-ethnic solidarity increases in situations where the contending groups are faced with a common threat and there is a multi-ethnic party to capture the moment.

Third, the return of democratic norms reintroduced ethnic

conflict as the minority group felt threatened with permanent disenfranchisement. The group that retained power after a long period of disenfranchisement is likely to close ranks in defense of its democratic right to govern while the aggrieved group makes it difficult for the government to function. Fourth, in these circumstances elections became sites of conflict, which eventually spilled over into the post-election period. Fifth, ceasefires were used by both parties as tactical maneuvers rather than genuine avenues for peace. The governing parties usually resort to business as usual as soon as stability returns.

The Discourse

The political discourse, in particular since the PPP's return to power has reflected one of the challenges of ethnically divided societies: Whose expression of history becomes settled history? Since there will always be ethnic narratives and counter narratives, it is difficult to conceive of a settled history that is accepted by both groups. Both groups will also resist the narrative of equal blame as can be seen from the discourse examined in this book. In fact it is the third narrative that causes the most discomfort. It becomes the enemy narrative as it threatens the basis and the logic of the ethnic narratives.

It is clear that proponents of the Indian narrative have been much more pro-active in expressing the Indian cause. As we have seen, some of these proponents are not members of the PPP. The dilemma is that while they despise the PPP leaders, they strongly support the right of Indians to govern. The PPP is, therefore, less pressured to advance an ethnic narrative in public. In fact it has the luxury of condemning ethnic narratives in public while reaping its benefits at the ballot box. Proponents of the African narrative have been less effective given the PNC's authoritarian past. Attempts to sanctify PNC founder-leader, Forbes Burnham, have been less forceful given his stewardship of the authoritarian government. In this regard, there has been more African Guyanese criticism of Burnham than Indian Guyanese criticism of Jagan. More importantly, while the Indian proponents have access to the state, party and independent media, their African counterparts are confined to the independent media.

Power Sharing

One of the principal reasons for the inability to form a power sharing government, despite expressions of support from the major political forces, is the belief by both major parties that once in power they would be able to manage ethnic tensions. They have also relied on wooing voters of the opposite group and enticing leaders of the opposite party to cross the floor. This strategy has not had the desired effect for two reasons. First, neither party has been able to win enough crossover voters to transform itself into a multi-ethnic party or to weaken the other party. This is due, in part, to the perception that the other party is the enemy and the fear of being ostracized by one's group. Second, the use of leaders of the opposite group or "ethnic window dressing" has not translated into votes. Such leaders bring little tangible benefits to the parties as they are often ridiculed by their own group as traitors. They are also forced to either endorse ethnic attacks on their group or remain silent. This dilemma was demonstrated in the exchange between Jerome Khan and Vincent Alexander of the PNC during the wave of violence against Indians during the period 2002 – 2004. This was the only occasion in which a leader actually publicly pushed back against the ethnic reflexes of his party. The Khan situation demonstrates the futility of ethnic window dressing.

The purging of African executives at the internal PPP election in 1959 and a similar purging of Indians from the PNC executive in 2004 further bears this out. No African has ever contested the leader's position in the PPP; there is an unwritten rule that the leader would be Indian or in the case of Ms Jagan, an honorary Indian. This is more overt at the level of government where the African Prime Minister is prohibited from becoming President after the embarrassment that followed Dr. Jagan's death in 1997. The PNC was similarly embarrassed when its longstanding Indian Chairman, Winston Murray, challenged the incumbent in 2008-- the first time an Indian competed for the top spot. Murray gained the support of other challengers and faced a relatively unpopular incumbent but the result was never in doubt.

Despite the failure to realize a power sharing government, there has been fourteen major proposals between 1961 and 2005 – an average of approximately one proposal every three years. Nine of these proposals led to talks among the parties. The WPA was associated with ten of the proposals and talks, making it the most consistent advocate of power sharing since its formation in 1974. This large number of power sharing proposals and talks point to the general acceptance of the idea as the most popular solution to the country's ethnic and other political problems.

Second, one of the reasons for the failure of the parties to agree on a power sharing government is the inability of all the major parties to compromise on key issues. In this regard the PPP's lack of flexibility on ideological considerations frustrated agreement during the period of the anti-dictatorial movement. Although the WPA was most flexible on ideology, it was initially less flexible on the issue of the PNC's involvement. This disagreement between the WPA and the PPP reflected the deeper political difference between the two parties. While the PPP was grounded in ideological orthodoxy and viewed alliances in terms of domination, the WPA was less wedded to ideological orthodoxy and viewed alliances as the highest form of political mobilization. Ironically, the PPP was less inflexible in power sharing talks with the PNC as evidenced by its willingness to either cede the top spot to the PNC or agree to an equitable distribution of cabinet seats.

A third trend to emerge from the Guyana case is the tendency of both the PNC and the PPP to embrace power sharing in opposition but reject it when in power. Both parties have also shown a preference to reach for power sharing when they sense that power was slipping away. This tendency was evident in the actions of the PPP in 1962 and the PNC in 1985 and 1990. During its second tenure in office, the PPP has shown a preference for engaging the PNC in dialogue when its hold on power was threatened. This tactic has worked well for the PPP largely because the PNC has been ambivalent about power sharing.

The political parties have shown a tendency to move to compromise when ethnic violence threatens to lead to civil war, only to retreat when the situation returns to normalcy. Ironically the absence of persistent overt ethnic violence has served as a deterrent to power sharing. In other words while the permanent threat of violence engenders calls for power sharing the fact that the violence more often than not abates causes the parties to retreat.

The parties have also shown a willingness to compromise whenever external mediators have intervened. This was especially evident during the PNC-PCD and the PPP-PNC negotiations in 1990 and 1998 respectively. However on both occasions the mediators did not wrest enough concessions out of the parties, in particular on the issue of a national government. President, Jimmy Carter, for example, took Dr. Jagan's word that he would lead a national unity government rather than making it an actual part of the agreement. His later attempts to persuade the PPP were rebuffed which had by then convinced the US authorities that it was a more reliable ally than the PNC. Similarly the CARICOM team that intervened following the outbreak of violence in 1998 erred in not getting all parties to commit to the immediate formation of a national government as part of the Herdmonston Accord. The preference for a dialogue between the two parties under the mediation of the CARICOM facilitator proved to be a disaster as the PPP, having consolidated itself in power, became less cooperative.

The use of violence and other forms of sabotage by both parties to force the other into a power sharing agreement has also failed. The PPP's use of industrial strikes and economic sabotage to force the PNC to engage its National Patriotic Front proposal in 1977 only succeeded in pushing the PNC government to become more authoritarian. Three decades later the attempt by some African Guyanese groups with the tacit support of the PNC to use military tactics to force power sharing on the PPP also failed. The PPP has successfully used the violence against Indian Guyanese to cement its electoral and other forms of political control of that community while even future militant protests by the PNC would be inevitably framed by the PPP in violent terms.

Appendix 1

An Open Letter to African Guyanese

I write this open letter to you out of concern for our collective future. Some of you will resent me for what I am about to say, but so be it. I am no expert on African Guyanese political behavior, but I am concerned about where you are headed. Since December 1997, I have watched you being demonized by your detractors, including some of your own race. You have been labeled everything that is bad: terrorists, hooligans, murderers, bullies, thieves, mobsters and sore losers. But what pains me most is that some of your actions have created the grounds for your demonization, and you don't seem to care.

You are correct about being discriminated against and forced to the margins of the society. You are also correct to protest against this condition and resist efforts to push you further out. After all, your history has been one of noble resistance and triumph against the odds. But most of your recent resistance, though noble in intention, has been less than noble in execution and outcome. Your protests and resistance have degenerated into unreason and hate. Why? Because you have been dishonest; allowed yourself to be abused by your political party; refused to sanction your party for its inability to effectively represent your interests; stopped believing in yourself, believing that the party will solve all your problems; mistakenly believed that Indians are responsible for your plight; selfishly believed that Guyana belongs to your race alone; and fought for the party rather than for yourself.

I have to remind you of a few things. Your marginalization did not begin in 1992; the PPP has simply continued the "marginalization" that your party, the PNC, perfected. The very young may not know this, but those of you who are over 30 years old know this. That is why I say you are dishonest. After 28 years in office, your party left you poorer and less educated than you were when it took office in 1964. It did not facilitate or encourage your entry into the business sector. It gave you jobs, but did not encourage you to accumulate wealth. In fact, by its policies, it pushed you out of businesses such as pig farming, poultry farming, cash crop farming, small and medium size cake shops and groceries, and pork knocking. You were forced to be totally dependent on the government for work, so when the government ran out of money and decided to downsize, you were downsized.

Some of you then turned to trading and saved Guyanese from starvation, but your own party treated you as criminals. And even today, they are still trying to get you off the streets. When Mr. Hoyte started his ERP in the late 1980's, you did not benefit; in fact, your situation became worse. The ERP trimmed government and froze wages, and since you worked for government you lost your jobs or your wages were frozen. The ERP also made it easier for businesses to grow, but you owned no businesses so you could not cash in.

In the meantime, you stopped sending your children to school because they had to help you sell or because you were so busy "hustling a dollar," you could not ensure that they went to school. Some of you were encouraged to seek the party card rather than a school certificate. Many good teachers left their jobs or left the country, because they were paid slave wages. Your villages, which were bought by your fore-parents, were left to rot. Roads became tracks, canals dried up, and your farms became useless. But most importantly, control over your villages was taken away from you as the villages were merged into neighborhoods. You could no longer make day-to-day decisions that affected your lives. Your party disempowered you economically, educationally and politically.

So when the PPP came to power in 1992, it, not unexpectedly, continued this disempowerment. In a small society where the pie is small and the society is divided, each side understandingly looks after its own. But when that is done totally at the expense of the other side, as the PPP has done, it is out of order. But let's be fair. The PPP in nine years repaired more roads and built more new schools in African communities than the PNC did in its last 25 years in office. That is a fact. But the PPP also did ten times more in Indian communities, and its policies on bauxite and the Public Service basically continued the marginalization started by the PNC.

I say all of the above to remind you that if marginalization means disempowerment you have been historically marginalized: by the colonizers, the PNC, and the PPP. So to blame the PPP alone for your marginalization is unfair and dishonest. And there is nothing like more marginalization and less marginalization: marginalization is marginalization. What is the mistake you are making when you blame the PPP alone for marginalization? You will fight to remove the PPP from office thinking your marginalization will end, rather than trying to change the system that causes your marginalization.

And it's on this score that you have allowed yourself to be abused by your party. By allowing yourself to be manipulated by the party, you have added to your own marginalization. What have you been protesting since 1997? First you were told it was rigged elections, and you believed. Then you were told it was marginalization, and you believed. What are you protesting for, or what do you want at the end of the day? At first you were not told anything, and you did not ask yourself anything. Then you were told it was inclusion and you have not asked what it means. You were brought on to the streets in 1998 and then taken off when they had enough. You were brought on again in 2001 and then abandoned again. You were told that your party would win the elections and you will be relieved of your burdens and you believed. You have surrendered your right to think and act in your own interest. Rather than fighting to end your marginalization, you are fighting to win elections. Bad business.

You voted for victory in 1997 and 2001, but you are still out in the cold. You have beaten and robbed Indians and you were neither told you were wrong nor urged to stop. You have fooled yourselves that the police will not beat you because they are black and you are black. And now you hate the police. But your party once instructed the very black police to beat black people who opposed the party. To what end have you protested since 1997 and assaulted Indians–to what end? Your party is now having dialogue with the PPP, but you are still jobless; you still can't get loans to start businesses; many of your children still can't read and write; crime, drugs, and disease still haunt your days and nights; your villages on the East Coast are still militarized zones; and your TV hosts are being charged for sedition. History repeats itself, for most of you were silent when your party once charged its opponents with treason.

You are told to apply "slow fire" and "more fire," yet nobody comes to sit with you and develop plans for your communities. You are fighting with guns and channa bombs rather than with development plans in your hand, as the WPA told you in 1992. But as usual you behave as if "stick bruck ah you hase." To be fair to you, sometimes you listen to reason and perhaps admire it, but you don't act on it. You act on unreason and so long as you continue to do that you will always be marginalized.

If you don't pull yourself together, you will be protesting elections forever. Do you want Guyana for yourself or do you want to share it with others? Common sense suggests that you have to share Guyana. So if you share the country you have to share the governance and the burden of the governance. This is part of what you ought to be fighting for -- Power Sharing. Those who tell you Power Sharing can't work are dishonest and don't have your interest at heart.

What really is the root of your current problem? Every civilized country has rules and laws that determine how it is governed. The British left us some rules in 1966 and the PNC upgraded those rules in 1980. The rules made by the PNC and PNC alone in 1980 state very clearly that governance of Guyana shall be determined by one person/ one vote and the party that wins the majority of the vote shall govern with its leader being head of government and state. According to those rules, the PNC will find it difficult to win a fair election, because in Guyana we vote along racial lines and you Africans are not the majority race. When another opportunity for review of these rules came in 1999, your party, the PNC, refused to change them. There was one of three reasons for doing this: (1) the PNC was hoping to do the impossible of rigging a victory while in opposition; (2) they thought that all Africans would have voted for the PNC and some Indians would have abandoned the PPP; or (3) they wanted Africans to remain out of government permanently. Since the last three elections did not result in the first two points, then it leaves us with the third one. The PNC, in its quest to regain power, cares very little whether you continue to suffer; in fact your suffering is a good election issue. And like "African Bees," you are used to do some stinging when the election plans don't come through.

I have recounted the above primarily to suggest to you that you are ignoring to your peril some glaring truths. You have no political and economic power. That is what you must be fighting for. You have to lift yourself. Stop the madness. Stop blaming Indians for everything. Start building your own future. Don't be fooled by promises of rehabilitation by the "dialogue." They will repair a few roads, but you need more than that. You need jobs, good education, business opportunities, bank loans, and drainage and irrigation. You need empowerment. Shouting "No Justice! No Peace!" is foolish. Nobody gives you justice; you have to fight for it. And the place to begin is in your communities, for only you can rehabilitate your communities. Here are my modest suggestions.

First, organize in your communities. Meet and discuss what you want and then set up committees to work out the different parts of your plan. Set up alternative Village and Town Councils to oversee the entire process. Come up with your development plans that will ensure your economic future. Your plans must include job creation, education, better infrastructure, health care and other necessary social services. Call in Clive Thomas, Eric Phillips, Kenneth King, Haslyn Parris, Eusi Kwayana and ACDA to advise you. These economists would be more useful to you in this way, than sitting on committees or going into the PPP's cabinet. When you have your plan in hand, then you can go to Freedom House and Congress Place and make your demands. Then you can take to the streets.

Second, form clubs and groups for young people in particular. Meet and talk and discuss and plan. Put out leaflets to publicize your views. Form ACDA chapters and then link up with ACDA. Invite David Granger; he knows the history. Third, demand your villages back; they are yours. Go to Congress Place and Freedom House and the Parliament and demand that they change the constitution to reintroduce the Village Councils. Fourth, start education/literacy programs immediately. Put your university students, teachers, and other professionals to teach during the holidays and in the afternoons. Work out your curriculum to include the following--reading, writing, agriculture, how to start and run a business, political organizing and leadership, parenting, conflict resolution, and African Guyanese history and culture.

Fifth, demand constitutional changes to protect you from discrimination and political marginalization. Include in your constitutional demands that your representatives sit in all branches of government and make decisions on your behalf. Insist that that they are part of the Cabinet, which makes decisions on jobs and contracts and how loans and grants are issued and your tax dollars are spent. Also demand that free university and technical education be reintroduced. Sixth, work out education and other plans to fight drug abuse, domestic abuse, HIV/AIDS, and violence. Your plan must seek government help but must not depend solely on government. Draw up grant proposals to send to NGO's and overseas Guyanese organizations to help fund these programs.

David Hinds
May 2002

Appendix 2

African Guyanese Marginalization is Real

When I first wrote on African Guyanese marginalization, I had hoped that it would raise the level of debate on this most important subject. Unfortunately, except for a very thoughtful Stabroek News editorial, the responses have had the cumulative effect of dragging the debate further into the mud. I was under the assumption that there was no argument over the fact that African Guyanese were economically and politically marginalized. So I intended to draw a clear line between those of us on the one hand who see African marginalization within the context of the larger class marginalization of the downpressed racial groups, including East Indians and Amerindians, and the wider global marginalization of non-white peoples and countries and those on the other hand who see it in exclusively racial terms. I also intended to cast African marginalization as a historical phenomenon whose evolution is reflective of the racial and class relations that have characterized the Guyanese political economy.

Insofar as the competition between Africans and Indians for political power over the last five decades has affected African marginalization, it has been the inability of the governments to seriously tackle the task of uprooting the historical causes of this problem. In this regard Indians cannot be charged with marginalizing Africans, for they have neither the power nor scope to do so. This does not take away from the fact that governments operating in the name of Indians have presided over the persistent marginalization of Africans. But so have governments operating in the name of Africans.

Asking me to provide proof of African Guyanese marginalization is somewhat defensive, but more importantly it exposes how unfeeling Guyanese have become to each other. If after 160 years of living together Indians cannot understand and acknowledge African pain and concerns and Africans cannot understand and acknowledge Indian pain and concern, then in a sense we deserve the society in which we live. In denying African marginalization, we are absolving almost five hundred years of slavery, colonization and neo colonization.

If the problem, as I explained it, is historical and systemic, then an examination of the historical development of the country's political economy and the location of the various groups in that process will reveal the evidence. If Africans, after more than 300 years of enslavement left the plantation with no compensation, then they began their post-slavery sojourn at a great disadvantage; they were marginalized from the beginning. If after initially developing their own democratic political forms in their villages, whereby they could and did directly make decisions that affected their lives, these were undermined by the autocratic Crown Colony System, then they were politically dispossessed. If the authoritarian organization of the economy located them in sectors that made them look "respectable" while imprisoning them as underpaid servants of the state, then their livelihood was determined by a state that has been hostile to their independence since emancipation.

The location of groups in Guyana's economic structures has been determined primarily on grounds of race and previous servitude. Contrary to what some people feel, Africans do not grope for slavery to explain the African Guyanese condition; slavery by necessity has followed the previously enslaved and continuously defines their relations to the rest of the society and vice versa. The very act of freeing themselves from slavery put Africans on an ongoing collision course with the powers that controlled the destiny of the state and society. Those who saw enslavement as the route to wealth and power could not and did not peacefully co-exist with those who saw their freedom as the route to wealth and empowerment. It is within the context of this struggle between these two forces, which has characterized socioeconomic and political relations in Guyana since 1834, that African Guyanese marginalization must be located and understood. Since independence, the skin color of those who control the levers of power has changed, but the authoritarian relations have remained intact.

I define marginalization in the following terms: (a) being on the periphery or "margins" of the political and economic power structures; (b) exercising no direct or indirect influence over national political and economic decisions; (c) not having equality of opportunity with other groups in the society; (d) inability to access resources needed to individually and collectively accumulate wealth; (e) having your labor power exploited without just compensation; (f) being most vulnerable to diseases, crime, drugs, bribery, and other forms of social violence; and (g) being most susceptible to cultural penetration from the outside on account of little or no internal cultural buffers.

Where are African Guyanese located and not located in the current political economy?

They are overwhelmingly wage laborers who work for the government. They are not in close proximity to the sectors that generate the accumulation of individual wealth.

They are overwhelmingly in the armed forces, which in economic terms is the equivalent of wage earnings. In political terms, they are outside of the power arena, as their elected leaders do not influence the decisions of the government. They have no direct control of their villages and wards, as they do not directly elect their local leaders. The villages are part of a larger "local" unit, which undermines ownership and control of ancestral space, something that Africans won for themselves after emancipation. They dominate the parallel market as retailers, drug pushers and enforcers.

What does this mean? First, as government workers, they are the most structurally adjusted in a structurally adjusted economy. Their wages are constantly contracted and they face layoff and a simultaneous diminishing of potential employment thanks to the IMF/World Bank/Globalization shrinking of government. But more than that, the very state of economic dependence on government engenders among other things fear of political bosses, while the low wages encourage theft. Second, because historically Africans have been deliberately placed on the fringes of the private enterprise network, they have not had access to the capital that is needed to even begin to compete in this exclusive arena. Except for Globe

Trust, there are no Black-owned banks, not many Black family businesses, and no sustainable government program aimed at allowing them access to loans on generous terms.

Third, although Africans dominate the armed forces, this is first and foremost a source of bread and butter. The ordinary rank is basically a wage earner. Many have pointed to this dominance of the armed forces as a source of African power. Well, it may be a potential source of power, but in actuality it is not. Guyana's military does not have an autonomous power base, as is the case in Latin America and some parts of Africa. The armed forces are constitutionally and institutionally civilian-controlled; they defer to the political directorate. African members of the armed forces have no way of translating this membership into African empowerment. They may refuse to pursue African contravention of the law or protect African bandits, but how do these translate into African empowerment? Why have the African police under both African and Indian governments continue to disproportionately kill Africans?

Fourth, the African masses, like all masses, have never legitimately held political power in Guyana. The 28-year PNC rule resulted from electoral fraud and by necessity shut out all groups, including Africans. It did not treat African empowerment as a first rate issue as it did not have to depend on Africans for its electoral legitimacy. Cover yes, but legitimacy no. Fifth, Africans have no direct control over their villages, the one symbol of power they had at the time of independence. They make no decisions over their immediate lives. Sixth, while others import Africans sell for them. Africans work for others even in the drug trade where they are the pushers, petty sellers and mules.

When one adds to this the cultural degradation that Africans continue to experience, the alienation and marginalization are complete. Robbed completely of language and culture, the African Guyanese must mimic others and deny or make excuses for his/her true heritage. Economic dispossession and political alienation lead to poverty, criminality, hopelessness, and cynicism. These are the symptoms of the larger monster called marginalization.

Is there a Black middle class? Yes. But that is a very small exception to the larger rule. Are the vast majority of Indians marginalized? Yes. Is it correct to say that Africans are not marginalized because Indians are equally poor? No. Indian poverty does not negate African marginalization. Some see the statement of African marginalization as an indictment of East Indians. On this score, they are at one with the African extremists. If Indians have had more access to economic opportunities and the political power structures, that is the function of history and location, and in the case of politics, population size.

Insofar as members of the PPP government deliberately discriminate against or alienate Africans, I think they do so primarily because Africans support their political rival. This is standard political behavior in the Third World, but in the case of Guyana, the racial element translates it into an explosive device. But the PPP does not have to overtly discriminate against Africans because it presides over a system that facilitates covert and overt discrimination of the down-pressed. By continuing to hold on to this system in the name of democracy, the PPP must face the charge of "democratically" marginalizing Blacks. But the truth is that the PPP is merely presiding over the marginalization of Blacks as previous regimes have done.

The charge that my attempt to explain African marginalization fuels black rage does not fly. To the contrary, the continued chorus that denies that there is African marginalization fuels the rage. It is arrogance of the highest order when the elite of your race group holds the levers of power and you insist on telling those who feel individual and collective pain resulting from the system that they are not hurting, that they are feigning pain. You are only angering them more. I don't have to tell Africans they are marginalized; they know it because they experience it every day.

Dr. Jagan acknowledged this when he said that blacks were at the bottom of the social ladder. In a 1988 speech, he also said: "What needs to be done is a recognition of the racial problem and the implementation of certain reforms. Apart from constitutional guarantees, these should include a Race Relations Board, an equal opportunity law, fair employment practices, and affirmative action as in the United States." I rest my case.

Some Black extremists are saying Africans are marginalized, Indians are in government and are marginalizing Blacks, and Indians came to Guyana after Blacks. So, with gun in hand, they argue that removing the PPP from power will solve the problem. I reject that view. I say Blacks are marginalized by a system. Blacks must fight to change the system; they must fight for the implementation of mechanisms, which will facilitate their freedom from marginalization. Don't fight the Indian masses, fight injustice, and there are many peaceful means still left to do so.

David Hinds
September 2002

Appendix 3

Indians Must Speak Out Against Indian Wrongs Also

I have said a fair bit about the violence emanating from Buxton, because I see it as a significant development for the black community and for race relations in general. Because the violence has been coming from the African community, African voices have a greater responsibility to engage the current situation, but I believe that Indian voices also have a responsibility to be more objective. We are in the midst of a racial conflict that involves both races. It is playing itself out at the level of crime and violence against Indians, but that is not the beginning and end of the scenario. In other words, while the African violence against Indians is abominable, it is not occurring in a vacuum.

While the perpetrators may be a relatively small band and the African Guyanese community has not openly encouraged them, neither have they condemned them. This is significant, for it points to something larger. There is something in the development of race relations between African and Indians that pushes Africans to abhor the violence but sympathize with what they see as a challenge to Indian domination. In racial and ethnic conflicts both sides look across the fence and act based on the perception and reality of what they see. In some cases they misunderstand what they see and overreact. It's then the responsibility of leaders to dissuade them from acting in an irresponsible manner.

I think that the reaction by the armed Africans is misplaced, even though their perception of the African condition is well placed. As is well known, I am unconditionally opposed to the violence, principally because I believe that violence should always be a last resort. I am not satisfied that we are near the point of last resort; there are many other peaceful means that have not been exploited. Even when violence is a last resort, its misdirection results in irreparable harm to all and I believe that the violence against the Indian masses is misdirected. The other reason I am opposed to the violence is that I am concerned about its negative impact on the psyche of African people. The resort to the type of violence we have witnessed could well lead to the development of a violent culture that could turn the African in Guyana into a slave a second time-- this time a slave to violence.

I have stated the above not to downplay the seriousness of the African cause, but rather to highlight it. I am pursuing this marginalization question because it is at the heart of the current national problem. Its mistreatment by some African leaders has resulted in our first racial-political "garrison" in the form of Buxton. I reject the view that discussion of African marginalization emboldens the perpetrators of violence against Indians. Rather, I think discussion itself is an alternative to violence.

There are three conversations that must simultaneously go on in relation to Black marginalization or the black condition: (1) a discussion among blacks; (2) a discussion among Indians; and (3) a discussion between the two communities. The absence of these conversations has in part fueled the current season of rage. Our society sits on the shoulders of almost 400 years of gross inhumanity in the form of slavery. History did not begin with slavery but, for the Caribbean and Guyana, our historical evolution has been largely influenced by the slave experience. Because the African was located at the center of slavery, the African condition has played a major role in dictating the post-slavery era. It is, therefore, a mistake to believe that African Guyanese can be ignored, disempowered, and manipulated without serious consequences. This is in no way a downplay of the roles and places of the other races nor is it an expression of the African as primary citizen. Rather it is recognition that our history places certain burdens on our society that must be acknowledged if we are to understand our existence.

The African condition is global. There is a reason that Africans all over the world are marginalized. There is a reason that the police shoot down Africans all over the world. There is a reason that the African is the victim of economic terror all over the world, including Africa. There is a reason that Africans more than any other race has to constantly affirm their identity. There is a reason that Africans all over the world run away from their Africaness. I am submitting here that the African condition in Guyana is part of a larger phenomenon with peculiar characteristics.

It is against the background of both the local and global factors that Africans must discuss their condition and in the process address the following questions: Is African marginalization simply political discrimination against African businesspeople seeking contracts or similar discrimination against the African elite or is it the historical discrimination against the African poor and the powerless? What are the economic and political causes of African marginalization? How have the post-colonial political and economic orders deterred or encouraged African marginalization? How the presence of other does races, in particular East Indians, affect this process? How have the internal structural and cultural weaknesses of the African community affected the process? What is the real meaning of the last ten years for African Guyanese? What is the meaning of 28 years of PNC rule for African Guyanese? What needs to be done by Africans themselves and by Africans in consort with others to deal with their marginalization? What should be the role of the African Guyanese political elite and the African Guyanese intellegencia in the process? What should be the relationship between these two groups and the African masses? What should be the relationship between African Guyanese and Indian Guyanese? Is the African view of Indians in Guyana a correct one?

The non-treatment of African marginalization by many Indians has been most unhelpful. For Indians in this day and age not to recognize that Africans have real historical, political and economic reasons to feel alienated, frustrated, and furious is totally insensitive and counterproductive for Indians themselves. There are times when we have to try to understand our adversaries in order to begin to understand our own condition. African violence against East Indians and African political reaction in general cannot be seen in the simple terms in which some Indian voices have been casting it.

This failure to grasp the real condition of Africans drives Indians to explain the current situation in the following terms: The PNC is behind the violence; Africans have always been bullying Indians; The PNC are sore losers and do not adhere to democratic rules; The PPP is not protecting Indians; Africans want to take what Indians have labored to achieve; Africans want to control Indians; African cry of marginalization is out of order.

There may be some truth in all of the above, but they do not get to the heart of the matter. The real truth lies in an examination of the conditions in which these tendencies have evolved. I now draw on Mr. Abu Bakr, whose recent writings have been misunderstood and so misrepresented. At the risk of being misunderstood, and bearing in mind the difficulty of asking Indians to engage in reflection when they have to daily bury their dead, I posit that Indians will better understand the Black condition and the current manifestations if they themselves were to engage in an examination of the Guyana in which they have lived and to which they have contributed. A major question that must be answered by Indians is whether the Indian attitude to Africans, both from a cultural and political standpoint, has always been positive. The question I am posing here is whether Indians, in the process of passively and actively responding to African disrespect and bullying and in their own perception of their place in the society, have not developed their own form of political degeneracy.

I repeat, violence against Indians and other defenseless people is abominable and must be stopped. But, it's a mistake for Indians to think that the violence is simply the work of the bully in the African. It's more complex than that. Those of us Africans who have spoken out against the violence do so at great risk to our own lives and those of our families and comrades as some in the Black community see us as traitors. But we are being consistent, for we spoke out, and later acted along with others, against the black PNC authoritarian regime. The point here is that we come from a tradition of confronting our own internal African weaknesses, without rejecting our Africaness. For us it is not just what is good for our race or party, but also what is good for the other races and for Guyana and the Caribbean as a whole. Solidarity with Indians and condemnation of African violence are not anti-African or pro-Indian; it's simply morally and politically correct.

But most Africans think we are crazy or naive when they do not hear Indian voices speaking out against the other type of violence that has negatively affected mainly Africans-- naked Indian corruption in high places; Indian triumphalism; the Indian drug connection; Indian cultural disrespect of Africans; Indian male sexual advantage of economically dependent African women; and Indian monopoly of government and state in the form of the Indianization of the top echelons of government and Indian control of public means of communication. Freddie Kissoon is the most constant in this regard.

Indianists must begin to look at the negative side of the Indian experience too. This is part of what I understand Mr. Abu Bakr to be calling for. Indians cannot seek to absolve themselves of all social and political degeneracy in Guyana because they are currently under unjust attack and are heroically refusing to hit back in like kind. Criminal violence for all its extremeness is just one type of racial violence.

There are other types of racial violence of which Indians are also guilty. The behavior of the Indian political and economic elite in and around the PPP cannot be ignored, for such behavior impacts negatively on Africans. In racial conflict blame is not always equally proportioned, but responsibility for the security of all must be equally shared. Just as the African elite and the masses are wrong in not fighting African violence, the Indian elite and masses are wrong in not fighting Indian political and other excesses.

At the moment the conditions present no incentives for the two races to talk with each other. Both sides have put up shutters: Africans hide behind Buxton and Indians hide behind the government. But should Indians and Africans begin internal conversations, this could well open the way for that larger inter-racial conversation.

David Hinds
October 2002

Notes

[1] For a detailed account of the actions of the plantocracy see Kwayana & Kwayana *Scars of Bondage* (1999).

[2] See Walter Rodney's *History of the Guyanese Working People* 1881-1905.

[3] See Cheddi Jagan's *West on Trial*

[4] See *Kwayana's "Guyana's Race Problem and my part in them"* Rodneyite September 1993

[5] For a fuller account so Jagan's *West on Trial*

[6] See Kwayana's *"Guyana Race Problems and my Part in them"*, Rodneyite September 1993

[7] For a fuller account see Jagan's *"West on Trial"*

[8] Dr. Jagan's 1956 Congress Paper *On the Way Forward*

[9] Personal Interview, August 2000.

[10] The other leading light in ASRE was HH Nicholson, an educator and committed Black Nationalist

[11] See *Next Witness*, Georgetown (1962 and 1999)

[12] For a fuller account of the politics see Eusi Kwayana's *Walter Rodney*

[13] See Walter Rodney "The Arnold Rampersaud Trial," based on a speech delivered in Georgetown in 1977

[14] The leaders were Brindley Benn of the Working People's Vanguard Party (WPVP) who was a former deputy leader of the PPP and a founding member of the WPA, Gunraj Kumar of the Liberator Party (LP) and Llewelyn John of the People's Democratic Party (PDM) and former PNC Minister of Government.

[15] She later explained her action as being motivated by what she saw as yet another attempt to deny power to the PPP.

[16] The team included three former Caribbean civil servants—Sir Shridath Ramphal, Sir Henry Ford and Sir Alister McIntyre.

198   Notes

[17] ROAR was one of a group of ethnic organizations formed since the return of electoral democracy in 1992. Other Indian organizations include the Guyana Indian Heritage Association (GIHA) and the Indian Arrival Committee (IAC). On the African side the leading organizations were the African Cultural and Development Association (ACDA), the Justice for Jermaine Committee and the Pan Africanist Organization.

[18] See the *GIFT Report* and Kwayana's *No Guilty Race*.

[19] Both the PPP and PNC were unwilling to go beyond minor reforms.

[20] Talk Show host Ronald Waddell was gunned down in front of his home. Although nobody was ever arrested for the crime it was revealed during the trial of Roger Khan, the leader of the Phantom, that he ordered the murder.

[21] The only non-PNC candidate was Keith Scott, a onetime WPA member who headed the small National Front Alliance (NFA).

[22] The data in this section is taken from a poll conducted in 2000 by political scientist Selwyn Ryan titled *Hopes and Aspiration: Political Attitudes and Party Choices in Contemporary Guyana* and commissioned by three prominent Guyanese—Clive Thomas, Hugh Cholmdley and Grantley Walrond.

[23] For a full analysis of these trends see Clive Thomas' "The situation of African Guyanese in the Economy"

[25] Khemraj Ramjattan claimed that leader and President, Bharrat Jagdeo, had accused him of leaking party secrets to the US embassy. All of the executive members, except Moses Nagamootoo, signed a statement denying the charge against Jagdeo. Ramjattan went on to form his own party while Nagamootoo was readmitted to the PPP in 2006.

[26] See Gift Report, January 1998.

[27] See *Revisiting Theories of Race (1993)*

[28] This is an interview I conducted with Thomas on July 14, 2005 for a television program, *Walter Rodney Groundings*.

[29] These programs were aired on a Black-owned TV station. Hosts included Ronald Waddell, who was later murdered allegedly by the Indian controlled Phantom Squad, Roger Moore and Mark Benschop who was charged for treason in 2003.

[30] Freedom Fighters" and "African Resistance" were used by some African spokespersons to describe a group of gunmen that since 2002 has operated out of Buxton, an African Guyanese village, from where they have terrorized Indians, policemen and later African Guyanese in the name of African liberation. "Phantom Group" refers to a group of rival gunmen sponsored by some Indian businessmen and supported by the government. The Phantom murdered a number of African Guyanese young men.

[31] See Hinds *Race and Political Discourse in Guyana* Gguyanacaribbean [31] See Hinds *Race and Political Discourse in Guyana* Gguyanacaribbean politics Publications (2004).

[32] Kissoon expressed these views in three articles written shortly after the 2006 election.

Bibliography

ACDA (2003) "ACDA says flawed electoral system is source of African repression" Stabroek News, June 10

Andaiye (2004) "Not in my name" www.guyanacaribbeanpolitics.com September 27

Andaiye (2004) "What is morally wrong is always wrong" www.guyanacaribbeanpolitics.com September 25

Andaiye (2004) "Notes on Women and Ethnic Conflict, Part 1" www.guyanacaribbeanpolitics.com September 26

Bakr, A (2010) "Rodney did not alone launch or lead the WPA" Stabroek News, January 3

Bakr A, (2010) "Us' versus 'them' should describe the divide between the corrupt and the clean, the competent and the inept" Stabroek News, January 3

Bakr, A (2010) "Dr. Rodney and the WPA have to be remembered for many reasons" Kaieteur News, January 6

Baghwan, M (2006) "Being Indian in Guyana: The challenges" Unpublished Paper

Boodram, A (2010) "We must eschew the Politics of Us versus Them," Georgetown: Stabroek News, December 31

Brown, M (1999) "The causes of Ethnic Conflict" in Michael Brown (ed) Ethnic Conflict and International Security : Princeton: Princeton University Press

Burrowes, R. A. (1984). *The Wild Coast: An Account of Politics in Guyana*. Cambridge: Schenkman Publishing Company, Inc.

Catholic Standard (1996) "What the President Said," November 24.

Danns, G. (1983). "Decolonization and Militarization in the Caribbean: The Case of Guyana", in H. Paget and C. Stone, eds., *The Newer Caribbean: Decolonization, Democracy, and Development*. Philadelphia: Institute for the Study of Human Issues.

Bibliography

Despres, L (1967). *Cultural Pluralism and the National Politics in British Guyana*. Chicago: Rand McNally and Co.

Dev, R. (1997) " Dr. Thomas presentation at the ACDA conference was misconceived, dangerous" Stabroek News, April 6

_____(1997) " Dr. Thomas has not answered my queries" Stabroek News, May 8.

(1998) "Aetiology of an Ethnic Riot" *Georgetown*.

_____(2002) "State and Societal Violence against Indians in Guyana: The Ethnic Security Dilemmas" Georgetown: GIHA Crime Report.

_____(2002) "Indians will have to stand up" ROAR, July 15

_____(2008) *For a New Political Culture in Guyana*. In Transition:. No. 38, September. Turkeyen: Institute of Development Studies.

Ellis, C (2001) "Notes on Power Sharing," in Guyana Commentary, Volume 1 No 4

Ellis, C (2002) " Hoyte must match words with deeds" www.guyanacaribbeanpolitics.com

_____ (2006) " Comments on the PNC Manifesto" www.guyanacaribbeanpolitics.com

Ellis, C and Phillips, E, (2001) "Power Sharing for Racial Harmony," guyanacaribbeanpolitics.com

Esman, M (2004) *An Introduction to Ethnic Conflict*, Cambridge: Polity

Ferguson, T (1995). *Structural Adjustment and Good Governance: The Case of Guyana*, Georgetown: Public Affairs Consulting Enterprise.

Gibson, K. (2003) *The Cycle of Racial Oppression in Guyana*, Lanham: University Press of America.

Guyana Chronicle (2002) "Constitution adequately addresses issue of shared governance" August 22

Guyana Chronicle (2003) "Towards greater inclusive governance in Guyana: Building trust to achieve genuine political co-operation'" February 9

Guyana Chronicle (2003) "Who becomes the Opposition with power sharing?" July 21

Hinds, D (2004) *Race and Political Discourse in Guyana* Georgetown: Gguyanacaribbeanpolitics Publications.

_____ (2010) "One must distinguish between Critique and Ridicule Especially in Ethnic Environments" Stabroek News, January 2

Horowitz, D (1989) Ethnic *Groups in Conflict*. Berkeley: University of California Press.

_____ (1994) "Democracy in Divided Societies" in Larry Diamond and Marc F. Plattner (eds) *Nationalism, Ethnic Conflict and Democracy*, Baltimore: The Johns Hopkins University Press.

Hoyte, D (1996) "Ethnic and Political Victimization in Guyana by the PPP: PNC Leader Writes the Press" Georgetown: PNC
_____ (2002) "Last Congress Speech," Georgetown: PNC
Huntington, S (1997). "Democracy for the Long Haul" in Larry Diamond et al, eds., *Consolidating the Third Wave Democracies: Themes and Perspectives*, Baltimore: Johns Hopkins University Press.
Jagan, C (1956) "On the Way Forward" Puerto Rico: University of Puerto Rico
_____ (1972) *The West on Trial*. Berlin: Seven Seas Publishers
_____ (1993) "Keynote Address" in Tilokie and Prem Misir The East Indian Diaspora New York: Asian American Center
_____ (1996) "National and Racial Unity: The Toronto Speech of President Cheddi Jagan" Georgetown: Guyana Information Services
_____ (1997) "An Interview with Dr. Cheddi Jagan" **NACLA** Report on the Americas, Vol. 31:1. New York.
Jaguar Committee for Democracy, "Indian Economic Power or an Excuse for African Political Dominance" V. 4 no1. August/September 1992.
Kaieteur News (2006) "Sherwood Lowe resigns from PNCR Executive Committee — says party's push for shared governance slow," October 25
Kissoon, F (2001) "The Window Opens Again," in Kaieteur News, April 6-13
_____ (2003) "Gibson's Book is Propaganda" www.guyanaundersiege.com
_____ (2003) " The Failure of the Buxton Conspiracy" www.guyanaundersiege.com
_____ (2006) "An amazing election " Kaieteur News, August 31
_____ (2006) "The day I was ashamed to be a Guyanese East Indian" Kaieteur News, September 4
_____ (2006) "The PNC's electoral losses" Kaieteur News, September 8
_____ (2009) "The narrative of a particular mind-set" Kaieteur News, December 22.
Kwayana (1956) "Reply to Dr. Jagan's Congress Paper" Puerto Rico: University of Puerto Rico
_____ (1961). *The Villager,* Georgetown: African Society for Racial Equality.
_____ (1978) "Racial Insecurity in Guyana," Unpublished Paper
_____ (1985) Forward to The Democratic Republic, Georgetown: WPA
_____ (1988) "More than Survival: A View of the Indo-Guyanese Contribution to Social Change," Unpublished Paper.
_____ (1992) "Guyana's Race Problems and my part in them" The Rodneyite: Vol. 2, no.3 August
_____(1999) *No Guilty Race*, Georgetown: Free Press

_____ (1999a) *Next Witness: An Appeal to World Opinion*, Georgetown: Free Press

_____ (1999b). "The Search for Politics Across Party Lines (1953-1990)" in Stabroek News, March 21

_____ (2001) "Common Sense about Power Sharing," guyanacaribbeanpolitics.com

_____ (2002) "Genocide in Guyana: Commentary on the Disturbances in British Guiana from January to July 1964" Free Press. Queenstown, Guyana.

_____ (2005) *Morning After*, Guyana: Guyanacaribbeanpolitics Publications

_____ (2009) "To rely on PPP sources alone is to give only one side of a historical narrative of guilt" Stabroek News, June 26.

Kwayana, E; Hinds, D & Andaiye (2002) "Buxton is a Terror Camp" Stabroek News September 1

Kwayana, E. and Kwayana, T. (2002) "Scars of Bondage: A First Study of the Slave Colonial Experience of Africans in Guyana" Georgetown: Free Press.

Lewis, A (1965) *Politics in West Africa*. London: George Allen and Unwin

Lijphart, A (1995)" Multiethnic Democracy" in Lipset, S et al eds The Encyclopedia of Democracy pp 853-865 Washington DC: Congressional Quarterly

_____ (1999) "Power Sharing and Group Autonomy in the 1990s and the 21st

Century", Presented at Constitutional Design 2000, San Diego, University of California.

_____ (1999a) *Patterns of Democracy: Government Forms and Performance in Thirty- six Countries* New Haven: Yale University Press

Majeed, H. (2005). *Forbes Burnham: National Reconciliation and National Unity 1984-1985*. Georgetown: Global Communications Publishing.

McGarry, J and O'Leary, B (2006) "Consociational Theory, Northern Ireland's Conflict, and its Agreement. Part 1: What Consociationalists Can Learn from Northern Ireland" in Government and Opposition

Milne, R (1981) *Politics in Ethnically Bipolar States*, Vancouver: University of the District of Columbia Press

Misir, P (1996) "The Legacy of Institutionalized Racism: The PPP/Civic's Response." *Guyana Chronicle* April 9

_____ (2001) "Power Sharing Proposals based on false assumptions in Guyana" *Guyana Chronicle*, August 13

_____ (2004) "Governance/Power sharing as buzz words" *Guyana Chronicle* May 10

Nagamootoo, M (2003)"Guyana Needs a new Strategic Vision and Focused Leadership" Guyana Chronicle, January 16

Narine, D and Singh, T (2002) " Power Sharing in a Plural Society," guyanacaribbeanpolitics.com

Norton, A, McAllister, J, and Lowe, S (1998) "Submission to the Constitutional Reform Commission" Georgetown." guyanacaribbeanpolitics.com

O'Donnell, G and Schmitter, P (1986) *Transitions from Authoritarian Rule: Tentative Conclusions about Uncertain Democracies*, Baltimore: Johns Hopkins University Press.

Ogunseye, T (2009) "The people's support for shared governance is of paramount importance if it is to succeed" *Stabroek News*, January 5

People's National Congress (August 1975) "Proceedings of 1975 Party Congress".

_____ (2003), PNC/R on Shared Governance, Georgetown.

People's Progressive Party (1977) "Fifteen Point Political Program".

_____ (1982) "All Party Talks"

_____ (1997) "History of PPP", Georgetown, PPP

_____ (2003), Towards Greater Inclusive Governance in Guyana, Georgetown.

Persaud, R (2006) "Randy Persaud responds to his Critics" Stabroek News, July1

Phillips, E (2002) "Moving Towards Democracy in Guyana: Shared Governance" Georgetown: Eric Phillips

Premdas, R (1993). Guyana: "The Critical Elections of 1992 and a Regime Change," Caribbean Affairs, Vol. 6 No. l

_____ (1995) *Ethnic Conflict and Development: The case of Guyana*, Brookfield: Ashgate

_____ (2007) *Trinidad and Tobago: Ethnic Conflict, Inequality and Public Sector Governance*, New York: Palgrave McMillan

Ramharack, B. (1992) "Conspiracy against the PPP" The Jaguar Committee for Democracy: v. 4 no.1 August/September

_____ (1992a) "The Failure of Indian Leadership," The Jaguar Committee for Democracy v. 4 no.2 October

Ramjattan, K, (2004) "The Khemraj Ramjattan Column" Stabroek News, August 28

Ramkarran, R. (2009) "You Cannot Expect Marriage without Courtship" in Guyana Chronicle, May 30

Ramsammy, L (2002) "The PPP/C's commitment to shared or inclusive governance," Guyana Chronicle, December 16, 2002

Rodney, W (1969) *The Groundings with my Brothers* (London: Bogle'L'Overture Press)

Rodney, W (1970) "Interview with Dr. Walter Rodney," Toronto: The Forum

_____ (1981) *Executing PNC Justice: The Arnold Rampersaud Murder Trial* Georgetown: Working People's Alliance

Roopnarine, R (2000) Proposal for a Consensus Constitution, Modification of the Herdmanston Accord, and a Transitional National Government, Georgetown :Working People's Alliance,

_____ (2002). "Thinking about Desmond" in Stabroek News, December 29

Ryan, S (1999) *Winner Takes All: The Westminster Experience in the Caribbean*. St. Augustine, Trinidad and Tobago: UWI Press

_____ (2002) "Guyana Needs a Power Sharing Formula" Trinidad Express, January 25

_____ (2002) " Why Power Sharing wont work" Trinidad Express, August 25

Stabroek News (2002) "Is power sharing viable?" February 28

_____ (2002) "Shared governance" December 10

_____ (2003) "Jagdeo rejects shared governance Proposes measures for building trust between parties" August 2

Seecoomar, J (2003) "Power Sharing: An Alternative to the Grand Coalition" guyanacaribbeanpolitics.com

Singh, R (1996) " Guyana and Race" Guyana Chronicle, November 24

Sisk, T (1996) Power Sharing and International Mediation in Ethnic Conflicts, Washington, D.C.: United States Institute of Peace

Taras, R and Ganguly, R (2008) Understanding Ethnic Conflict, New York: Longman Publishing Group

Thakur, R. (2008) "Crime, Ethnicity and the Political Impasse in Guyana" in "Transition" No.30 September. Turkeyen: Institute of Development Studies, pp102-125.

Thomas, E (2006) "Critique of Dr. Hinds' work deemed intellectual dishonesty" www.guyanacaribbeanpolitics.com

Thomas, C (1997) "The Situation of African Guyanese in the Economy" Georgetown: ACDA

_____ (1997a) "Mr. Dev has not read my paper" Stabroek News, May 7

_____ (2000) "Revisiting Theories of Race and Class" in Kampta Karran (ed) *Race and Ethnicity in Guyana*. Georgetown: Offerings Publications.

_____ (2003) "Time Ripe for shared Governance" Stabroek News, July 3

_____ (2005) "Interview on Walter Rodney Groundings" Georgetown July 14

Trotz, A (2006) "Race-baiting only benefits two main parties" Stabroek News, July 13

Wilkinson, B (1996) "President in Hot Water" Associated Press, November 26

Working Peoples Alliance (1978) "WPA on National Patriotic Front"
_____ (1979) " Government of National Unity and Reconstruction"
_____ (1982) " A WPA Response to the PPP's 'All Party Talks"
_____ (1985) An Appeal From Guyana, Georgetown.

Index

A

African Cultural and Development Association (ACDA), 75, 88; conference on African Guyanese and the economy 97-99,110; as advocate of power sharing 137, 139, 183

African Guyanese, and racial construction of ethnicity 29- 31; ethnic insecurity 31-33; ethnic attitudes to politics 34- 38; and the economy 38- 40, 97-101; and dominance of the military 40-42, and party affiliation 42-44; and marginalization 94-97; African self-criticism 101-111

African Society for Cultural Relations with Independent Africa (ASCRIA), 12, 13, 44, 53, 66, 75, 162

African Society for Racial Equality (ASRE), 8, 9

Alexander, Vincent, 27, 109, 176

Alliance for Change (AFC), 25 26, 27, 44, 47, 54, 55, 56, 92,113, 135, 136

Andaiye, 13, 98; and African self-criticism 101-108

B

Bakr, Abu, 92, 194
Baptiste, Violet Jean, 75,
Benn, Brindley, 13
Bhagwan, Moses, 12, 15,111,113
Black Nationalism, 8, 12, 29, 60, 70, 71, 74, 85, 86, 94
Boodram, Annan, 89, 90, 91, 92
British Guiana Labor Union (BGLU), 3
Burnham, Forbes, 4,5,6,7, 12, 17, 18, 31, 43, 51, 63, 69, 78, 85, 91, 92, 93,113, 130, 133, 155, 157, 175
Buxton, 24, 25; as center of political violence101-110; 195

C

Caribbean Community and Common Market (CARICOM), ix, 22, 23, 178
Carter, Jimmy, 19, 80, 156, 178
Carter, Martin, 4, 5
Chase, Ashton, 4
Committee for the Defense of Democracy (CDD), 125, 126, 127
Corbin, Robert, 27, 88
Critchlow, Hubert Nathaniel, 3

D

Darke, Father Bernard, 17
Dev, Ravi, x, 23, 32, 33; and narrative of Indian suffering 81-86; and criticism of Clive Thomas 97-99; and Buxton violence 110-111; 113,114, 135, 141
Dublin, Edward, 17

E

Ellis, Clarence, 142

G

Georgetown, 3, 10, 14, 16, 21, 25, 62, 81, 91, 123,126, 157
Gibson, Kean, 96, 97
Good and Green Guyana (GGG), 44, 157
Granger, David, 183
Greene, Hamilton, 21, 44, 156, 157
Guyana Action Party, (GAP), 25,135, 136
Guyana Agricultural Workers Union (GAWU), 10, 14
Guyana Indian Heritage Association (GIHA), 75, 76, 84, 85,103
Guyanese Indian Foundation Trust (GIFT), 82

H

Hinds, David, as target of Indian critique 86-89; criticism of Indian narrative 90- 92; and African self-criticism101-108
Holder, Sheila, 25
Hoyte, Desmond, and the decline of the PNC authoritarianism18-19; 37, 38, 40, on maximum leadership 51-52; on African marginalization 94-96; on the Buxton violence 106-107; 115, and PPP-PNC unity talks130-131; and WPA's interim government proposal 151-153; and the transition to PPP's rule 156-157; 164
Hubbard, HJM, 4

I

Indian Arrival Committee (IAC), 85
Indian Guyanese, ethnic insecurity, 31- 33; ethnic attitudes to politics 34-38, and the economy 39- 40; ethnic affiliation 44-48; ethnic narratives 78-87; Indian self-criticism 111-114
Indian People's Revolutionary Associates (IPRA), 13, 44,163
International Monetary Fund (IMF), 38, 40, 100, 128, 188

J

Jagan, Dr. Cheddi, and the early PPP 3-6; and the split of the PPP 6-7,10, 17, 20, 21, 32, 43, 45, 48, 51, 52, 57, and Indian narrative of suffering 58- 62, 63, 64, 65, 66, 78, 79, 80, 81, 84, 85, 86, 90, 91, 92, 93, 94, 100,104,113,115,122, 125, 130, 132, 133, 135, 138, 154, 175, 176, 178, 189
Jagan, Janet, 4, 21, 22, 23, 51, 52, 95, 133, 153, 176
Jagan, Joey, 91, 135
Jagdeo, Bharrat, 52, 143, 164
Jaguar Committee for Democracy (JCD), 76, 85, 86, 89

K

Khan, Jerome, 109, 176

Kissoon, Freddie, 87, 97,110,113, 144, 195
Koama, Ohene, 17
Kwayana, Eusi, viii, x; and the early PPP 1-5; and the 1956 split 7-8, and ASRE's Joint Premiership 9-10; and ASCRIA-PNC relationship 12, 43-44; 15, 16, 23, on Racial Insecurity 31- 32; and African narrative of suffering 57-65; and multiethnic narrative 66-69; 74, 75; and No Guilty Race thesis 81-84; 88, 89, 93, 95, 99, and African self-criticism 101-107; 108, 117, and 1961 power sharing proposal 119- 121; 122, 130; on power sharing discourse 137- 140, 152, 156, 183

L
League of Colored People (LCP), 5, 42, 43
Lewis, Arthur, 121
Lewis, Lincoln, 108
Lowe, Sherwod, 142

M
Majeed, Halim, 130
Manpower Citizens Association (MPCA), 3
Misir, Prem, 97,114, 143
Movement Against Oppression (MAO), 13
Murray, Winston, 27,176

N
Nagamootoo, Moses, 138, 139
Narine, Dhanpaul, 141
National Democratic Party (NDP), 5
National Front Alliance (NFA), 135, 136

National Patriotic Front (NPF), 123, 124, 178

O
Ogunseye, Tacuma, 108, 140, 156
Omowale, 17

P
Parris, Haslyn, 98, 183
Patriotic Coalition for Democracy (PCD), 18, 20, 55, 131, 150, 151, 152, 153, 154, 156, 158
People's Progressive Party (PPP), Early years 4-6; splits 6-7; and the 1957 and 1961 elections 8-9; and ethnic violence 10-1; in opposition 11-19; return to power 20-28; overtures to the PNC 121-122; National Patriotic Front 123-126; and PPP-PNC 1985 unity talks 130-131; Inclusive Governance 130-132; betrayal of national reconciliation 149-159
People's National Congress (PNC), birth of 8; in government 11-19; return to opposition 20-28; rejection of PPP overtures 121-122; rejection of National Patriotic Front 123-126; and PPP-PNC 1985 unity talks 130-131; Shared Governance 133-134; and Big Tent politics 134-136; and the transition to electoral democracy 147-158.
Persaud, Randy, 86, 88,114, 143
Phillips, Eric, 139 183
Premdas, Ralph, 155

R
Rai, Balram Singh, 8
Ramjattan, Khemraj, 25, 55, 144

Index

Ramkarran, Boysie, 4
Ramkarran, Ralph, 114, 144
Ramsammy, Joshua, 13
Ramsaroop, Peter, 135
Ratoon, 13
Rise Organize and Rebuild (ROAR), 22, 23, 25, 45, 47, 75, 76, 84, 135, 136, 137
Rodney, Walter, x; and the WPA 14-17; 44, 58, 66; Multi ethnic narrative 69-74; 79, 89, 91; target of Indian narrative 92-96; 117, 127, 162, 163
Rodrigues, Malcolm, viii
Roopnarine, Rupert, 13, 17, 134, 139, 151, 153
Ryan, Selwyn, 145

S
Singh, Tara, 141

T
Thomas, Clive, x, 1, 13, 16, 39, 53; on African Guyanese and the economy 97-100, 117; on power sharing 139-140; 156, 158, 183
Thomas, Evan, 88
Trade Union Congress (TUC), 10, 18, 123, 124, 130, 137
Trotman, Raphael, 25, 55
Trotz, Alissa, 87

U
United Democratic Party (UDP), 8, 12, 32, 61
United Force (UF), 9, 10, 123

V
Vanguard for Liberation and Democracy (VLD), 16, 127, 128

W
Westmaas, Nigel, 91
Westmaas, Rory 4
Wiggins, Dennis, 98
Williams, Eric, 121
Working People's Alliance (WPA), opposition to PNC regime 12-19; opposition to PPP government 20-27; 44, 45, 47; as a multiethnic party 52-55; 58, 65, 66, 69, 77, 78, 85, 86, 87, 88, 89, 90, 91, 92, 93, 94, 95, 97, 98,101,105,110,111,116,117,118, 124, and power sharing proposals 126-130; 131, 134, 135, 136, 137, 139, 140, 147; and the PPP's betrayal of National Reconciliation 150-159; 162, 171, 174, 176, 182
Working People's Vanguard Party (WPVP), 13

www.ingramcontent.com/pod-product-compliance
Lightning Source LLC
Chambersburg PA
CBHW031312150426
43191CB00005B/192